THE DISABLED, THE MEDIA, AND THE INFORMATION AGE

Recent Titles in
Contributions to the Study of Mass Media and Communications

The Disabled, the Media, and the Information Age

EDITED BY
Jack A. Nelson

Contributions to the Study of Mass Media
and Communications,
Number 42

Greenwood Press _____
WESTPORT, CONNECTICUT • LONDON

Library of Congress Cataloging-in-Publication Data

The disabled, the media, and the information age / edited by Jack A.
Nelson.
    p. cm.—(Contributions to the study of mass media and
communications, ISSN 0732–4456 ; no. 42)
   Includes bibliographical references (p.   ) and index.
   ISBN 0–313–28472–5 (alk. paper)
    1. Handicapped in mass media—United States. 2. Handicapped—
United States—Social conditions. I. Nelson, Jack A. (Jack
Adolph). II. Series.
HV1553.D564   1994
302.23′087—dc20   93–7700

British Library Cataloguing in Publication Data is available.

Library of Congress Catalog Card Number: 93–7700
ISBN: 0–313–28472–5
ISSN: 0732–4456

First published in 1994

Greenwood Press, 88 Post Road West, Westport, CT 06881
An imprint of Greenwood Publishing Group, Inc.

Printed in the United States of America

The paper used in this book complies with the
Permanent Paper Standard issued by the National
Information Standards Organization (Z39.48–1984).

10 9 8 7 6 5 4 3 2 1

Copyright Acknowledgments

The author and the publisher are grateful to the following for granting the use of material:

Transcript from news broadcast © CBS Inc. 1988. All Rights Reserved. Originally broadcast on
March 8, 1988, over the CBS Television Network on CBS "Evening News with Dan Rather."

Transcript from "ABC News World News Tonight with Peter Jennings" reprinted by permission.
Copyright © ABC News 1988.

Transcript of portion of NBC News Broadcast originally broadcast on March 7, 1988. Reprinted
by permission of NBC News.

Material from the Winter 1990 issue and short pieces from other issues of *The Disability Rag*
used by permission.

Contents

Preface

As Americans look toward the twenty-first century, a new world for those with a disability may be waiting just beyond the horizon. Technology has already altered the way most Americans live. In one way, computers have proved the great equalizers, and apparently technological advances are just beginning. Coupled with those advances, the passage of the Americans with Disabilities Act of 1990 promises new attitudes in a society that is rapidly changing.

A hundred years ago, at the end of the nineteenth century, the United States was in a state of flux too—due not only to industrialization but to the influence of the media on society. Those were the times when the muckrakers of the press—especially the magazines *McClure's, Cosmopolitan,* and *Munsey's*—exposed national corruption and when the robber barons and other industrial giants were keeping the public twisting on a string, at the mercy of their financial and political manipulations. Through the efforts of such journalists as Lincoln Steffens, Ida Tarbell, and Upton Sinclair, Americans were made aware of the abuses of public trust. The result was improved and safer living conditions. The Pure Food and Drug Act, for instance, put an end to abuses of the meat-packing industry. A reform mood swept the country, resulting in new attitudes, new guidelines, and new bodies like the Federal Trade Commission that were aimed at protecting the public from the blatant misrepresentations and fraud that had flourished for decades.

Now, as the twentieth century comes to a close, another major change is taking place. Along with the lot of other minorities, life may be improving for those with disabilities—those who for centuries have been hidden away in back rooms or shunned in genteel society. It is still early yet to judge, of course. But the passage of the Americans with Disabilities Act of 1990 is undoubtedly the most important step forward in the history of this nation for those with physical and mental limitations. Not only does this act guarantee rights in employment, housing, and transportation, it also signals a new awareness of the general populace that those with disabilities have a right to equal treatment and consideration.

For centuries, negative images have persisted, burned into people's minds by mindless portrayals in the media. But in recent years a new attitude has surfaced. It began with the civil rights battles for racial minorities following World War II. Americans became aware that constitutional guarantees ought not to apply only to selected citizens. As those battles were won, media focus began to turn to other minorities, including the millions of people with disabilities. Movies and television, as this book shows, were among the worst offenders of stigmatizing this significant minority. Yet in the 1970s, 1980s, and 1990s, writers and producers who mold so many attitudes of viewers began to show disability in a new light, featuring real human beings with feelings and goals and talents and personalities—people with something to offer. Movies dealing with these people began to gather audiences and win Academy Awards and, most of all, to win understanding—not without some mawkishness, of course, and a certain amount of condescension and even stupidity at times, but the direction has been clear: toward a greater closeness of the human condition, a sense of belonging and brotherhood.

Perhaps even more important, this significant minority has slowly become aware of their own empowerment. They have grown more militant. Like others who demanded their civil rights earlier in this century, they march with wheelchairs, they parade with placards before legislatures, they invade and sleep in government offices. Blind people, deaf people, people on crutches and in wheelchairs—they come. They protest not only unfair treatment but abuses by telethons, nursing homes, segregated institutional facilities, and inaccessible buildings. They represent a new attitude among their number, a new sense of worth, a new commitment to fair treatment for themselves and others with disabilities. They no longer are willing to be shunted aside and ignored. As a group, they sense new power and newly recognized rights, and they recognize that at times those rights must be wrested and seized from bodies that only reluctantly want to give up power.

There is a growing pride among those with disabilities. A new disability culture is growing. "We're proud of who we are," it says. "We're not inferior—just people who are different." And most of all, they proclaim that those differences are not great or important and that they are more like than unlike all other Americans. That may be the key to expanding the quality of life for those with disabilities. There will be setbacks, problems, even betrayals. But the avalanche has begun. There is no going back now. The world is changing.

THE DISABLED, THE MEDIA, AND THE INFORMATION AGE

1

Broken Images: Portrayals of Those with Disabilities in American Media

Jack A. Nelson

A few years ago in an episode of "Little House on the Prairie," children from the town's school for the blind were being transferred to another town because the school was moving. The children, tied to a wagon and instructed to hold onto a rope, walked stiffly, like wooden robots, staring straight ahead, totally dependent and stigmatized. That is not how blind children behave, but it is the way the audience was led to believe they behave. The episode was not an isolated instance.

The American media have shown a preponderance of negative stereotypes when depicting persons with disabilities. These people are often portrayed as evil, or as pitiable victims doomed to an unsatisfying life, or in an array of other roles that in the main tend to strengthen prejudices, fear, and loathing among audiences. In a time when powerful media influences are molding society's attitudes and bringing about social change, it is important to understand more about the role of media portrayals of this group that has been called the "invisible minority."

President Franklin D. Roosevelt, who led the nation during the wrenching depression years and World War II, provides a good example of the importance of media portrayals. No other person was more idolized by the majority of Americans during those trying times; he was elected to four presidential terms. That this larger-than-life figure had been hit with poliomyelitis during his term as governor of New York was well known, but in his terms as president, he almost never was shown in his wheelchair or struggling to stand in braces. Indeed much of the public assumed that Roosevelt had recovered from the effects of polio. The White House laid down strict guidelines about what pictures might reveal about him, and through a tacit agreement, his disability was not portrayed in the media. Even political cartoonists honored the agreement. Throughout his terms, the image of a vigorous, active president was believable and accepted by the public. Apparently those in the White House felt that depiction of a strong leader, especially in wartime, was important enough that the manipulation of the image was justified.[1] The point, however, is that it was felt necessary to shape the image—as if a president who used a wheelchair could not provide strong, energetic, and active leadership.

More recently, the impact of new laws, combined with more enlightened portrayals in the media, have changed public perceptions about groups. The best known example is of the civil rights laws of the 1960s and the changes in ensuing media portrayals of minority racial groups that helped shape how Americans view all races. The standard stereotypes of African-Americans in films thirty years ago, for instance, would not be tolerated today, yet the portrayal of these people as subservient, near illiterate, and frightened in the face of danger was standard fare for movies of that earlier time, and prejudices endured partly because they were reinforced and legitimized by these media portrayals. As laws changed to legislate fairer treatment for minorities, however, and as the public became conscious of the unfairness and damaging potential of such stereotypes, society's attitudes began to change, and the new attitudes were reflected on the screen. Now, with the Americans with Disabilities Act of 1990 mandating a change in the treatment of another minority, those with disabilities, it is time to examine how they are treated in the media.

Do the media have the power to change public attitudes? Sociologists tell us that children learn most of their attitudes toward others through personal interaction or through portrayals seen on television. "People's values, attitudes, and perceptions are based not only on their real-life experiences but on the perceptions created and shaped by the media, primarily television," explains Tari Susan Hartman, a former actress who holds a master's degree in social work.[2] Indeed, the values, perceptions, and ideals portrayed as correct or predominant have an impact on viewers' values. In 1991, a massive study of television viewing in America demonstrated that television has been a major force in changing attitudes. "Television started as an agent of social control," wrote the authors of the study, "but became an agent of social change."[3]

It is important, in order to help remove the stigma that has been attached to disability, that those in control of writing and producing what America absorbs on television not do so out of prejudice, fear, or ignorance. "Unfortunately," writes Keith Byrd, "whether the information is correct or not, the fact remains that TV is one of the major ways that many of us learn about people with disabilities."[4]

A PREJUDICE WITH DEEP ROOTS

The roots of prejudice against those with disabilities run deep. For centuries, fairy tales have portrayed evil people as afflicted; the witch in "Hansel and Gretel" limps, Rumpelstilskin is a midget, and Pinocchio's nose grows. Indeed, these classic authors suggested that evil inevitably goes along with a disability. Shakespeare gave Richard III—who in real life was not disabled—a twisted and deformed body to go along with his evil personality. One was seen as an extension of the other:

> I, that am curtail'd of this fair proportion,
> Cheated of feature by dissembling nature,
> Deform'd, unfinished, sent before my time,
> Into this breathing world, scarce half made up,
> And that so lamely and unfashionable,
> That dogs bark at me as I halt by them,
> Why, I, in this weak piping time of peace,
> Have no delight to pass away the time,
> Unless to spy my shadow in the sun,
> and descant on mine own deformity,
> And therefore, since I cannot prove a lover,
> To entertain these fair well-spoken days,
> I am determined to prove a villain,
> And hate the idle pleasures of these days.
>
> (Act 1, scene 1)

But we do not have to go to times past to find reasons for prejudice against those with disabilities. Anyone who read comic books while growing up will recognize the view that people with disabilities usually have some evil about them. In the fictional world, a long literary history has seen a strong connection between criminality and disability; deformity of body and deformity of soul have gone hand in hand: we see the pitiable character of Phillip in *Of Human Bondage*, Captain Ahab in *Moby Dick*, and the evil character of Long John Silver in *Treasure Island*. When we first meet Long John Silver, only casual note is made of his wooden leg. Later, after his perfidy is revealed, his "timber" leg becomes a symbol of his evil, and we hear it thumping across the deck. On almost any evening, a crime show on television pairs disability and evil. Such negative depictions burn deep into viewers' and readers' vision of the world and dictate their reaction to those with disabilities whom they encounter.

Why have the media focused on such negative stereotypes? The number of Americans with physical limitations has been placed at around 43 million, roughly one out of every seven people. Why don't movies and television programs present these citizens in a more realistic way, perhaps even focusing on the real problems that confront them, such as access and job discrimination? One explanation is offered by critic Michael Wood:

Movies bring out our worries without letting them loose and without forcing us to look at them too closely. . . . It doesn't appear to be necessary for a movie to solve anything, however fictitiously. . . . Entertainment is not as we often think, a full-scale flight from our problems, not a means of forgetting them completely but rather a rearrangement of our problems into shapes which tame them, which disperse them to the margins of our attention.[5]

Centuries of tradition that regarded anyone with a disability as malevolent or cursed by a vengeful god might help explain why such deeply held prejudices have endured. In addition, deep-seated anxieties exist in each of us as to our own vulnerability: "Disability happens around us more often than we generally recognize or care to notice, and we harbor unspoken anxieties about the possibilities of disablement, to us or to someone close to us. What we fear, we often stigmatize and shun and sometimes seek to destroy," says Paul K. Longmore, a specialist in the program in disability and society at the University of Southern California, whose bout with polio left him without the use of his arms.[6]

Longmore's statement may partly explain why, in the past, media portrayals of people with disabilities reflected those fears, anxieties, and prejudices. From screen criminals whose evil is symbolized by an obvious physical defect to telethons that elicit funds by capitalizing on the pitiably afflicted, to featuring "heroic cripples" doing daring deeds, the media have presented a picture of a stigmatized minority. The media themselves have contributed to the negative sociopolitical consciousness about disabled people. Only in recent years have the media begun to show a sensitivity to the prejudices that have dominated coverage of this minority group for decades. The recent emergence of a new sociopolitical consciousness about disability, as evidenced by passage of the Americans with Disabilities Act of 1990, may portend changing attitudes in the media as well.

THE MAJOR STEREOTYPES

The stereotypes that have barraged the public through the years—the ones that reinforce limiting attitudes in society—fit a pattern. For convenience, we may look at seven major stereotypes—what Robert Bogdan and Douglas Biklen call "handicapist stereotypes"—that over the years have dominated film and television.[7]

The Disabled Person as Pitiable and Pathetic

One source of continuing negative stereotyping on television is the omnipresent fund-raising marathons, better known as telethons. These feature syrupy mixtures of tearful appeals from Hollywood stars and the appearance of those with disabilities as examples of the need for funds for further research. Viewers watch the telethons partly because they are on for so many hours and partly because they usually feature major talent acts in an informal setting. As popular as these telethons are, they perpetuate the image of those with disabilities as objects of pity. Disabled people are usually depicted as childlike—as in Jerry Lewis's Kids—or as incompetent, needing total care, as nonproductive in our society, and as a drain on taxpayers.

Telethons rarely point to the accomplishments of those who carry out their lives in ways that are mostly normal and who contribute greatly to society. As Paul Longmore points out, "Disabled people are not characterized [in telethons] as a social minority with civil rights but as victims of a tragic fate."[8]

In 1992, when it was time to air the most famous telethon—actor Jerry Lewis's annual muscular dystrophy Labor Day appeal—protests from disabled groups were held around the country. The spokesmen for these groups were vehement that such appeals demeaned, degraded, and dehumanized all disabled, showing them as passive and in need of care and pity. Lewis had especially angered disability advocates in 1990 when he said that if he had muscular dystrophy, he would feel like half a person. Nevertheless, in spite of the protests, the 1992 muscular dystrophy telethon raised $45.8 million in viewer pledges—up half a million dollars from the previous year.

In the same way, movies too have often featured those with physical limitations as victims and as removed from the societal mainstream. This perpetuation of the stereotype of the disabled as objects of pity or praise when they accomplish a worthwhile goal has brought considerable scorn from the disabled. When Mary Johnson, a disability rights activist and editor of *The Disability Rag,* visited a journalism class at the University of Minnesota, she was appalled when students showed her a text that recommended stories showing the disabled triumphing over great odds—"One of the most god-awful 'heartwarming-cripple' stories I have read," she says.[9] She reminded students that reporters who solicit pity for people with disabilities do more harm than good. Her point was that maudlin news stories reinforce passive images that some disabled people have of themselves, and they reinforce that image in the public's mind, distracting attention from the important issues of access and discrimination. *The Disability Rag* is an advocate for those with disabilities and a critic of the social forces that often seem determined to block their progress toward better-quality lives. For years, Johnson has argued with editors about coverage of the disabled. Her publication has had some success with getting editors of various publications to avoid using offensive terms such as *victim, cripple,* or *wheelchair bound.*

The Disabled Person as Supercrip

Inevitably the supercrip portrayal deals with a heartwarming struggle of someone likable facing the trauma of a disability, who through great courage, stamina, and determination either succeeds in triumphing or succumbs heroically. Television especially focuses on such battles as one of its most popular dramas. Their heroes' actions are inspirational—and often superhuman. The television movie "The Terry Fox Story" featured the account of a young Canadian who, after he lost a leg to cancer, hopped across his country on one leg to raise money for cancer research.

"Sure, it raised money for cancer research and sure, it showed the human capacity for achievement," says actor Alan Toy, who walks with a brace and has appeared in television shows ranging from "Airwolf" to "Trauma Center." "But a lot of ordinary disabled people are made to feel like failures if they haven't done something extraordinary. They may be bankers or factory workers—proof enough of their usefulness to society. Do we have to be 'supercrips' in order to be valid? And if we're not super, are we invalid?"[10] Toy's feelings echo the objections that the focusing of public attention on the heroic struggles of a few—the "disability chic" approach that some disabled label as another adventure of a supercrip—diminishes the attention needed to access, transportation, jobs, and housing to improve the status of all those with disabilities.

The Disabled Person as Sinister, Evil, and Criminal

The image of a threatening, evil character who also has a prominent disability plays on subtle and deeply held fears and stereotypical prejudices. Modern movie and television portrayals abound in villains whose evil and threatening presence is exemplified by a deformity of body. It was no happenstance that the movie characters Dr. Strangelove and Dr. No both had hands and forearms of black leather. In innumerable movies, disabled villains rail against their "fate" and vow to destroy a world inhabited by "normals."

The tendency to show disability accompanying or even causing criminality has continued unabated on television and in movies, perhaps until recently. The long-running television series "The Fugitive" featured a one-armed killer who slayed the protagonist's wife in the first episode. The numbers of maimed and amputee bad guys are so great on the silver screen that when a character shows up with a physical defect, the audience's assumption must be, "Oh oh! Look out for this guy!"

"One wonders about the psychosexual significance of the connection between blackness, badness, amputations and artificial arms," writes Longmore. He suggests that part of the reason for moviemakers' giving disabilities to villainous characters so often is that "the unacknowledged hostile fantasies of the stigmatizers are transferred to the stigmatized."[11]

In depicting those with psychiatric disorders, the media have an even worse record. These portrayals, inevitably negative, occur more than any other disability on the screen. E. Keith Byrd and Timothy Elliot noted, "It seems apparent that psychiatric disorders provide interest and give the viewer the opportunity to view abnormal behavior in a context that is entertaining and in a fashion that is generally nonthreatening. Television programs tend to portray mental patients as dangerous, unpredictable, and evil, and these portrayals may lead to unwarranted apprehension and ostracism of people who have such disorders."[12] Not only do such depictions do great damage to the public perception of those with mental illness, but institutionalized psychiatric patients spend a good deal of time watching television—and learning from the portrayals the community's attitude toward them.

These common portrayals of the disabled person as a criminal or as a monster reflect what Erving Goffman calls the fundamental nature of stigma in which the stigmatized person "is seen as somehow less than human." That is, the person is identified by this trait, which dominates other aspects of his or her being, robbing him or her of social identity.[13]

Although this association of physical handicaps with evil is a holdover from medieval attitudes, through the centuries the media have done more than their share to perpetuate the fear and loathing that have accompanied such stereotypes.

The Disabled Person as Better-Off Dead

Perhaps the most vivid and frightening evidence of societal attitudes that are threatening to persons with disabilities is the "better dead than disabled" syndrome. At the heart of this is the attitude that because anyone with a serious physical impairment is unwhole and incapable of a fulfilling life, he or she would be better off dead. In the mid-1980s three dramas reflected this position: the play and movie *Whose Life Is It, Anyway?*, the television movie "An Act of Love," and the play *Nevis Mountain Dew*. In each of these dramas, paraplegics or quadraplegics request that they be assisted in suicide because they apparently find life unbearable. A subtext is that medical care is out of control in its costs, and there is an exorbitant cost to keeping alive people who would be better off dead anyway. This portrayal also harks back to the fear and loathing mentioned earlier—that for many, the sight of serious physical disability is an unpleasant reminder of mortality and vulnerability. Longmore suggests that in these dramas, disability alienates a person from society and deprives the individual of self-determination. Death is shown as preferable, particularly since it relieves society of the problem of dealing with the long-term needs and rights of those with such disabilities.

The chilling implication is that this attitude is a step toward justifying euthanasia for those whose "lives are unworthy of life." In prewar Nazi Germany, the official policy of the Third Reich was that "defectives" were killed in order to improve the so-called Aryan race. More than 100,000 mentally and physically disabled Germans died in gas chambers. The criteria for killing children and adults continually expanded and came to include various minor handicaps. The rationale for such an approach was contained in *The Permission to Destroy Life Unworthy of Life*, published in 1920 by Alfred Hoche, a professor of psychiatry at the University of Frieberg.[14] Hoche wrote that if only the fit were preserved, the nation would constantly grow more perfect.

The Disabled Person as Maladjusted—His Own Worst Enemy

For the popular media, the maladjusted disabled person has been a mainstay in recent years, especially in television dramas. These persons are bitter and full of self-pity because they have not learned to handle their disability. In the standard formula, a friend or family member sets the pitiable character straight in a confrontational scene, informing him or her to "buck up" and take control. Rarely is any mention made of social prejudice or the role of society in helping with the problems. Almost always the nondisabled person is shown to understand the problem better than the one with the problem. For example, during the 1980s on a television episode of "Night Court," a young woman without legs asks Harry, the judge, on a date. He is busy, and she is devastated, so he sets her straight. Her disability, he tells her, is in her attitude. A few minutes later, she walks in smiling on the artificial legs she had had with her all the time. What she needed, it seems, was Harry's insightful advice to get her on the right track.[15] Such stories imply that if only disabled characters were not so bitter and would accept themselves, they would have better lives.

The myth is maintained that persons with disabilities need greater insights about themselves and the world. Those insights are provided by others; therefore, says this myth, those with disabilities need guidance, since they are unable to make sound judgments themselves or to shape their own destinies.

The Disabled Person as a Burden

Another concept promoted through the years is that those with physical limitations need to be taken care of. Depicting such persons as a burden reflects the view that duty impels family, friends, or society to meet these needs. At the same time, the implication is that a burden is difficult to bear and is to be avoided. Thus, this portrayal dehumanizes those with disabilities.

The word *handicap* itself is judgmental, probably originating from the age-old practice of beggars who held cap in hand to solicit charity. It reflects the dependent position in which persons with disabilities are viewed. As a dramatic concept, this stereotype is often used on screen as a device to show the nobility and generosity of those who furnish care, making the disabled person little more than a prop rather than a human being capable of interacting with others to the profit of both. We see Heidi in Johanna Spyri's 1881 novel, *Heidi,* hired as a companion to the "rich little cripple" Clara. Through the loving and attentive care of Heidi, along with considerable doses of mountain air and goat's milk, the pathetic crippled girl gets well. Clara serves as a prop to show Heidi's giving nature. Tiny Tim in Dickens's *A Christmas Carol* serves the same function.

The Disabled Person as Unable to Live a Successful Life

Overall, the media have portrayed those with limitations as unable to live full and happy lives. Instead, they are shown as defined by their disability. Rarely, at least until recently, have they been shown as useful and happy members of society: workers, members of families, lovers, teachers or students, or any of other numerous roles by which human beings are usually defined.

In the past, the portrayals have mostly been of inferior persons, stigmatized by their disability, and unworthy of attention. In fact, in most dramas, those with a disability rarely are shown at all unless there is a dramatic reason for their presence. Although this is beginning to change, they are seldom seen in normal situations such as the workplace, carrying out their daily affairs, as they do in reality. The result is that over the past decades, the media have been major offenders in maintaining these unhealthy and distorted stereotypes that have little relation to reality.

A LEGACY OF NEGATIVISM

An increasing number of plays, films, novels, and television dramas have been concerned with the topic of disability in recent years. Before determining whether this means attitudes have changed, we need a measuring stick of television offerings of a few years ago. In 1980, for instance, *Newsweek* magazine reported that most approaches to advertising and stories informing the public about disabilities were "degrading and dehumanizing."[16] A significant study in 1978 found that television stigmatized people with disabilities. The personality traits most depicted were "dull, impotent, selfish, defensive, and uncultured. They [those with disabilities] were regarded as objects of pity and care. Overall, they were considered not quite human, and virtually immobile in society."[17]

A 1979 study by Joy Donaldson provides more insights. Her examination of eighty-five half-hour prime-time television shows noted that, although what were called "handicapped characters" were sometimes seen in major roles, they seldom appeared in incidental roles. In fact, in the entire study, not one handicapped character appeared in a minor role except in juxtaposition with other handicapped characters; none were visible in groups of shoppers, spectators, jurors, customers, or workers. Handicapped people were thus invisible among the thousands of people in the background of the eighty-five television shows studied.[18]

As might be expected, Donaldson found that positive portrayals appeared less often than negative portrayals. When they were portrayed positively, those with a disability were shown valiantly struggling against a dominating facet of their life, such as blindness or paralysis. In a sense, these portrayals are positive, but they also strengthen the stereotype that the disability is the central focus of a person's life. What was absent was the portrayal of a person who lived a full and rich life in which a disability was an incidental facet: a successful lawyer or professor who happened to use a wheelchair, for instance.

Just as important, those with disabilities were seldom shown in interaction with those who did not have disabilities. "The absence of positive portrayals that belie stereotypes and depict comfortable interaction between handicapped and nonhandicapped people suggests that prime time television is not exerting a significant influence in shaping positive societal attitudes toward individuals who are handicapped, nor is it facilitating comfortable relationships by providing models of interaction," Donaldson wrote.[19] Interestingly, those with disabilities were often shown in "extremely negative roles." And, when they were shown as evil threats to society, their disabilities were only incidental to the plot. In other words, their disabilities were not shown to dominate their lives, as was the case in the positive portrayals.

There have been exceptions to this dominant image. One prominent early example was the portrayal by the noted actor Lionel Barrymore as Dr. Kildare in a series of movies. Even after Barrymore began to use a wheelchair in real life and on the screen, he was shown in that same problem-solving role of a doctor, living a full life and helping to guide others from his wheelchair. After World War II, partly because of the number of disabled veterans, a few movies presented sympathetic portraits of these men adjusting to life. Most poignant was the role of the soldier who had lost both hands in battle in the award-winning 1946 film *The Best Years of Our Lives*. For the role the producers chose Harold Russell, a veteran who had actually lost both hands in battle. For his performance, Russell won an Academy Award as best supporting actor, along with a special Oscar for inspiring other disabled vets. In addition, Marlon Brando as a returning paraplegic in *The Men* was a powerful example of the travails of a proud youth finding his life changed forever by war. Nevertheless, the preponderance of the portrayals on screen was overwhelmingly negative, and mostly remains so today. These portrayals both reflect and form public attitudes.

RECENT PROGRESS

There are positive signs that considerable progress has been made over the past decade or so. A *Denver Post* columnist recommended in 1989 that the time had come for the physically and mentally handicapped to take their place among television's "types" in positive portrayals.[20] It might be argued that being depicted as "types" rather than as individuals is exactly what those with disabilities do not need, but nevertheless most would recognize this attitude as at least a step forward in the right direction.

During the 1980s and early 1990s, show business began to take a new look at disabilities. This new attention is reversing some of the traditional stereotypes. In the fall of 1991, NBC television's "Reasonable Doubts" broke new ground by featuring Marlee Matlin as a deaf district attorney who delivered some lines in sign language. Most important, the series was not about a disabled person but a district attorney who incidentally is deaf. "It's not that we don't take into account Marlee's hearing impairment, but that's not where the story line comes from," said Charise McGhee, the network's vice-president of dramatic programming.[21]

The trend is clear. Jeri Jewell, an actress who has cerebral palsy, was a regular on the NBC series "Facts of Life." Actor Alan Toy, who is unable to walk without crutches, was appearing widely in such television series as "Simon and Simon" and "Airwolf." Actor Jim Burns, who played the character Lifeguard in a wheelchair on the early 1990s CBS show "Wiseguys," lost both legs in an automobile accident in 1972. Hugh Farrington, a paraplegic, has played a police lieutenant on ABC's "T. J. Hooker."

In the area of mental retardation, television took one of its boldest steps in the fall of 1989 when ABC presented a series about a family with a teenager with Down syndrome, played by a mentally impaired actor. Before the show's appearance, *TV Guide* labeled it "the most likely to flop the fastest," giving as the reason that some viewers might find its subject depressing.[22] Much of the focus on the hour-long show deals with problems any family faces: Mr. Thatcher, a construction worker, dreams of starting his own construction company, while his wife struggles with turning forty. Corky Thatcher, played by Christopher Burke, is having his own crisis: dealing with entering a regular high school after years of attending a special education school. His personality sparkles through the show. After four full seasons, "Life Goes On" appears to have won public acceptance. In the fickle land of television, it has made a place for itself—at least for the time being.

One of the most significant characterizations of disability has been the movie *Coming Home*, in which Jon Voight played a veteran returning home from Vietnam as a paraplegic. Although somewhat idealized, the role was shown in a nonstereotypical way, partly because Voigt spent many days at a rehabilitative hospital learning how paraplegics deal with the world. Undoubtedly that movie helped prepare the public for other movies about disability, such as *The Elephant Man* and *Ordinary People*. In 1986 the world of the deaf was portrayed in *Children of a Lesser God*, in which Marlee Matlin won an Academy Award. Many deaf viewers were critical of the film, however. One of these, comparing the film to the earlier Broadway play, wrote: "Little remains of Marlee Matlin's Sarah except sexual heat. Disconnected from the real-life struggles of deaf people, her anger has no clear source. Her outbursts seem unrelated to the misunderstanding and devaluation that harass deaf people in the real world so relentlessly."[23]

In the early 1990s, two critically acclaimed films were released that featured disabled characters and helped raise disability consciousness in this country. *My Left Foot* dealt sympathetically with Christy Brown, a bright young Irish man with severe cerebral palsy. Almost totally frustrated in his need to communicate not only creature needs but ideas, Christy rages gloriously and from a rough-and-tumble upbringing learns to fight back, culminating in a barroom brawl that he starts. "When Daniel Day-Lewis accepted the film industry's highest award for his portrayal of Christy Brown, I cried . . . with joy," wrote a disabled woman. "I wanted to take to the streets and celebrate. At last, recognition! Thanks to Brown and Day-Lewis . . . I rejoice. I can feel proud to be disabled."[24] Not everyone was so thrilled with the representation of those with cerebral palsy, however. Some people pointed out that the tantrums of Christy Brown in the restaurant showed the antics of a spoiled child rather than a frustrated adult.

Another popular movie, *Born on the Fourth of July*, recounts the true story of the disillusionment of Ron Kovic, who through a Vietnam War wound became a paraplegic. It is a very powerful story, called "an important film" by critics. Although the film is actually a portrayal of the futility and injustice of the Vietnam War, Kovic's disability and the problems it brings offer a constant refrain. The blocked catheters and the cavalier attention the patients receive in the Veterans Administration hospital raise concerns about how those with disabilities are treated in all institutions.

It is true that neither the role of Brown nor Kovic was played by a disabled actor, and it is true that both films ignore the larger social context of disability. Nevertheless, the new awareness of disability issues they show stands in contrast to earlier films characterized as tearjerkers or cure sagas. For instance, when Kovic returns home in a wheelchair, there is a very visible ramp up the front steps of the family home, and his father notes that he has widened the bathroom door—points that would probably have been missing in earlier films. Both movies are films with disability treated realistically. And to see both receive Academy Awards—one for best director and the other for best actor and best supporting actress—indicates that the general public is ready for new attitudes about those who face limitations.

MEDIA ACCESS OFFICE: CHANGING PERCEPTIONS

One positive influence at work for people with disabilities is the Media Access Office (MAO), which since 1978 has operated in Hollywood to exert pressure in favor of the disabled. Made up of approximately 250 actors and actresses with varying disabilities, the group advocates the use of actors with disabilities to portray characters with disabilities and the more "normal" treatment of people with disabilities by writers, producers, and directors of movies and television. They particularly encourage roles in which the disability is seen as incidental. For instance, former MAO chairman Alan Toy recalls a television commercial he made in which he portrayed an ordinary businessman carrying a briefcase—and walking on crutches, which is how he gets around. "If only we could get that image of normality projected more," he says, "the more audiences would get used to seeing us as human beings, and the less aghast they'll be when they meet us in the street."[25]

The Media Access Office does not take lightly its role as watchdog representing disabled Americans. When actress Joan Collins made disparaging comments about the character with cerebral palsy in *My Left Foot*, MAO spoke out. Collins had characterized the Oscar-winning performance of Daniel Day-Lewis in the difficult lead role as "brave" and "difficult." Then she added, "For somebody as good-looking as he is to make himself look as ugly as he is in every way is . . . a total art."[26] Media Access Office responded with a tart letter to Collins: "Daniel Day-Lewis did not make himself look 'ugly,' . . . he made himself look as if he had cerebral palsy," wrote MAO operations director Marta Russell. "The disability community is insulted and disappointed at your inference that the ability to take on mannerisms that make one look disabled was equated with the ability to look 'ugly.' "[27] The negative myth and stereotype were being perpetuated, Russell wrote later.

The pressure that this group brings on producers and writers to avoid the negative stereotypes that are so damaging to public perceptions is having an effect. The activism of this group has had a major impact on casting and even plot lines. Longmore believes that such groups may hold the key to achieving desired changes: "It is *organized* constituencies, of whatever size, that have brought about changes in broadcasting and advertising. Although the disability community and civil rights movement have slowly been becoming more media conscious, concerted efforts to alter media images have thus far remained on a comparatively small scale."[28]

CONTROL OF THEIR OWN DESTINIES

The disabled community has begun to recognize what is most needed is empowerment—control of their own destinies rather than to be at the mercy of institutions. Their recent demonstrations are reminiscent of the civil rights protests two decades earlier. For instance, in 1992 when the governor of Utah announced cutbacks in funds for aiding disabled persons, pleading that the state was broke, an army in wheelchairs and on crutches, plus others with various disabilities who were receiving such aid occupied the governor's office. The local media jumped on the story, and it made front pages. The cutbacks were rescinded.

ADVERTISING: LEADERS OF CHANGING IMAGES

Paradoxically, it is in television commercials, generally regarded as the conservative part of television, that the most progress in showing people with disabilities has occurred over the past decade. Until 1983, anyone less than perfect was practically invisible on these commercials. It was a case of "only the most attractive need apply" as advertisers tried to ally their products to the most seductive life-style.

In 1982, however, CBS television used for a promotion a montage of quick shots showing facets of the new season—including a paraplegic wheelchair racer and a deaf couple expressing their love in signs. Next, a Levi jeans ad showed a paraplegic doing wheelies on the sidewalk with a group of friends without disabilities; a McDonald's commercial showed a crowd applauding that included a man on crutches and a child in a wheelchair; and a Plymouth Voyager ad included a man on crutches explaining the virtues of the vehicle.

Since then, a veritable flood of television commercials has shown those with various disabilities carrying out normal activities in happy settings. The most common subject is attractive, young wheelchair athletes. In early 1992, for instance, a Budweiser commercial featured a muscular athlete flat on a workout bench lifting weights as his attractive girlfriend is duly impressed. He then swings into his wheelchair, and they go down the sidewalk laughing. There is a quick cut to a wheelchair road race in which the hero is among the top finishers. In the final shot, they are celebrating in a fancy restaurant—with a glass of Bud.

The significance of the Budweiser commercial is twofold. First, of all television commercials, beer commercials are among the most expensive and the most sophisticated. To entice young Americans, only the most masculine-appearing, attractive men are shown, inevitably in a setting that implies the ultimate in enjoyment. "It doesn't get any better than this," is the way one company identifies not only its beer but the setting in which it is shown. For paraplegics to begin showing up in such advertisements implies that even with a limitation, one can still be one of the beautiful people featured in the beer commercials. Second, less than ten years after some advertisers somewhat hesitantly tried such commercials because they were concerned with the public's reaction, the response appears overwhelmingly favorable. By 1993 the roles were more frequent and more varied. Many of these commercials show disabled workers in the background, often in law offices and such high-profile places as newsrooms, carrying out routine tasks without fanfare—exactly like other workers in these offices. The message is that those with disabilities have a place on the job like all other Americans.

These ads represent a changing acceptance of those with disabilities as real people who only incidentally have a disability. Some humor has even begun to creep into the ads, a sign that disabled advocates see as healthy. For instance, one television commercial shows Ray Charles, the blind musician, being handed a Diet Coke instead of the Diet Pepsi he had asked for. In this commercial Joe Montana, the noted San Francisco Forty-Niner quarterback, is shown laughing at Charles's consternation. A few years ago, that reaction would probably not have been deemed appropriate; now such responses seem to be a healthy sign of increasing public acceptance.

The growing trend to realistic and positive portrayals of persons with disabilities in commercials as happy and hip and a normal part of society is in part a reaction to the increasing tendency to regard them as a minority group, partly brought about by the impact of the disability civil rights movement. Whether this trend continues may depend on the actions of the disabled community itself. Yet there is solid evidence that the public is accepting this new approach. In the 1980s, an ad for Target discount stores included a photograph of a child in a wheelchair in a sales circular. This occurred at the suggestion of a vice-president of marketing whose daughter was born without a left hand. With some trepidation, company officials approved the ad. The reaction of the public was enthusiastic. The company received more than 2,000 letters of praise.[29]

Although people with disabilities sometimes irreverently refer to these as "crip commercials," this new approach represents an acknowledgment that those with disabilities are part of mainstream life, living normal, enjoyable lives in interaction with mainstream people. That is the ultimate goal that disability activists see for the role of the media in changing public perceptions.

THE GOAL: SEEING PEOPLE AS PEOPLE

One of the most frequent complaints is that the media have difficulty seeing disabled people as people. "Whatever complex human psychology is responsible, the disabled are often left confined, not to wheelchairs, but to negative stereotyped labels which are both inaccurate and damaging," writes actress Lindsey Smith.[30] Disability activists would like to see an approach that neither denies nor emphasizes the disability portrayed. Certainly most of the 43 million Americans with physical or mental limitations lead lives that do not center on their disabilities. Only when those with disabilities are shown in the workplace, at cocktail parties, at fine restaurants, and everywhere else as a routine matter will attitudes change.

The comparison between the portrayals of those with disabilities and the portrayals of minority racial groups is a valid one. For the same reason that objections were made when black people were portrayed in "Step'n Fetchit" roles or constantly subservient characters, there is concern in showing those with disabilities as victims dominated by a disability.

In time, the elimination of negative stereotypes that serve to maintain society's prejudices and fears may change those attitudes and decrease reactions of fear and discomfort in interacting with persons with disabilities. Perhaps even more important, those with disabilities now have role models who more and more are shown carrying out normal lives. As the awareness has grown that they are part of a group that has been stigmatized and denied rights, they have become more vocal and visible in campaigning for changes.

The mass media have an opportunity to build a greater understanding between society and this emerging minority group that is clamoring for its rights. If they are aware of that tremendous power and responsibility they bear, the media can make a difference not only in portrayals and perceptions but eventually in the quality of life for these millions of Americans. Ultimately, considering the powerful impact of the American media abroad, that impact may have positive reverberations worldwide.

NOTES

1. See Betty Houchin Winfield, "FDR's Pictorial Image, Rules and Boundaries," *Journalism History* 5:4 (Winter 1978–1979): 110–14.

2. Libby Slate, "The Able Disabled," *Emmy Magazine* (November–December 1985): 28.

3. Robert S. Lichter, Linda S. Lichter, and Stanley Rothman, *Watching America: What Television Tells Us about Our Lives* (Englewood Cliffs, N.J.: Prentice-Hall, 1991), p. 4.

4. E. Keith Byrd, "Television Programming: A Rating of Programs' Disability," *ALABAMA Personnel and Guidance* 5:2 (1979): 19–21.

5. Michael Wood, *America in the Movies* (New York: Basic Books, 1975), p. 17.

6. Paul K. Longmore, "Screening Stereotypes: Images of Disabled People," *Social Policy* (Summer 1985): 32.

7. Douglas Biklen and Robert Bogdan, "Media Portrayals of Disabled People: A Study in Stereotypes," *Interracial Books for Children Bulletin* 4:6, 7. (1982). These authors have identified ten major media stereotypes of those with disabilities. I am indebted to them for their terminology.

8. Libby Slate, "The Able Disabled," *Emmy Magazine* (November–December 1985): 32.

9. Louisville *Courier-Journal*. (October 23, 1988): 1B.

10. Joanmarie Kalter, "Good News: The Disabled Get More Play on TV, Bad News: There Is Still Too Much Stereotyping," *TV Guide*, May 31, 1986, p. 43.

11. Paul K. Longmore, "Screening Stereotypes: Images of Disabled People," *Social Policy* (Summer 1985): 32.

12. E. Keith Byrd and Timothy R. Elliot, "Disability in Full-Length Feature Films: Frequency and Quality of Films over an 11-Year Span," *International Journal of Rehabilitation Research* 11:2 (1988): 146.

13. Erving Goffman, *Stigma: Notes on the Management of Spoiled Identity* (Englewood Cliffs, N.J.: Prentice-Hall, 1963), p. 8.

14. Mary Johnson, "Life Unworthy of Life," *The Disability Rag* (January–February 1987): 24–30.

15. Kalter, "Good News." p. 42.

16. *Newsweek*, August 25, 1980, p. 13.

17. B. D. Leonard, "Impaired View: Television Portrayals of Handicapped People" (Ph.D. dissertation, Boston University, 1978), reported in T. R. Elliot and E. K. Byrd, "Media and Disability." *Rehabilitation Literature* 43 (November–December 1982): 350.

18. Joy Donaldson, "The Visibility and Image of Handicapped People on Television," *Exceptional Children* 47:6 (March 1981): 415.

19. Ibid.

20. *Denver Post*, February 19, 1989.

21. *New York Times*, September 23, 1991.

22. Meg Cox, "Show with Retarded Actor Breaks New Ground on TV," *Wall Street Journal*, July 19, 1989, p. B-1.

23. Judith Treesberg, "That Wasn't for Deaf People!" *Disability Rag* (January–February 1987): 22–23.

24. Rebecca Bates, "The Oppressed as Oppressor," *The Disability Rag* (July–August 1990): 23.

25. *Christian Science Monitor*, March 2, 1989.

26. *Kansas City Star*, April 20–26, 1990.

27. Ibid.

28. Longmore, "Screening Stereotypes," p. 37.

29. *New York Times*, September 23, 1991.

30. Lindsey Smith, "Disability Cool: The Real Plight of the Disabled Performer." pp. 209, 266–68.

Frightening Theory

"Practically every year there's at least one movie, based on a true-life account, in which the hero or heroine overcomes some frightful physical disability. . . . Triumph-of-the-Human-Spirit movies tend not to vary any more than the bran breakfast cereal. . . . One symptom of the genre is that the actor/ actress who plays the afflicted hero-heroine does such a bravura job as to automatically earn a shot at an Oscar, and so it is with *Born on the Fourth of July* and *My Left Foot*. In the former, Tom Cruise plays a reasonably embittered veteran Ron Kovic, confined to a wheelchair. . . . In the latter, Daniel Day-Lewis plays Irish painter-writer Christy Brown, who performs in both arts with just his big left toe—the only part of him spared the crippling effect of cerebral palsy." Newhouse News Service's Richard Freedman, trotting out of the old clichéd ideas and phrases.

From *The Disability Rag* (July–August 1990)

Joan Collins to Daniel Day-Lewis: "Ugly in Every Way"

Last spring's [1990] Academy Awards marked the second year in a row the Oscar for Best Actor has gone to someone playing the part of a disabled man. Last year it went to Dustin Hoffman for his role as an autistic man in *Rain Man*. This year it went to Daniel Day-Lewis for his portrayal of Christy Brown in *My Left Foot*. Was Hollywood starting to understand disability?

In the afterglow of this spring's Oscar ceremony, during a chance Los Angeles KABC-TV interview with celebrity Joan Collins, reality quickly set in.

"I'm thrilled about Daniel Day-Lewis," Collins said. ". . . For somebody that is as good-looking as he is to make himself look as ugly as he is in every way is . . . a total art."

Ugly? "Ugly as he is in every way?"

At a press conference held to protest Collins's remark, Nancy Becker Kennedy demanded Collins apologize. Without an apology, insisted Kennedy, "the message of *My Left Foot* is lost."

Marta Russell, Director of the Media Access Office, wrote Collins that "the disability community is insulted and disappointed at your inference that the ability to take on mannerisms that make one look disabled was equated with the ability to look 'ugly.' "

But Collins never apologized. "I deeply resent your implication that I insulted the disability community by referring to Daniel Day-Lewis as ugly," she wrote back. "I assure you that in no way at all do I have any prejudice against the disabled people whatsoever, as I myself know only too well what it is like to experience the disability of a loved one. As you may or may not know, my own daughter was severely brain injured."

But having a disabled daughter, as Barbara Faye Waxman points out, does not make a parent immune from fostering prejudice about disability like Collins has done.

"Whether or not she apologizes to us," said Waxman, "as long as non-disabled people express prejudice toward us, we are going to respond."

The National Stuttering Project was able to get a public apology from Kevin Kline for poking fun at stuttering in *A Fish Called Wanda* only by hiring a fulltime consultant to go after Kline. Without the financial resources to hire someone to go after Collins for a public apology, the disability community had to settle for little more than righteous indignation this time.

From *The Disability Rag* (July–August 1990)

Television's Concept of People with Disabilities . . . Here's Lookin' at You

Ninety-eight percent of us own one. We average six hours a day in front of it. Ownership of it cuts across every economic and social level in the United States. It is a friend, a nuisance, education and entertainment. It is Television.

TV is a bonafide modern-day miracle. Through its eyes we saw a leader felled by bullets and watched man take his first steps on the moon. We were close enough to the Prince and Princess of Wales during their wedding to hear the nervous bride stumble over her new husband's name. The magic of satellite telecommunications permitted the world access to the XXIIIrd Olympiad. People from Bangor, Maine, to Hilo, Hawaii, have been able to share in common experiences, laugh at the same jokes and cry at the same emotional moments.

Fiction is the most popular televised commodity. Dramas and comedies created in the United States offer entertainment to the world. "Dallas" and "Dynasty" are as big in the United Kingdom as they are at home. "Hill Street Blues" is a favorite in Italy. "The Love Boat" has an international following. Despite diverse markets, the majority of TV productions are conceived, written and produced in one area: Los Angeles County, California.

Watchers of the Tube recognize the danger of a small society of creators. Ideas repeat themselves. A hot movie clones a TV series, a beloved character sets up shop in a spin-off show and one successful crime drama with cars trashed at every turn leads to another.

A formula used prolifically in fiction is a genre of work called the "affliction drama." Various approaches to disability and disease are a staple story idea. How does the TV treat physical difference?

Mabel: I'm deaf. Men aren't interested in a deaf wife.

Travis: That's just sympathy talking because I'm different.

Father: She's broken! She's twisted, inside out!

Doctor: Right now, Susan is stone deaf.

It is a little unfair to take these scripted lines out of context but they express the general mood used by writers to approach physical disability.

Approximately 71 percent of the fictional network programming created is beamed into our homes each week. Disability programs pop up at the average of one a week.

According to my ongoing survey of 327 different fictional "cripshows" (covering 10 years' worth of watching for these images), blindness is featured in 23 percent, making it TV's Most Popular Disability. Close behind in second place at 22 percent are people using wheelchairs. Nipping at two's (w)heels in third at 21 percent are deaf characters. Fourth-place amputees account for 10 percent of the programming. Shows about developmental disabilities, short-satire, brain-injuries, cerebral palsy or "other" make up the rest.

As with most TV characters fictionalized disabled people are depicted as being white. Few blacks are smattered across the categories, less than five Hispanics and one Asian-Pacific. Sixty-four percent of TV's disabled are male, 36 percent female.

When one views numerous cripshows, reliable images begin to appear. Blindness, as seen on TV, is accepted almost exclusively as lightlessness. Titles express that all too clearly, "Journey from Darkness," "Seven in Darkness," "Love's Dark Ride" are just a sample. Twenty-six percent of blind programs display "face-feeling": the blind person touching the faces of strangers or loved ones to "see" them. Like darkness, this "trait" appears enough to be identified as a characteristic of blind people. Nineteen percent of these shows represent blind people as having ultra-sensory perception. In the 1982 "T. J. Hooker" episode "Blind Justice," a blind witness to a murder detected Vince Romano's accent from South Philly, recognized Hooker's cologne, identified (from a sentence spoken at the hold-up) one killer as a black man from Louisiana and the other as a white man from Oklahoma. The sound of one man's shoeheels was, she assured Hooker, cowboy boots. And a smell she noted was liniment—the kind used by bodybuilders.

The 1983 "Simon and Simon" story, "I Heard It Was Murder," had the blind witness to the crime trailing the bad guys as they left the scene. She heard and smelled the getaway vehicle. Later, riding between detective brothers Rick and A. J. Simon in a pick-up truck as they passed the suspect's car, Rebecca identified the sound of the engine. "I smell the same exhaust fumes, too!"

This is not to suggest that some people, regardless of visual capacity, do *not* have heightened sensory perception. However, when 70 fictional programs about blindness are looked at as a whole, this is seen as a trend. It becomes another characteristic like "face-feeling" or "darkness."

Wheelchair users on TV are generally unemployed, sedentary in personality, lackluster and, on the whole, miserable. They often mope about sex, commonly stating to a spouse, "I can't give you that kind of love anymore." Episodes of the popular "Hotel" and the cancelled "Fantasy Island" both featured this theme in the spring of 1984. Only 5 percent of the wheelchair stories have mentioned accessibility.

Television's deaf are often uncanny lipreaders. Although experts on deafness maintain only 40 percent of English is visible on the lips and the best speech readers only get 80 percent of that, any screenwriter knows this is bunk.

Deaf people on film have lipread people through binoculars from a few flights up (*The Man Who Played God*, 1932) or "overheard" extortion 20 feet from a man in a phone booth ("The Hardy Boys," "Mystery of the Silent Scream" episode 1977). "Mannix's" "Silent Cry" episode displayed a deaf woman lipreading a man plotting his wife's murder—as he stood in a phone booth—across the street—at twilight—in the rain!

Arm amputees have a very poor screen image. They are evil, vengeful types wanting to get back at society. On "Hawaii Five-O's" "Hookman" episode, a man who lost his hands when the bomb he was holding went off in a heist sought revenge on Steve McGarrett for interrupting the robbery. He had a special pair of hooks waiting with McGarrett's name engraved on them. The hookman also used a prosthesis to nail someone in the back, causing a "transection of the spinal cord" with a "metal, heavy clublike" object, diagnosed the coroner.

Amputees have scarred their cheeks with prostheses ("Gilligan's Island"), or used the mounting base as a terminal to attach hideous implements to create all sorts of mayhem ("Chamber of Horrors," 1968, "Starsky and Hutch," 1975, "V," 1984). The dexterity illustrated by double hand amp Harold Russell in the "Trapper John, MD" 1982 "Days of Wine and Leo" episode may have been pushed to the back of the viewers' minds when he reluctantly held a woman in his arms. "Can you imagine the scar tissue my wife would develop being hugged by me?" The light statement could easily create a chill in those unfamiliar with the functions of the prosthetic hooks.

Leg amps, fortunately, do not seem to have the same criminal bent as those who have lost upper limbs.

"Until someone comes along with something different," stated a producer with whom I spoke regarding the misportrayals, "this is the way it's gonna be." *Coming Home*, the 1978 Hal Ashby film starring Jane Fonda and Jon Voight was, in the opinion of many, "something different." Yet, only five months after release of the movie that portrayed a paraplegic veteran as vital, energetic, passionate and sexual, came "Thou Shalt Not Commit Adultery." This TV picture depicted a variety of attitudes about important moral issues: when a paraplegic husband gives his wife permission to seek an affair. "You don't have to be faithful to me for the rest of your life." The man Sally has an affair with agrees. "It's just not right for one person to ask another person to give up sex for the rest of their life." A friend tells her, " . . . in the real sense, you don't have a husband. You're a widow . . . " Sally spills all to a stewardess on an airplane who dutifully reports to her coworkers. "Her husband is a paraplegic. She just cheated on him." The other stewardesses nod understandingly. "Now the guilt, huh?" asks one. "Uh-*huh*," says the first. "Now the guilt."

The film was blasted by the California Association for the Physically Handicapped and catalyzed that organization to seek legal support to protest to the Federal Communications Commission.

"Something different" happened in 1977. Citizens with disabilities sat in at the Old Federal Building in San Francisco, an action which persuaded then-secretary of the U.S. Department of Health, Education and Welfare Joseph Califano to sign the regulations implementing Section 504 of the 1974 Rehabilitation Act.

The event received national coverage. Despite the far-reaching consequences to people with disabilities, the sit-in and its issues were reflected in only one program. "All That Shatters," a 1977 episode of "Baretta," revolved around disabled protesters' seeking enforcement of their civil rights. A 1979 "James at 15" story, "Actions Speak Louder," alluded indirectly to P.L. 94-142 when a deaf teen wanted to attend James' high school. It would seem safe to say that Hollywood's creativity personnel, as a whole, had no idea what was happening with the *actual* disabled community, continuing to flood TV with the same old formula concepts.

Creativity using people familiar with disability or individuals who have limitations in creating and performing in TV drama is one solution to the proliferation of "cripshows." As with ethnic minorities, creative persons with disabilities find Hollywood a hard nut to crack, but various sources have begun to help. The Media Office Regarding Disability, run by Tari Susan Hartman in Hollywood, is helping showcase talent to industry professionals and casting directors. The office acts as a casting clearinghouse for performers with disabilities. Three hundred performers with limitations have membership in a combination of the 5 performing unions—Screen Actor's Guild, AFTRA, Equity, Screen Extras Guild and AFM Local 47; less than half a dozen members of the Writer's Guild identify themselves as having disabilities.

Writers who have physical limitations themselves created two of the most memorable stories regarding disability during the 1983–1984 television season. The "Hill Street Blues" "Midway to What?" episode was based on a story by Darryl Ray and Alan Toy. Detective Belker, on a stake-out, parks in a handicapped zone. Outside he finds an angry young man in a chair spray-painting the offending vehicle. Belker arrests "Jerry" and gets a crash course in accessibility when he discovers the bathrooms at the station weren't made for wheelchairs. In the "St. Elsewhere" "Hearing" episode, actor/writer Bob Daniels created and performed in a story about a deaf x-ray technician whose boss blames every shortcoming of his department on the fact he has to hire "*one of them*."

Positive portrayals are increasing as more people become aware of performers with disabilities and utilize the services of the Media Office. The most positive step by the networks is the use of these performers in casual "incidental roles"—roles not contingent on a limitation. For example, in a 1983 "Cagney and Lacey" episode, the man at the messenger service the female cops tapped for information was a man in a chair. More actors who themselves have disabilities are portraying the disabled characters in a drama or comedy, but are often bound by staple "affliction drama" lines. "In every show," athlete/director Kim Knaub said in 1984, "there are some things I have to say. They just won't let me change [the lines]."

Despite the increasing visibility of these performers, clear-cut, honest "featured" depictions of people with disabilities are few and far between.

Notable in recent years are two TV films. In 1979, "And Your Name Is Jonah" depicted a family who discovers their institutionalized son is not retarded, "just deaf." The introduction of a ten-year-old without language into a family ill-equipped to handle him creates havoc. The subject was explored with compassion. In 1982, "The Ordeal of Bill Carney," a quadriplegic man's actual battle to retain custody of his sons, was delivered without moralizing or tears. A writer's willingness to explore these matters and approach them realistically can result in sound, entertaining fare—which also serves to educate the public about some people they admittedly "don't know how to talk to."

TV stereotypes can be fought. Network executives can be made aware that the lack of identification of active, interesting people with disabilities is noted by the public. "Above-the-line" personnel need to understand that the barrage of "He's got nuthin' to live for" attitudes are creating solid, predictable—and false—pictures of the nation's disabled.

"No one takes TV seriously." Perhaps. But in March, 1983, NBC broadcast the well-done "Special Bulletin," a chillingly real videotaped movie about terrorists threatening to detonate a nuclear bomb. Police stations received calls from worried viewers. A man in Chicago even offered to lead a commando raid against the terrorists! This, despite 15 televised disclaimers reminding the viewers that the show was only fiction! TV *does* affect viewers.

The Corporate Affiliations Directory lists TV advertisers and can be found in any library. If a show offends or pleases you, let the "brought to you by" people know. Write to the Advertising and Promotion Department of the company. Sponsors have a lot of clout in determining what gets on the air. NBC's highly acclaimed "St. Elsewhere" averages a mediocre 50 in the national Nielsen television ratings. Still, it was renewed for the 1984–1985 season, its third. A contact at CBS Fox Studios where the show is filmed told me marketing research revealed the majority of viewers were highly educated, white-collar workers with high incomes to buy the advertised products. This convinced the sponsors to back the series despite the dismal rankings. Demographics dictated the show's survival—not its touted "high-quality."

The ranks of performers with physical limitations are growing and gaining recognition. The artistic struggle for acceptance as professionals who can play a diversity of roles not contingent on physical differences will be a long one. But their presence reminds us that people with disabilities are a viable, natural resource—and television should reflect that. Their lives and experiences offer a wealth of ideas that Hollywood would be well-advised to note to use to enhance their products. It would help break away from the old "affliction drama" perpetuation and dissolve some of those attitudinal barriers.

Maybe when we get a Clark Gable or Tom Selleck who uses a chair . . .

From *The Disability Rag* (January–February 1985)

2

Sticks and Stones: The Language of Disability

Mary Johnson

Early in 1991, the National Cristina Foundation, a group that provides computers to disabled people, announced a new term to use to refer to people we call "disabled" or "handicapped." The term, chosen from what the foundation said were over 50,000 entries in a widely publicized contest, was said to be the unanimous choice of a panel of judges that included Jonathan Latimer of Houghton Mifflin, publisher of the *American Heritage Dictionary*. *People of differing abilities* was the new term. "I hope it helps us look at what we all have in common," said B. Freer Freeman, the Arlington, Virginia, special education teacher who had come up with it.

Bruce McMahan, founder and chair of the Cristina Foundation, had provided the contest's $50,000 prize (a likely reason there were so many entries) from his own wallet, so intent was he on finally getting a word "for the abilities, not the disabilities," as he put it. A professional public relations firm ensured that the contest received wide publicity when announced in 1990. Articles appeared in scores of newspapers nationwide. "There have been a lot of attempts to deal with this linguistic shortfall, the lack of a good word," McMahan said in explaining why he underwrote such a contest. "But most of them have focused on the disabilities side and not the abilities" (*The Disability Rag*, Winter 1990, p. 14).

Shortly after the contest was announced, many disabled people publicly criticized what they considered McMahan's misplaced priorities. A number of them told the *Detroit Free Press* the prize money could be spent better, for example, on public education. Some felt another word might just "further confuse the public." McMahan, sensitive to criticism that the contest wasted money and that words to describe a group of people are not created by a contest, eventually started saying that the real purpose of the contest was "basically an attempt to stimulate debate." Still, the contest left a sour taste in the mouths of many in the disability rights movement who viewed the approach as a kind of slap in the face. They felt that a contest was no way to name a group that struggled with common discrimination and oppression. How would it look if such a contest were held to pick a new monicker for African Americans or Native Americans? Did anyone think the gay rights movement would resort to a contest to get a new term for itself? The fact that it was sponsored by a nondisabled man who seemed to have little understanding of the disability rights movement (despite having a daughter with cerebral palsy) only added to the outrage.

Terms that define any subgroup or minority with any degree of pride must arise out of that group's culture; they cannot be imposed from outside. This point may seem obvious to anyone who has had any experience with minority culture, but it was a point the instigators of the Create a New Word contest seemed unaware of. It seems to be a point most people—both within the disability rights movement and in society at large—miss when it comes to disability terminology. There seems to be little understanding as to how words that stand for a subculture and its attributes emerge and become adopted by a society.

Disability rights activists were particularly irritated by the assumption that all words used heretofore to stand for disabled people were negative. The Create a New Word contest wanted "to avoid the 'negative' at all costs," a contest brochure put out by the foundation said. "Avoid a word that is negative in any way," instructed the entry form. "The goal of this contest is to invent a new word . . . for a group of people who in the past have been described in negative or exclusionary terms. A great many people with disabilities have clearly demonstrated their ability to be productive. . . . The words we have available in the English language are not adequate to describe these people in a positive manner. . . . The new word must recognize that a person's disability acts as a guiding force in developing special skills, attitudes and understandings, bringing successful living."

In a letter to the Cristina Foundation, independent living consultant Maggie Shreve, who has been involved in disability rights issues for years, wrote:

The disability movement has struggled for some time now to eliminate the cute phrases and euphemisms which detract from what our struggle is all about—creating a sense of pride . . . *based upon having a disability*.

There is nothing negative about the word "disability." Your contest is a total waste of energy and a shameful waste of money. I know of about 50 ways that $50,000 could be better spent to assist people with disabilities gain their rightful place in our society.

Other disabled people offered cheekier remarks. "How about 'person' or 'human being?' " a reader of *The Disability Rag* suggested, only half in jest. "Heck, I'd even let them call me an 'American.' " "The best response I have heard so far to this contest is 'severely euphemized,' " wrote *The Disability Rag* reader Andrew J. Washburn of the Granite State Independent Living Foundation in New Hampshire.

The flip remarks belied a deep dissatisfaction—and one that is steadily growing—among activists in the disability rights movement that got the Americans with Disabilities Act passed in 1990. The dissatisfaction is two-fold: activists are indeed weary of many of the words and terms used to describe them and their lives, but they are equally—perhaps more—irritated at recent, to them coy, attempts to "solve" the problem by coming up with ever-more-ridiculous words and terms to try to get rid of the "negativism" of disability. It is an attempt that will not work, they insist, pointing out that language is not imposed on a culture but emanates from it. The fact that new terms keep getting coined is nothing so much as a sign that few people understand the reality of the emerging disability rights movement or its culture.

In this chapter, we will look at a number of terms that have been used in the past or are currently being used and discover what the disability rights movement has to say about them. We also will look at emerging trends as a nascent movement begins to create its own culture and develop a sense of pride and power.

A survey on disability terminology in the July–August 1987 issue of *The Disability Rag* asked readers to comment on a list of common words used to describe disabled people. In addition to the standard identifiers *handicapped* and *disabled*, the publication asked for comments on the terms *wheelchair bound* and *victim*. The editors also sought comments on the term *crippled*, as well as the newer *differently abled, handi-capable, physically challenged,* and *person with a disability*.

Responses were remarkably consistent, perhaps signaling that a common language and culture was starting to emerge within the disability rights movement, which much of the general public was unaware of. Responses gave a picture of a community almost on the point of consensus on terminology—but in a way far different than outsiders might assume.

Few who responded liked *handicapped*, though they agreed it was not too offensive—certainly not as bad as the euphemism *handi-capable*. A number of respondents noted that it was a legal term, enshrined in the 1973 Rehabilitation Act's Section 504 regulations and the Education for All Handicapped Children Act. Nevertheless, many activists dislike it because they believe it hearkens back to the term *cap in hand*, for "begging." However, this etymology of the word is dubious. The term *handicap* comes from a betting game, called "hand in cap," as early as the fourteenth century. By the end of the seventeenth century, the concept—of giving items additional value or compensation—had been extended to horse racing, where today it retains that meaning—a disadvantage imposed on a superior competitor to even chances in a competition ("Handicap," *The Atlantic*, May 1992, p. 131). It appears to have been appropriated in the earlier part of this century by well-meaning but paternalistic social workers who wanted a term to indicate what they saw as an additional burden placed on an individual who had some sort of physical or mental difference. The statement the appropriated term was supposed to make was that the individual was "handicapped" by society, the disability, or something external to the individual.

Although this term seems precisely in keeping with the disability rights movement's analysis of the situation—that the individual is okay but society has put him or her at a disadvantage—the term was nonetheless rejected when disabled people began wresting the power of the programs that controlled their lives from social workers and began to run their own programs. This was the time when the independent living movement was starting in California, and a number of disability activists instrumental in starting independent living programs began to refer to themselves as "consumers." *Handicapped* was disliked if for no other reason that it was a term imposed on them by agencies. They rejected it and chose instead a heretofore medical term—*disabled*—using the somewhat tortuous reasoning that *disabled* may be what they were considered clinically, but this term, at least, unlike *handicapped*, did not mark them as people who could not function in society. They proclaimed that they were not, in fact, "handicapped." One could argue precisely the opposite, of course—that oppression, not one's physical condition, "handicaps" one.

Until quite recently, the principal debate over terminology within the movement was whether the term of choice was to be *handicapped* or disabled. Today that argument has been all but won. For purely political reasons, *disabled* and *disability* became the terms of choice; a number of those who were seen as leaders in the movement said that *disabled* was better than *handicapped*. The reasons they conjured up to validate this were of less importance than the fact that those who were decreeing it were perceived to be leaders.

In this, the disability rights movement is no different from any other group; this is precisely how the nomenclature of any minority group gets decided on. Although each term has its supporters who come up with rationales for the term's being the "best" one, the real truth is that it has to do with politics and power within the minority. That is why the issue of whether a term is "negative" is really not germane to which word will define a group, and has not had much effect with the disability rights movement, either.

"DISABLED" VERSUS "PERSON WITH A DISABILITY"

Substantiating what was occurring in the disability rights movement, respondents to *The Disability Rag*'s language survey selected *disabled* over *hand-*

icapped as their term of choice by a fairly wide margin. This was to be expected and not surprising to observers of the rights movement. There was not much rationale offered by respondents for their choice. "It just seems more contemporary," one respondent noted. This reader had honed in on the precise point: today people who are "in" simply use *disabled*, and that's that.

Once the movement had keyed in on *disability* rather than *handicap*, a more sophisticated debate ensued. Political correctness advocates decreed that the correct term to use was not *the disabled* or even *disabled person* but *person with a disability*. Though few can argue with the rationale behind the term—putting the person first is something everybody thinks is morally correct—word mavens remain uncomfortable with the fact that the result is awkward on the page and on the tongue. Corroborating this, a number of respondents to *The Rag*'s survey noted that *person with a disability* was better than *disabled person* in that it "put the person first." They knew the rhetoric surrounding the term. Nobody had anything bad to say about *person with a disability* politically, but a number of respondents were quick to pick up on the term's shortcomings.

"It's the best of a not-so-great list of possibilities," acknowledged Richard Skaff of San Francisco. Someone else called it "forced"; to another it was "awkward." "Technical," said Jim Parrish of Miami. "Politically correct but clumsy," said yet another respondent. "Too long," charged another. "Windy and overly sensitive" was the opinion of James P. Sullivan of Chicago. Lisa Coyne of Sacramento noted that it is "hard to use in long sentences." And Barbara Duncan of New York pointed out, "Journalists will never use it consistently—due to length."

Anthony Tusler, head of Sonoma State University's Disabilities Resource Center, dealt with the difference eloquently when he explained a transition he had gone through personally:

For the world at large, I called myself a "person with a disability." Irv Zola [Irving K. Zola, a professor of sociology at Brandeis University and an editor of *Disability Studies Quarterly*] has said that the significance is more grammatical than the word choice. He's right. It was a liberating day when I identified myself as a person with a disability. I felt I was reclaiming my personhood from a society that treated me as "less than" solely on how I walked. That was almost 10 years ago.

It is now 1988 and I am struck by how [Dr.] Paul Longmore [a historian and expert on disability culture] calls us. He says things like, "I'm disabled," "my disabled brothers and sisters," and "the non-disabled."

"No, no, no," I think. "We're 'people with disabilities.' Didn't we solve that years ago?" But, as I think about it, listen to the rationale, and discuss the rationale, I find merit in this seemingly regressive phrase.

Here's how I see it. I wish to be recognized, by the world, as a "person with a disability." But I am proud to be "a disabled person." I am proud, now, to be seen as "disabled" first and foremost. I am proud to have persevered, to have triumphed, transcended, and learned with the help of my brothers and sisters who are "disabled."

I have long felt that we need to find a phrase and rubric that matches "black is beautiful." Defining myself as a "person with a disability" helped to free me but it didn't resonate. Being a "disabled person" does. (*The Disability Rag*, September–October 1990, p. 32)

What Tusler has gotten in touch with in himself is disability pride, something new that has emerged among disability rights activists. Because it is so new a phenomenon in the movement, its real significance in relation to terminology has yet to be felt, but already its presence can be noted. It is at the basis for Maggie Shreve's anger at the Cristina Foundation's daring to assume that the terms that define disabled people are, ipso facto, negative. It is also the basis for the rights movement's irritation at—and frustration over—the euphemisms that continue to crop up and gain misguided popularity with the public at large who, say activists, have no clue as to why the seemingly positive terms are so anathema to rights activists.

THE NEW EUPHEMISMS

In recent years, there has been an attempt to generate "positive" terms. What none of the generators seem to have caught onto is that the reason a term identifying a disabled person is negative has nothing at all to do with the word and everything to do with the existence of oppression and prejudice against a group of people who, no matter what they are called, are believed to have dismal existences. The reality seems negative; any word will take on that reality until the reality itself changes—and then any word will do fine as an identifier. The clearest example is *black*, which used to be so negative that to call an African-American *black* was "fightin' words." Many minorities, when they perceive their own internal power, adopt a once-negative word as their word of choice; this is starting to happen in the disability rights movement as well. People who do not know this, though, continue to come up with euphemisms.

"Physically Challenged"

Perhaps the quickest of the new euphemisms to catch on is *physically challenged*, which continues to gain popularity. One of the nation's largest dailies in the fall of 1991 reported that "more mentally and physically challenged people are showing up on the small screen" (*Toledo Blade*, September 29, 1991). A little later, the same term popped up in the paper's report of a speech. A year earlier, a story in the *Washington Post* reported one disabled person saying that "my challenge is getting up steps." "Challenges," the story went on to note, "can be as basic as bending down to reach electrical outlets" (*Washington Post*, November 15, 1990). A recent Harris poll on public attitudes toward the disabled used *challenge* in this way, too: "The public recognizes that . . . disabled people face many more challenges than the rest of the population" (*The Disability Rag,* January–February 1992). Some newspapers seem to be starting to use the term routinely.

Most of the activist segments of the disability rights movement disdain the term. Brochures put out by many groups pan it. The widely distributed *Guidelines for Reporting and Writing about People with Disabilities,* published by the Research and Training Center on Independent Living at the University of Kansas, called it "condescending." It "reinforces the idea that disabilities cannot be dealt with upfront." Yet other groups think it's fine, including the group that named itself the New York State Parks Games for the Physically Challenged.

"Until you've tried to make it your own responsibility to get a job, only to find you can't get in the company's front door because of their steps and your quadriplegia, you may not understand why 'challenge' is no good as a description of what we face," said an unsigned article in *The Disability Rag* in 1983. In its January 1992 issue, *The Rag* discussed *physically challenged* again:

Some suspect that the term "challenged" has gained in popularity because it appears more "positive." Another way of phrasing this would be to say that it gives society a word that removes the concept of discrimination from the picture. One can maintain that the term "physically challenged" attempts to conceal the crucial fact that the reason physically disabled people can't do lots of things is not because they're lazy, or because they won't accept a "challenge" but because many things are simply beyond our control—like barriers. The person who won't accept a "challenge" is refusing a chance for heroism, and this, too, plays into the myth of the disabled person as being responsible, somehow, for surmounting the barriers, individually. People who favor "physically challenged" can be said to be making the statement that barriers—and, by extension, discrimination—are not *problems* for them. They're *challenges.*

They want those barriers, by golly, they seem to be saying—because by overcoming them we'll become better persons! Stronger. More courageous. Etc. After all, isn't that what *challenges* are for?

Perhaps those who favor the term "physically challenged" are unaware of this message. But that message can be seen in a comment David Braddock, director of the University of Illinois' Affiliated Program in Developmental Disabilities, made to a syndicated health columnist recently that "many children with disabilities . . . are more mature and more able to sustain strong friendships because of the uncommon *challenges* they have faced" [italics ours].

Until a person has had to make it their responsibility to get downtown—only to discover there are no buses with lifts running on that route—he or she may not fully comprehend that it isn't a personal "challenge" they're up against, but a system resistant to change. A challenge is something one solves by oneself. The term conjures up lone mountain climbers, trekkers across the frozen wastes, the woman sailing alone across the Atlantic. Many people who like to refer to disabled people as being "challenged" by their disabilities wouldn't think twice about telling us that, when we can't get in that restaurant door or can't nail down that job interview, we are merely facing another "personal challenge"—ours to overcome if we're person enough to do it. The implicit message: that disability is really just a self-actualization test, architectural barriers and discrimination conveniently there for us to work out our own personal enlightenment through. As a philosophy for a rights movement, this sucks.

When are we ever going to believe, in our hearts, that our problems are not "challenges" we have been assigned by some new-age buddha as our personal-growth karma, but failings of a society that we personally have done nothing to cause (except to remind those in power of their own mortality, something they heartily do not want to be reminded of). Calling ourselves "physically challenged" shows we buy into that up-by-your-bootstraps crap that wars against the fight for common justice. Disabled people, like all oppressed minorities, have been handed that bill of goods since time immemorial. We ought to wise up.

Physically challenged came in for a solid drubbing by *The Disability Rag* readers in its survey. Some called the term an "insulting trivialization" of disability. It "robs us of the right to be mad as hell when confronted with injustice," wrote Julie Osborn. "Stairs don't 'challenge' me, they infuriate me," said Jack Prial. Besides, Jeanette Seitz of Bluff City, Tennessee, pointed out, " 'Physically challenged' is too hard to say." Many shared the sentiments of Arthur Campbell of Louisville, who merely considered the term silly. Campbell had the same criticism of the term *handi-capable*. To Mary McKnew of Olympia, Washington, *handi-capable* sounds like "a kitchen utensil." Maybe you "get one at the Tru-Value Hardware," quipped Bill Henderson of Dorchester, Massachusetts.

The late Jim Neubacher, who wrote the *Detroit Free Press*'s "Disabled in Detroit" column, thought words like *physically challenged* and *handi-capable* too "Californiaish." They tried to "prettify" disability, said Ginger Lane of Highland Park, Illinois. "Who are we kidding?" asked Rose Wilson of Illinois. "I think their purpose is to distance the truth and make non-crips feel more comfortable," said Cheryl Wade. Unfortunately, added Lucy Helm, they were "too often used by people trying too hard to do the right thing."

Differently-abled was among the cutesy terms *The Disability Rag* readers wanted banished. "Why not be real without being labelly?" asked Moira Mumma of Pennsylvania. Vanessa Tompsett of South Yorkshire, England, insisted they were "stupid Americanisms—trying to avoid saying 'disability.' " "Why? What for? Is it something to be ashamed of?" she asked.

Complaints about *physically challenged*, *differently-abled*, and other new terms generally center on the fact that such terms trivialize the disability experience. That is particularly true of the term *inconvenienced*, which *The Disability Rag* reader/activists called a "masterpiece of understatement" and "laughable in its inadequacy." It reminded reader Barbara Devore "of a hangnail." Barbara Aiello, founder of the "Kids on the Block" puppet program, which teaches about disabilities, wrote, "If the public sees a person with a disability as merely 'inconvenienced' when she/he can't get into stores, a college dorm, a school or a bank, then they will lose sight quickly of the necessity of basic civil rights for persons with disabilities." "Most disabilities deserve more serious language than a word used for a late plane or poor restaurant service," David Gerber complained. Steve Brown had the same criticism of *physically challenged:* It "discounts the deprivation of rights," as he put it. Michigan's legally correct *handicapper* has the same effect on many disabled people.

"Special"

Many disability rights activists today are challenging the use of the word *special* to refer to what they say really means "segregated." John R. Woodward wrote in the November–December 1991 *The Disability Rag* that *special* "implies differentness and apartness"; "it's the label [we put] on segregated programs, . . . a euphemism, a word introduced by do-gooders to sugar-coat their control of our lives." Woodward reiterated the movement's complaint about trivialization: " 'Special' infantilizes and trivializes the identity of a disabled person," he wrote. "If you are disabled, you are not 'special'; you are disadvantaged and oppressed."

Woodward points out a key problem with such euphemisms: by sugar-coating the problem, disabled peoples' oppression can continue to be denied. That, say a host of critics, is the real problem with such "invented" terminology. "We need to deny there's anything special about being disabled, so we can stop getting 'special treatment' instead of justice," Woodward wrote. To illustrate this point, Woodward, writing in the May–June 1992 issue of *The Disability Rag,* told of an experience he had had at a town meeting at which he confronted a local school official about problems:

When my turn came to join in the discussion, I asked [a member of our school board], "When are you going to stop busing Southside students up to the Tharpe Street area?"

She looked puzzled. "Oh, we don't do that."

"Yes you do," I told her. "Dozens of Southside kids are bused up. . . . I've met lots of them."

"No, sir, you are mistaken," she persisted.

I looked at her sadly. "You don't even know the students I'm talking about," I said.

"Well, perhaps you could tell me," she snapped.

"Any student who uses a wheelchair is bused . . . ," I said.

"Ah, I see!" she said, relieved. "But that's not *busing.* They just go to Tharpe Street [School] because that's where the physical therapists are.

Woodward's point is that

the trouble is, we call it "mainstreaming." We've had "mainstreaming" for 17 years and most disabled kids still aren't educated in their neighborhood schools alongside their nondisabled peers.... If we'd called it "integration" back in 1975, at least people would have understood what we meant....

So the next time you get into an argument about the use of the word "disabled" instead of "handicapped" or the terms "wheelchair bound" vs. "wheelchair user," and the person you're arguing with tells you it's "just a matter of semantics," tell them about "mainstreaming" and "integration." Let them know what a difference a word makes. Tell them that "mainstreaming" has set us back a decade or more. And ask them how far they think they'd get swimming against the "mainstream."

CHANGING THE WORDS IN THE NEWS

In 1987, the Associated Press style book, one of the most widely used in the news profession, for the first time listed a new entry under "Handicapped." The entry read, in part, "Do not describe an individual as *disabled* or *handicapped* unless it is clearly pertinent to the story" (*The Associated Press Stylebook and Libel Manual*, Chris French, ed., New York: The Associated Press, 1987). The term *handicap*, it said, should be avoided in favor of *disability*. The entry also told reporters and editors not to use *wheelchair bound* or "variations" (the most common being *confined to a wheelchair*).

Getting the terms *wheelchair bound* and *confined to a wheelchair* out of the language has proved a formidable task. Michael Jones, head of the effort at the Research and Training Center for Independent Living at the University of Kansas (R&T Center) in the mid-1980s, contacted Chris French, editor of the AP style book, to get the ball rolling. French was eventually persuaded that the argument made sense.

As many disability language mavens point out in letters to the editor, the terms *wheelchair bound* and *confined to a wheelchair* are inaccurate, if nothing else. "Wheelchairs liberate us, they don't confine us" is a popular rejoinder of activists. Others point out that the terms are trite and clichéd and that replacing them with *wheelchair user* is both more accurate and shorter. Many of these watchdogs so dislike the terms that they have taken to mailing offending reporters bookmarks that show cartoon characters chained into wheelchairs, underscoring the ridiculousness of the term's meaning.

The effort to get an AP style book entry discussing disability terminology was but one of a number of coordinated or individual efforts that have been tried by people in the disability rights movement to change the way reporters and editors write about disability issues. Few of these efforts have focused on discussing actual coverage of disability and disability rights issues (perhaps because this seems a fairly difficult task). Most have attempted to change terms.

As a result, many groups have issued lists of "appropriate" terminology to use when writing about disability. The R&T Center's brochure, *Reporting and Writing About Persons with Disabilities*, is probably the most widely distributed of these materials, with a reported 50,000 copies disseminated annually. The National Easter Seal Society has produced a set of guidelines (*Portraying People with Disabilities in the Media*); disability syndicated columnist Dianne Piastro collaborated with disability scholar Dr. Paul Longmore on one ("Unhandicapping Our Language," Los Angeles: Criptography, Inc., 1988); even a disabilities committee of the American Society of Newspaper Editors has come up with a terminology brochure for its members (which was published in the December 1990 *ASNE Bulletin*), drawing heavily on these other published brochures.

Critics of these efforts find in all of them a bent toward an effort to please many divergent groups. The editor of the R&T Center guidelines, Susan Elkin, pointed out when producing a revised edition that such a task was made doubly difficult by internal disagreement—something to be expected in such a diverse movement that was still in its infancy ideologically and politically. Elkin found some groups insisting that she tell editors to use *blind*, whereas others petitioned her to avoid *blind* at all costs in favor of *visually impaired*. There is a political battle over *deaf* versus *Deaf* too: Elkin wisely reported it and explained the difference (*Deaf* is used by deaf individuals who see deafness as a cultural distinction; most of these are American Sign Language users) and let editors make the final judgment (*The Disability Rag*, July–August 1987, p. 17).

CONSENSUS

There is little wonder that people bristle at such efforts to impose political correctness on a reality that contains little of it. On the other hand, certain changes have occurred, and consensus has emerged among those in the disability rights movement who are sensitive to the effects of language. Almost all of these people are trying to eradicate *wheelchair bound* and *victim*.

These efforts have had some effect. "People here would say 'confined to a wheelchair' is a phrase out of the past, and is a stereotype—it's a cliché," Dick Johnson, assistant city editor of the *Kansas City Star* told *The Disability Rag* in 1987 (March–April), after a disability rights group in Kansas City had worked for a number of months with reporters and editors about problems with terminology like this. "I think if anyone on our copy desk came across a phrase like 'confined to a wheelchair,' they'd change it."

Johnson's lesson is one not all newspaper editors have learned. Though many reporters who have covered disability issues have been confronted by their sources about using the terms and now understand and seem to agree that they are to be avoided, their copy editors still reinsert the term or use them in captions and headlines. Understanding has not penetrated very far.

Adding to the frustration is the existence of those who continue to refer to themselves as "wheelchair bound" and "confined to a wheelchair," including some fairly influential writers and columnists who use wheelchairs. Because the disability rights movement has not devoted more than scattershot efforts at eradicating these terms, they continue to plague news and feature accounts of disability issues.

It may be that people who fight for better coverage of AIDS issues and of people with AIDS, being more activist and better organized, have had more success with *victim*. *Victim*, like *afflicted*, serves no real purpose in writing about people with disabilities other than to add color and drama. A number of AIDS activists have pointed out that AIDS is not a sentient entity with a will and therefore does not have "victims" in the same way a rapist or murderer has "victims"—and that using the term *AIDS victim* perpetuates that myth of a volitional monster rather than a disease. This is a point the disability rights movement was making in the mid-1980s about all disabilities. "Diseases aren't rational; they don't have a will. They don't seek out people to harm in the way a rapist seeks out someone to overpower," wrote Anne Peters in the March–April 1987 issue of *The Disability Rag,* in an article entitled "Victim's Baggage."

Editors do not see anything wrong with using *victim*, Peters pointed out; they argue with those who want the word banned that "it's accurate." Peters pointed out that *victim*, when used to refer to someone who has multiple sclerosis, AIDS, or polio, is not accurate at all, but that it is in fact being used symbolically. *Victim* is a metaphor with emotional baggage that editors covet, she wrote:

The phrase "John Doe, a victim of multiple sclerosis" *does* carry a different flavor than, "John Doe, who has multiple sclerosis." The one has "emotional baggage."

What's in that baggage? Helplessness. Powerlessness. Dependency. A need to be "saved" . . . from . . . the diseases they're "victims" of. [The media resist abandoning *victim* because the term] really describes . . . their perception of us. The word's emotional overtones are, in their eyes, right on target. They believe we *are* victims— helpless, dependent; our victimizer a disease or bodily imperfection. . . .

The phrase "victim of multiple sclerosis" puts the blame on the wrong party, obscuring the argument that solution lies in social changes for access and rights more than in cure.

METAPHORS OF OUR TIMES

When *victim* is used to refer to someone with a disability, it is actually being used as a metaphor. That is true of other words as well. Common disability words have been appropriated for use as metaphors in a way that no other minority group would tolerate. This common metaphoric use of terms is an enormous hurdle to developing a strong image of people with disabilities. While groups raise justified complaints about terms like *victim* and *afflicted*, the metaphoric use of *blind*, *crippled*, and *paralyzed* to refer to everything from bigotry to bad economic times has avoided scrutiny by the disability rights movement almost altogether until quite recently.

Use of disability terms as metaphors is rampant. "Strike by Blacks Paralyzes South Africa," read the *New York Times* on November 5, 1991. "Soviet Pledge on Cuba Leaves U.S. Paralyzed," said the *Times* on September 13, 1991. "Czech Book Industry Paralyzed by Freedom," it announced on February 17, 1991. "A new turn in the Serb-Croat conflict paralyzes federal rule," wrote a *New York Times* editor in the May 16, 1991, issue. The *Times* uses *paralyzed* in this manner regularly, as does every other news publication. "We've been paralyzed by our politeness," Bishop William Frey, president of Pennsylvania's Trinity Episcopal School for Ministry, told *Time* magazine on February 18, 1991, referring to a church debate. These were only a few references noted in a brief period of time.

Crippling also is used as a metaphor: from the *New York Times*, "Overcoming a Crippling Fear of School" (September 4, 1991) and "Lawmakers Deal a Crippling Blow to the B-2 Bomber" (November 1, 1991); from the *Washington Post*, "Lean Times Cripple Agencies" (January 28, 1991); from the *Detroit Free Press*, "Doctors say care facilities inside Iraq are crippled" (March 16, 1991); and from the *Louisville Courier Journal*, "Crippled Generations" (April 4, 1991). Ten days later, the *Times Herald Record* of Middletown, New York, told readers that a "railroad strike threatens to cripple country."

This is a metaphoric use of *cripple*, to mean "washed up," or "injured." Headline writers are fond of *crippled*. They use it even when the word is not in the story at all and use it metaphorically. "Crippled Airliner Lands," wrote a suburban weekly; "Crippled Tanker Spills Oil" is from the *New York Times*.

Of all the appropriated metaphors, none is used more readily than *blind* to signify something bad. In 1991, we got: "In Financial Scandals, Is Blind Greed Meeting Sightless Watchdogs?" (*New York Times*, September 15) and "Some fear blind pacifism has replaced militarism" (*New York Times*, January 26). The *New York Times*'s Andrew Malcolm on March 4, 1991, wrote of "society's blindness to abuse." Another *New York Times* reporter referred to March 30 to "the legal concept of 'willful blindness.' " The *New York Times*'s Anna Quindlen, in a November 9, 1991, column on Magic Johnson and AIDS, showed exactly how blindness is used for this purpose; she referred to "the horrible *bigotry and blindness* [italics ours] that has accompanied the [AIDS] epidemic." She was using *blindness* metaphorically, to mean "refusal to face facts." In another newspaper, another Quindlen column was headlined, "In Time of Plague, Some Parents Remain Blind to Reality." The *Detroit Free Press* headlined Mitch Albom's March 16, 1991, sports column, "Blind Ambition Wins Iditarod."

Few disability groups seem particularly bothered by such metaphors. The National Federation of the Blind reprinted a December 10, 1990, *People* magazine story headlined, "Armed with a White Cane, Sightless Robert Toye Tapped His Way to the Teller and Robbed Seventeen Banks Blind" and raised no complaint about this headline.

"Blind justice" and "color-blind society" may have positive connotations.

But what about "blind greed"? "blind ambition"? "blind pacifism?" "blind to reality?" "willful blindness"? All of these phrases mean something bad. The "bad" connotation comes from being paired with the word *blind*.

Deaf is also used frequently in headlines and stories: "deaf to her pleas"; "turning a deaf ear"; and *Time* magazine's "Dialogue of the Deaf" are only a few examples.

Blind, deaf, paralyzed, and *crippled* are words that in real life describe real people, who are trying against huge cultural odds to maintain dignity in a society that uniformly denigrates them to worse than second-class status. Yet these same identifiers—*blind, deaf, paralyzed,* and *crippled*—are used in a negative sense in the metaphoric world of words. In that metaphoric world, they carry negative messages all their own, so much so that they serve as today's most common synonyms for *incapable* and *unable*.

The belief persists that the words themselves are negative, rather than the concepts attached to them, because of our beliefs about the reality of the disability experience, which we are convinced is solely negative. Because the words assigned by culture to signal disability have been appropriated by pundits and artists to mean "bad," the words themselves have come to signify something bad. They work powerfully as metaphors because they make a connection with the reality of what society believes about a person who is blind, deaf, paralyzed, or crippled.

The more that the disability rights movement reclaims those words and breathes dignity back into them, the less need there will be for new words. Many disability activists make the point that words like *cripple, blind,* and *deaf* (with a capital D when referring to the cultural concept of Deafness) describe human conditions well and that it is those who have appropriated them for metaphoric purposes that have made them negative. They point to other words that can do the double duty writers have been requiring of *blind, paralyzed,* and *crippled.* Instead of *paralyzed, frozen, stuck, stalled,* or *stopped* can be pressed into service. Instead of using *crippled,* they can use *broken* (which is what they are trying to say anyway). In many places, there is no need for any word to replace the gratuitous use of *blind.* Any effort to make this point publicly is still in its infancy, and it may be a long time before these words will be reclaimed by disability activists and given power.

THE PERSISTENCE OF THE NEGATIVE

Retarded and *mentally retarded* are intensely disliked by many people who have been labeled as such. Some of them insist they prefer *people with mental retardation,* stressing the *people* first. The stress on "people first" is so important to many activists in this arm of the disability rights movement that they started an organization, People First, that has chapters in most states. "Label jars, not people" is a poster many of its members are very fond of.

Trying mightily to avoid *retarded,* nondisabled advisers have helped spawn what can only be considered euphemistic substitutes. The newest of these is the term *self-advocate,* which is rapidly replacing the catchall *developmentally disabled* (person, or *person with developmental disabilities),* a bureaucratic word meant to identify people who became disabled during their developmental years (before age twenty-two). It was enshrined when the Developmental Disabilities Act was passed. Although anyone who had acquired a disability at birth or in youth that affected development was in fact developmentally disabled, in practice the term came to be synonymous with *mentally retarded,* and because it signified something people felt was a stigma, it, too, became a stigmatized word. The same fate will probably befall the term *self-advocate.* In line with the current throw-out-*retarded* fervor, the former Association for Retarded Citizens changed its name recently to The Arc (no acronym).

These recent developments in response to the dislike of *retarded* may be read as a kind of cautionary tale. Words like *retarded* and *crippled* (or *blind* and *deaf)* become words to be reviled because that which they stand for is reviled by society. When people like Bruce McMahan deplore the lack of "positive words," they fail to recognize that the words convey only what society loads them with. They carry whatever current baggage disability carries in society. Until the perception of disability changes, any word saddled with the meaning of disability—*retarded* or *crippled* or *deaf*—eventually will acquire a stigma of its own. The reason much of society thinks *physically challenged* and *differently abled* are positive is that they have not been around long enough to soak up the negative connotations of *crippled.* People who used to be called "retarded" and are now called "developmentally disabled" have picked this point up fairly quickly on an emotional level; they are beginning to dislike *developmentally disabled* as much as they dislike *retarded.*

If this is the case, is there any solution? The solution is the same one other oppressed groups have found: reclaim the negative and use it with pride. The pride, and the power, makes the word a proud one. That is what happened with *black,* and it is happening to those who are now using *queer* with pride.

THE FUTURE OF DISABILITY TERMINOLOGY

A number of those responding to *The Disability Rag'*s language survey wrote that they wished people would quit coming up with new terms. "We don't need any more words!" Penelope Whitesall of Pennsylvania insisted. Some concurred with Walter Kiver of Acton, Massachusetts, who felt that "either 'handicapped' or 'disabled' says it like it is—let's not play around with other words." There are words that avoid euphemism and seem to be contenders for what disabled people in the movement want to be called. One is *survivor.*

"Survivor"

Survivor has found favor with many disabled people. People who have had cancer have adopted it almost exclusively. Many disabled people today refer to themselves as "polio survivors" or "spinal cord injury survivors."

The word "survivor" is uniquely suited to . . . people who survive accidents, diseases, who survive what would have been almost certain death just a few short decades ago. . . . No other word could unite us quite as clearly as the word "survivor."

It finds common bonds among so many different people, in so many different physical conditions. For it does not deal with the state of our bodies at all but with a political reality: survivorship. . . . We are not alike in our physical conditions—as we know too when looking for coalition. But we are alike in experiencing oppression—an oppression focused on the status our bodies signal to our oppressors. We are different because of our bodies; but for that reason we are also alike. And we are all oppressed the same way, for the same reason our bodies are different, therefore we are oppressed the same way, for the same reason: our bodies are different—therefore we are not normal. This one fact unites us. Our status throughout our oppression is as survivors.

Attempts have been made before to unite us with a word that recognizes the social reality of our status. That's how "handicapped" was born. It attempted to unite us by stating that we were all "handicapped" (or put at a disadvantage) by society. But it soon acquired a negative ring to it: it made us sound like so many social service cases. And the fact that it was an adjective—"handicapped"—didn't help things, either: "Handicapped" what? That has always been a problem. The solution was always to call us "THE handicapped"—something that grates on our ears and means, really, nothing at all.

"Disabled" was our own way of fighting this label. But "disabled" is in many ways even worse: it is, itself, a negative word. True, we can look to the success of "Black," which was also originally a pejorative term. But black, as a word, is neither negative nor positive. It's only a color. True, in white culture, "Black" has been used to convey evil, but that meaning was thrust upon the word; it was not inherent in the word itself. But you cannot get away from the fact that "disable" means "not able." There is no other meaning.

"Survivor" is a real word. It is not negative; it always conveys a sense of wholeness, of skill in just those ways we have had to be skillful. And it defines us both socially and politically within the framework we have had to live all these years. We have survived medically, morally, politically and economically. Those of us who are involved in the struggle to end our oppression are, simply, survivors.

There is no better word to define the reality that belongs uniquely to us. We persist in enduring continuous medical humiliation, lack of privacy, lack of respect, constant tooling around on our bodies; blithe promises of cure, prohibitively expensive devices for moving about, confinement in nursing homes, confinement in back rooms, dependence on the mercy and good will of people who take care of us (because we are not allowed the technology to take care of ourselves), deplorable economic conditions, life on SSI [supplemental security income], blockage from buildings. And yet we continue to work for change. What are we if not survivors?

There has been a move recently to coin "cute" words: "handicappers," "exceptional" and "physically challenged" come to mind. What are we trying to do? The intention is good: we're looking for a way to make it all sound so positive. But it ends up sounding like pablum.

It is no good to invent an identity. If we do not choose an identity freely, it has no meaning for us. We will still be defined by the oppressors. And how can we build a pride if we are defined by our oppressor, if our existence is plotted by our oppressors?

Until we define our existence, in a word we ourselves have chosen, we will never be free. (S. L. Rosen, "I call myself 'Survivor,' " *The Disability Rag*, May 1983, p. 8)

"Cripple"

The word to watch, though, is *cripple*. It may have an astounding future. By a wide margin, respondents to *The Disability Rag*'s poll panned *crippled*. "Medieval," said Alice Sporar of Ohio. "The 'nigger' of naming," Alice Levenson of Springfield, Massachusetts, called it. Others complained it was "loaded with old baggage" and "politically passé."

Yet those on the disability cultural avant-garde make strong cases for its use. To Mark O'Brien of Berkeley, it "packs more punch." Performance artist Cheryl Wade said, "It's visual, strong—feels like a good, gnarled fist." *Gimp* has much the same élan among the avant-garde. Penny Gillett of Fresno thinks of *gimp* as "a cool disabled person." Both are trendy words only among the cognoscenti, however. Like *queer*, it can be used only by those in the know; an outsider calling a disabled person a "cripple" still "shows ignorance and insensitivity," according to Robert Mauro of Levittown, New York. It is "for use only among *us!*" stressed Kim Christensen of New Rochelle, New York. "Otherwise it's very offensive!"

Barry Corbet of Golden, Colorado, editor of *Spinal Network* magazine, said that *crippled* was "okay when used by a crip." (*Crip* is an even trendier term.) Wade added, "Crips can call themselves anything they want to." Jack Prial of Baltimore agreed: "It's for use by disabled persons only—as in 'Yo, Crip!' " he said. Susan Nussbaum of Chicago agreed with Prial. Both words were good only "if used in a militant manner." "I learned to use 'gimp' in a militant way in college," said Juliet Duncanson of Indianapolis, noting that she enjoyed "the discomfort it causes."

For Wade, *cripple* was "a personal identity," though she admitted it was an accurate term only for some people. One of the acknowledged problems with the word, even among its adherents, is that it does not apply to everyone. *Disabled* has evolved to serve that purpose. But "it's boring," said Wade. "We need a generic term we can apply to ourselves as a group, a community and a culture."

Ann Landers has always used *cripple*. She refers to a disabled child as "a crippled child" (1981) and tells readers about "a woman who is an emotional cripple." As a window into society, Ann Landers's column provides insight into the way society still uses *cripple*—a way that disability activists detest. People who write to Ann Landers use *cripple*. Some of them do not know another word to use. "Chicago Closet Case" wrote that people with panic attacks were "paralyzed by this crippling condition." She saw nothing wrong with using *paralyzed* in this way. A reader in 1981 wrote that as a youngster she was embarrassed by her father. "He is crippled," she wrote. In 1984 a reader wrote, "We have three crippled children."

Crippled is "in and of itself not a terrible term," writes Barbara Aiello in *The Disability Rag*, "but the use made of it over the years leads me to choose not to use the word. I am reminded of the 'Give to Crippled Children' posters I saw growing up."

In 1985, Anthony Tusler, Director of the Disability Resource Center at Sonoma State University, wrote in his office's newsletter, "Before I came to the disability rights movement I facetiously called myself a cripple. I guess I figured that if I was gutsy enough to call myself a cripple then I wouldn't be one. In retrospect, it didn't add to my self esteem. . . . When I first became exposed to the movement I found that not only were my newfound peers defining what our reality was to us, but that we called ourselves 'people with disabilities' when talking to the world and 'crips' amongst ourselves."

CONCLUSION

While the issue of what one is to be called rages within the disability rights community, the general public is generally unaware of any difference between *handicapped, disabled,* and *crippled.* Editors still do not understand why disabled people get angry at *victim* and *confined to a wheelchair.* This is a debate within a tiny, closed community of activists in a civil rights and cultural movement most of the nation knows little about. Most people whom the Americans with Disabilities Act defines as having disabilities would themselves feel no compunction about using the words interchangeably.

The effort to reform words and terms and to create new ones arises from a basic misunderstanding about how words develop in a culture. The disability movement has been particularly vulnerable to this because there is no strong internal culture to protect against it or to develop a sense of its own identity, style, and name. That, however, is coming from the avant-garde of the disability movement. Those who make up this group are a tiny number of people; they and their thinking are largely isolated and unknown to society at large. Until their understanding of disability and the disability experience are better known, little will change. The disability rights movement has a long way to go in getting a consistent terminology accepted by the media and the greater society.

Watt, Did He Say?

Everyone knew Interior Secretary James Watt had done it again.* People were furious. But one group was strangely silent: us.

We should have raised hell, but we didn't.

The man Watt referred to with the slur didn't seem to understand that it was a slur. He was concerned about Watt's reference to Jews.

Senator Robert Dole was upset, but the public never heard him deplore the word "cripple." We *should* have heard him deplore it. We *should* have heard him tell this nation that the word "cripple" is as unacceptable as "nigger." But we didn't hear that.

Senator John East, who uses a wheelchair, didn't see anything wrong with the remark at all.

Where were the national disability groups that should have been calling for an apology for the handicappist slur "crippled"? Silent.

"It's not that important," some would say. But think of it this way:

If Watt had said, "A nigger," do you think blacks would have raised a cry?

If Watt had said, "girl," do you think leaders of the women's movement would not have lashed out at the sexist term?

But there was no complaint about the term "crippled." No clear denunciation that would have let the public know that "cripple" is as unacceptable as "nigger."

Until we begin to raise a public outcry about the terms used to demean us, the public will never know why such terms are wrong. It's up to us to tell them. We missed a big chance with James Watt.

From *The Disability Rag* (November 1983, p. 7)

*In 1983, President Reagan's Secretary of Interior James G. Watt apologized for a remark to the media in which he characterized an advisory panel as ideally balanced because it included "a black, a woman, two Jews and a cripple." (See *New York Times*, September 23, 1983.)

Now It's One Word

"Wheelchairbound vet (Tom Cruise)." Phrase from February 26 *Newsweek* "Periscope" column, ensconcing the ridiculous "wheelchair-bound" phrase as newspeakese in one of those trendy hyper-adjectives newsmagazines like to flaunt. Why not "wheelchairrider," *Newsweek?*

From *The Disability Rag* (May–June 1990)

3

Disability Coverage in American Newspapers

John S. Clogston

Disability rights activists and others have criticized newspaper coverage of those with disabilities as being stereotypical, paternalistic, and inaccurate in the areas of issue coverage, role portrayal, and language (Biklen 1987; Cooke and Reisner 1991; Elliott 1989; Johnson 1990; Johnson and Elkins 1989; Krossel 1988). Their pieces provide a rich and detailed picture of the short-comings of disability coverage, but the case studies and anecdotal evidence do not tell us what American journalists are writing about disability on a day-to-day basis.

Empirical studies of newspaper coverage of persons with disabilities also have concluded that coverage tends to be negative. Yoshida, Wasilewski, and Friedman (1990) found that the traditional issues of budget expenditures, housing, and treatment in institutions were the most prevalent topics. Keller and others (1990) found that persons with disabilities were covered in feature stories rather than as hard news and that these articles presented the negative impact of disability on people's lives. Haller (1992) noted that portrayal of deaf persons in the *New York Times* and *Washington Post* was progressive—based on a political or cultural perspective of disability—when covered as part of a civil rights protest, but they were portrayed traditionally—conforming to medical or social stereotypes of disability—when covered in general news and features. Clogston in 1992 found that the *New York Times* had become more progressive since 1941 in the issues it covered but was still somewhat traditional.

Do newspaper reporters view the topic of disability as something more than medical cures, government support programs, and charity telethons?

How often do they include such issues as access to public buildings, disability protests as part of a drive for civil rights, and the disabled person as a consumer? What images of those with disabilities are portrayed by newspapers? Do they show a group of poor, powerless unfortunates who depend on society for physical and economic sustenance? Or do media images of disability include those of a minority group demanding equal rights and full participation in society? Do newspaper reporters use stereotypically offensive language such as "confined to a wheelchair," "deaf and dumb," or "suffering from blindness"? Or do they employ less offensive and usually more accurate descriptions, such as "wheelchair user," "deaf individual," and "is blind"?

Clogston's 1991 study of disability coverage in sixteen prestigious and high-circulation daily newspapers during the first three months of 1990 provided an empirical look at how some of the most respected and widely read newspapers covered the topic.[1] The study examined 363 articles dealing with physical disability written by staff reporters at the newspapers and evaluated them in terms of language used, issues covered, and portrayal of individuals with disabilities. In addition, the reporters who wrote the stories were surveyed about their attitudes toward and experiences with those with disabilities and were questioned about other newsroom and demographic information.

Disability coverage can be divided into two distinct types: traditional models, which focus on the disabled individual's differences from others in society, and the progressive viewpoint, which focuses more on how society deals with a population that includes those with various disabilities (Table 1).

The traditional perspective views persons with disabilities as dysfunctioning in a medical or economic way. Seen this way, they are to be cared for medically or economically by society (Gliedman and Roth 1980; Hahn 1982), or they might be looked upon in awe as "supercrips" when they perform workaday tasks "in spite of their disabilities" (Covington 1989; Zola 1985).

The progressive outlook consists of the minority civil rights and cultural pluralism perceptions of disability. These view the dysfunction as lying not within the individual with a disability but in society's inability or unwillingness to adapt its physical, social, and occupational environments to accommodate all of its members (Bogdan and Biklen 1977).

A story that exemplifies how misleading traditional newspaper coverage of persons with disabilities can be was a personality profile in the *Denver Post* headlined, "Falling into a Nightmare: Accidents Frustrate Wheelchair-Bound Woman." The story chronicled the mishaps of a "helpless hemiplegic—paralyzed on one side," who was described as "a prisoner of her own immobility, trapped by her nightmares as much as her paralysis." The story's subject was quoted as saying, "Being unable to walk and then unable to work, to get around, has really been hard." Although the story ostensibly was about unsafe sidewalks in a suburban community, its traditional language

Table 1
Traditional and Progressive Models of Disability

Traditional

Persons with disabilities are viewed as malfunctioning; the source of their disability-related limitation lies within the individual. Society's role is either to cure or maintain the individual medically or economically. In extreme cases, the individual is considered to be deviant or less than human because of the disability.

Medical Model

Emphasis is on the individual's physical disability as an illness. The individual is portrayed as dependent on health professionals for cures or maintenance. Also included in this model are stories that focus primarily on the physical aspects of an individual's disability.

Supercrip Model

As in the medical model, individuals are focused on because of the physical characteristics of their disability. Individuals are portrayed either as "superhuman" because of physical feats (e.g., rock-climbing paraplegics) or "amazing" because they function "normally, in spite of their disabilities."

Social Pathology or Economic Model

Individuals with disabilities are portrayed as disadvantaged clients who look to the state or society for economic support, which is considered a gift, not a right. The individuals are portrayed as passive recipients of government or private economic support.

Progressive

This perspective views the major limiting aspect of a person's disability as lying in society's inability to adapt its physical, social, or occupational environment, as well as its attitudes, to accept those who are physically different.

Minority/Civil Rights Model

The person with a disability is shown as member of a minority group dealing with legitimate political grievances, usually involved in disability rights political activities, actively demanding political change.

Cultural Pluralism

The person with a disability is considered a multifaceted individual whose disability is just one aspect of many. No undue attention is paid to the disability. The individual is portrayed as are others without disabilities.

and portrayal of the wheelchair user as a helpless victim put the focus on the individual's travails rather than on society's inability to maintain sidewalks.

Newspaper reporters can, and do, do better. A story in the *Detroit News* early 1990 noted that accessibility battles in Berkeley, California, could be joined nationwide with the passage of the Americans with Disabilities Act (ADA). An accompanying article noted how the ADA would affect the already strong local and state laws regarding access and accommodation. The language referred to "persons with disabilities" and "wheelchair users." Sources, both with and without disabilities, were quoted for the information value of their comments rather than the emotional impact. One member of Berkeley's transit board said, "I'm not seen only as a disabled politician; I'm seen as a politician. And that's when you are really starting to change perceptions."

The 1990 study found newspaper coverage of persons with physical disabilities to be traditional in four categories: types of disability issues covered, roles of individuals with disabilities, language used to refer to persons with disabilities in headlines, and language used in the text of the stories.

Traditional issues—medical treatment and institutionalization, government and private support programs, and victimization of disabled persons—predominated in nearly 60 percent of the stories; while progressive topics—discrimination, access issues, integrated education, and employment and consumer issues, for example—were covered in slightly more than 40 percent of the stories. The traditional stories covered, for example, a trial over who was to blame for a New York man's paralysis from a diving accident (in *Newsday*); another was the *Detroit News*'s weekly feature, "Helping Hands," which solicits donations for selected persons with disabilities. Examples of progressive stories are a *Chicago Tribune* piece on a handicapped products directory, a story on a backlog of disability cases before the Kentucky Commission on Human Rights in the *Louisville Courier-Journal*, and numerous papers' coverage of a protest by disability activists in Washington, D.C.

Persons with disabilities were portrayed in traditional roles nearly as often as traditional issues were covered. Recipients of medical and economic support and supercrips were the rule in 55 percent of the stories. The disabled person as political activist or member of a pluralistic society was the subject of only 45 percent of the stories.

Many of those portrayed traditionally were young people. For example, the *Los Angeles Times* reported on sixteen-year-old Seung Bok Kim, who was in California from Korea for surgery to rearrange muscles and ligaments and remove bone, which would offer the "teen-age sufferer of cerebral palsy a chance to leave his wheelchair." A ten-year-old former poster child was the focus of a *Louisville Courier-Journal* column that portrayed the disabled person as the recipient of charity support. Another teenager, seventeen-year-old David Palmore, was portrayed as a supercrip by the *Miami Herald*. The story told of how the high school athlete was able to return to interscholastic wrestling after several vision impairments.

Larry McAfee, a Georgia man who after winning the right to die chose to live and advocate disability rights, was often portrayed in the minority civil rights model, as were protesters who left their wheelchairs to crawl up the steps of the U.S. Capitol to call attention to the Americans with Disabilities Act. Individuals with disabilities who were portrayed simply as members of a pluralistic society ranged from Vietnam veteran Ron Kovic and singer Stevie Wonder to Lisa Santiago, a consumer of closed-captioned television programs interviewed in the *New York Daily News*, and Dr. Herbert M. Gale, an eighty-two-year-old author with Parkinson's disease.

The language in story headlines was traditional to the same extent as roles were: 55 percent traditional and 45 percent progressive. Some of the most traditional headlines were in the *New York Daily News*—"Crippled, He Fends Off Teen Attack"; "Coma Victim's Hubby Starts Head-Injury Fund"— although other newspapers' headlines used negative language—"Stricken Acrobat Continues Fight to Overcome Cancer" (*USA Today*)—or referred to persons with disabilities with adjectives substituting for nouns (*disabled, blind,* etc.).

Progressive headlines used these adjectives appropriately to modify nouns—"Blind Rights Activists Fight Proposal by FAA" (*Detroit News*), "Deaf Consumers Aren't Ignored Anymore" (*Wall Street Journal*)—or used nonpejorative terminology—"Curbs Present Roadblocks to Wheelchair Users' Independence" (*Washington Post*).

Traditional language was used to refer to persons with disabilities at least once in the text of nearly 60 percent of the stories. Although more than half the stories (62.7 percent) used progressive language more often, only about 40 percent of the stories contained no traditional language. To put this issue into perspective with coverage of other groups, one cannot imagine even a single instance of racially or sexually derogatory language escaping condemnation by the affected groups.

The survey of those who wrote the stories found that these reporters had progressive attitudes toward those with physical disabilities but their attitudes had no connection with how they wrote about disability. The same held true for reporters' gender, age, education, and number of years on the job.

Two factors, however, did correlate with whether stories were progressive or traditional: newsroom style guidelines regarding disability coverage and whether the reporter had a co-worker with a disability. In newsrooms that had style guidelines dealing with disability, more stories portrayed those with disabilities in progressive roles and used more progressive language than stories from newsrooms without such guidelines. The effect was opposite with issues, however: newsrooms using such style guidelines had more stories covering traditional issues.

Reporters who reported contact with a co-worker with a disability wrote more stories on progressive issues and more stories with progressive roles than did those reporters without such contact. Their story language, however, was more traditional than for reporters who did not know a disabled co-worker.

For newspaper journalists, the question of what amount of traditional coverage is acceptable should be addressed differently for each of the content categories.

With language, the case can be made for avoiding any use of traditional terminology to refer to individuals with disabilities, as has been done with women and racial minorities. But lack of consensus among those with disabilities themselves on what constitutes acceptable language makes reliance on rigid guidelines risky. Making journalists aware of the issues and ensuring that they avoid using some of the more offensive terms may be the most that can be hoped for in terms of making newspaper language more progressive.

Coverage of roles may be more difficult because some disabled people in traditional roles may warrant news coverage. It would be inaccurate and unethical for reporters to ignore individuals who fit into medical, social pathology, or supercrip roles, or to portray them inaccurately as fitting one of the progressive models. The real problem arises when reporters rely on traditional stereotypes to describe individuals with disabilities because, even as journalists, they are not aware of the diversity of people who have disabilities. The goal of journalists should be to portray the uniqueness of individuals rather than the similarity of their disabilities.

The toughest area is with issues. Not covering traditional aspects when they are an integral part of the story would be poor journalism. But covering traditional disabilities with no awareness of nontraditional disability issues is just as bad. A goal for journalists should be an awareness of the variety and scope of disability-related issues.

The effect of contact with a disabled coworker and of style guidelines suggests that one of the most effective ways a news organization can make coverage more progressive lies within the working environment itself. The professional values that reporters learn in the newsroom need to be made more accommodating to acceptance of persons with disabilities.

Newspapers should make an effort to include all aspects of disability coverage in style guidelines and to ensure that reporters are aware of those guidelines. Since presence of style guidelines on covering disability was associated with traditional issue coverage, it might be desirable for those guidelines to go beyond the do's and don'ts of language and to include a discussion of what disability issues and roles are considered to be traditional or stereotypical and what ones are progressive.

It is unlikely and undesirable that guidelines would impede coverage of breaking stories that deal with the traditional aspects of disability. But reporters who are more aware of the progressive issues and roles might be more likely to include them in nonbreaking stories that might otherwise not include the impact of an event or issue on those with disabilities.

Another way newspapers can improve disability coverage is to take the Kerner commission's advice of twenty-five years ago and hire more members of the minority group whose story is being told inadequately (National Advisory Commission on Civil Disorders 1968). Having contact with a co-worker with a physical disability has a strong association with progressive roles and issues. Newspapers should make a concerted effort to hire staff members with physical disabilities—not simply to have a token expert to cover a particular beat but to provide other reporters with colleagues who may, overtly or subtly, influence the way reporters cover all stories, not just those that obviously involve persons with disabilities.

A story covering the Jerry Lewis 1992 Labor Day muscular dystrophy telethon is a good example of how newspaper disability coverage remains stuck between traditional and progressive coverage. The telethon has come to represent the epitome of portrayal of persons with disabilities in the traditional social pathology model—that is, showing them as pathetic and as objects of charity. Because of this, disability activists have protested the annual event. The story, "Telethon Sets Record Despite Flap over 'Pity,' " that appeared in the *Chicago Tribune* on September 8, 1992, provided equal coverage to Lewis and the telethon itself and to the protests by disability activists and antitelethon statements by the head of the U.S. Equal Employment Opportunity Commission. The article covered both the charity event (traditional) and the protests (progressive), and it portrayed disabled persons as both passive charity recipients (traditional) and progressive disability activists (progressive). It utilized progressive language when referring to "disabled people" and to Lewis's envisioning himself "with muscular dystrophy." But traditional language was also used twice: when persons with disabilities were described as "stricken" and as "afflicted" with muscular dystrophy. The story did use the word *pity* in quotation marks, diminishing the legitimacy of the assertions by the protesters that Lewis's approach looks at muscular dystrophy in a negative and stereotypical way.

As evidenced by the 1990 study of sixteen newspapers and exemplified by the story about the telethon, the state of disability news coverage is not completely traditional or completely progressive. But the fact that these newspapers, among the best in the country, contain a considerable amount of traditional coverage indicates there is plenty of room for improvement in coverage of those with disabilities. By improving coverage, journalists can provide less limited, nonstereotypical coverage of members of this last minority as they move toward full participation in society.

NOTE

1. Stories from the following newspapers were analyzed: *Atlanta Constitution*, *Baltimore Sun*, *Chicago Tribune*, *Christian Science Monitor*, *Detroit Free Press*, *Detroit News*,

Los Angeles Times, Louisville Courier-Journal, Miami Herald, New York Daily News, New York Times, Newsday, St. Louis Post-Dispatch, USA Today, Wall Street Journal, Washington Post.

REFERENCES

Biklen, Douglas. 1987. "Framed: Print Journalism's Treatment of Disability Issues." In Allen Gartner and Tom Joe, *Images of the Disabled: Disabling Images*, pp. 31–46. New York: Praeger.

Bogdan, R., and D. Biklen. 1987. "Handicapism." *Social Policy* (March–April).

Clogston, John S. 1991. "Reporters' Attitudes Toward and Newspaper Coverage of Persons with Disabilities." Unpublished doctoral dissertation, Michigan State University.

Clogston, John S. 1992. "Fifty Years of Disability Coverage in the *New York Times*." *News Computing Journal* 8(2):39–50.

Cooke, Annemarie, and Neil Reisner. 1991, December. "The Last Minority." *Washington Journalism Review*, 13(10):14–18.

Covington, George. 1989. "Washington, D.C. The News Media and Disability Issues: A National Workshop—News Media Education Project." National Institute on Disability and Rehabilitation Research.

Editor & Publisher International Yearbook, 1989. 1989. New York: Editor & Publisher Co.

Elliott, Deni. 1989. "Media and Persons with Disabilities: Ethical Considerations." In Mary Johnson and Susan Elkins, eds., *Reporting on Disability: Approaches and Issues*, pp. 59–66. Louisville, Ky.: Avocado Press.

Elliott, Timothy R., and E. Keith Byrd. 1982, November–December. "Media and Disability." *Rehabilitation Literature*, 43.

Gliedman, John, and William Roth. 1980. *The Unexpected Minority: Handicapped Children in America.* New York: Harcourt Brace Jovanovich.

Hahn, Harlan. 1982, July–August. "Disability and Rehabilitation Policy: Is Paternalistic Neglect Benign?" *Public Administration Review*. 73:385–389.

Haller, Beth. 1992. "Paternalism and Protest: The Presentation of Deaf Persons in the *New York Times* and the *Washington Post*." Paper presented at the Mass Communication and Society Division of the Association for Education in Journalism and Mass Communication Annual Convention, Montreal, Canada.

Johnson, Mary. 1990, May–June. "Opportunity Lost." *The Disability Rag* 11(3):30–31.

Johnson, Mary, and Susan Elkins, eds. 1989. *Reporting on Disability, Approaches and Issues.* Louisville, Ky.: Advocado Press.

Keller, Clayton E., Daniel P. Hallahan, Edward A. McShane, E. Paula Crowley, and Barbara J. Blandford. 1990. "The Coverage of Persons with Disabilities in American Newspapers." *Journal of Special Education* 24(3):271–82.

Krossel, Martin. 1988, May–June. " 'Handicapped Heroes' and the Knee-jerk Press." *Columbia Journalism Review* 27(1):46–47.

National Advisory Commission on Civil Disorders. 1968. *Report of the National Advisory Commission on Civil Disorders.* New York: Bantam Books.

Yoshida, Roland K., Lynn Wasilewski, and Douglas Friedman. 1990, February.

"Recent Newspaper Coverage about Persons with Disabilities." *Exceptional Children* 56(51):418–23.

Zola, Irving K. 1985, October. "Depictions of Disability—Metaphor, Message and Medium: A Research and Political Agenda." *Social Science Journal* 22(4):5–18.

Drivel in the Press: Covering the Americans with Disabilities Act

As disability groups across the country celebrated the anniversary of the Americans with Disabilities Act [ADA] signing and prepared to take advantage of millions of dollars available to begin the arduous process of educating disabled people in how to use their new-won rights, complaints about the ADA from business continued.

A new vibration is appearing in the anti-ADA saw these days—one calculated to divert the energy of the disability community from enforcement monitoring to self-absorption. The new cry is that the ADA is going to hurt disabled people themselves. Because they're not in any way job-ready, goes this new tune, they'll need much more training. (Business is willing to hire *qualified* disabled people, but there are so few of them!) And because advocates insisted on including even people with slight disabilities under the law, it's those who will be hired first. The more seriously disabled people will go begging.

The first part of this argument is seductive because, on the face of it, it's true enough: many disabled people *do* need more training. But the current argument is designed to serve another end: to convince the public, Congress and the courts that the ADA was premature, ill-timed; and to develop a public climate in which lawsuits by businesses alleging they're overburdened (not just by making modifications, but now having to train disabled people, too!) can flourish.

National Public Radio's "All Things Considered" for July 26, [1991], the anniversary of the ADA signing, featured a long segment with this spin.

The [Disability] Rag has seen no less than a dozen stories since the ADA was passed explaining just how the ADA will harm capitalism in America. Here's a taste of the latest version we've encountered, this from the June issue of the *Free Market*, a publication of the far right-wing Ludwig von Mises Institute in Auburn, Alabama:

The Americans with Disabilities Act will burden the economy and do harm, in this case to many disabled people. . . .

The new law requires nearly every business in America to invest heavily in accommodations for the handicapped. Restaurants must print menus in braille. . . . Theaters must provide "integrated seating"; undertakers cannot refuse to handle AIDS-infected corpses. . . . Retail outlets must widen their aisles, lower their shelves, and employ special store personnel to wait on the handicapped. . . .

Such mandated "benefits" are sure to reduce employment opportunities for the disabled [emphasis added]. Consider a situation where two equally qualified employees, one of whom has a physical handicap, are being considered for, say, an accounting position. Even though both employees can perform the job equally well, hiring the handicapped person will be more costly because of the government mandated accommodations. Consequently, the rational employer will not want to hire the hand-icapped individual.

Furthermore, as increased unemployment of disabled persons becomes more ap-parent, the government will institute a system of employment quotas. . . .

In order to fulfill the quotas, employers will seek out individuals with only the mildest handicaps. . . . It will also be in the interest of employers (and of empire-building bureaucrats) to lobby to expand the definition of disability to include more of their current employees (i.e., hangnailism, golfaholism, etc.).

The end result will be fewer employment opportunities for individuals with more severe disabilities. . . .

There'll be more of this drivel to come. Count on it.

From *The Disability Rag* (September–October 1991)

1990 . . . and No Disability Sensitivity? The News, and All the News

Editors like to argue that news merely reflects the opinion of the day. If true, there is still no real disability sensibility in this country.

In examining several months' worth of stories about disability that have appeared in the nation's biggest newspapers—as well as those in a scattering of smaller and community papers—[*Disability*] *Rag* readers continue to be struck with the lack of context. Each story, each time, invents the wheel all over again. It is as if there are no such things as disability "issues" in this country—issues over which the movement has fought; issues which the movement agrees on, such as the need for integration, the problems with access, the need for more captioning. Each story says "this is a new thing!" to its readers. When a disability angle doesn't seem "new" to an editor, the story isn't done at all.

Editors do not yet see the issues of inaccessibility, disability discrimina-tion, the attendant services need, the suicides of disabled people, as "real news."

There are oases of understanding. Some reporters listen and put things into context.

The *Village Voice*'s Amy Virshup reported on the discrimination faced by Joe Gibney in trying to find a job after graduating from Columbia Law School. "The endless trial of Joe Gibney," which ran August 7 [1989], was the first story to describe for readers the chasm that yawns between the rhetoric of the politicians promoting the ADA and the reality disabled people continue to face. Not too long after the beginning of her story, Virshup, after throwing in a few paragraphs talking about the ADA and what it will allegedly mean, adds this: "Clearly, rhetoric and Little League's Challenger division won't suddenly move the disabled into the social and economic mainstream. And although the ADA will build protections into federal law, New York State already has antibias laws on the books and they haven't done Joe Gibney much good."

What follows after this remarkable staging is the detailed report of a man who, by his own count, sent out 400 letters and had 70 interviews for jobs and was turned down for every one and who has begun to internalize the belief that disabled people can't get jobs, after starting out in law school with the belief that "I could educate myself out of a wheelchair."

What's new in this story isn't the tale of a man; it's the facts the reporter has chosen to put into the story, seeing their significance to the overall picture: "Joe went to a public sector job fair for 'disabled college graduates' seeking positions 'at the technical professional and administrative career entry levels.' The average salary: $6,000."

"I called the people at Just One Break (JOB), a nonprofit employment agency for the disabled. Yes, Joe had been a client, said spokeswoman Jennifer Reilly, and no, JOB hadn't been able to help him. Incidentally, did I know how much *money* Joe wanted to make? And did I know about his *grades* [average, not outstanding]? But his ablebodied classmates . . . , I began, launching into the argument that I thought *she* should be making. Finally, I stopped myself and asked, 'Don't you think there's some discrimination at work?' Reilly answered, 'I haven't come across any blatant discrimination.' "

She looked into complaints by law firms that it might cost "perhaps $20,000" to modify a workplace, including the restroom, but didn't drop it there but quoted Mark Leeds with the Mayor's Office for People with Disabilities, who pointed out that this shouldn't seem a bad investment "when they're paying starting lawyers $80,000 a year."

Virshup did what too few reporters do: She put her story in context. She saw not just Joe Gibney and his problem; she saw the disability issue as well. And she recognized that some disability sources—in this case, JOB—weren't as good as others.

Joe Shapiro of *U.S. News and World Report* was one of the first reporters to realize that disability rights was about issues, and that those issues were ongoing stories. His stories routinely appear in the newsweekly.

A short time after some California disability activists complained to *The [Disability] Rag* that the *Los Angeles Times* refused to cover their demonstrations on budget cuts, *Times* reporter Edmund Newton took an in-depth look at those same activists' complaints, not only with budget cuts but with the ADA. "But for all the 1960s-style passion with which members of this growing new civil rights movement have pushed for the Americans with Disabilities Act," he wrote, "many believe that the law probably won't amount to a hill of beans in the grinding struggle for survival that is the lot of many disabled people."

In interviewing many of those who were active in the movement, Newton gave an overview of the problems disabled Californians faced. He discussed the effects of budget cuts. He discussed the problems many poorer wheelchair users have obtaining motorized chairs, and reported on the lawsuit filed against the state.

Two weeks later, *Los Angeles Times* reporter Marlene Cimons, also using the ADA as a jumping-point, fashioned a story about the ADA's spawning of consultants—including a warning from Disability Rights Education and Defense Fund's Pat Wright that the new law will "spawn an industry of get-rich-quick consultants," and that businesses should instead "hook up with the disabled community."

The disability perspective: That's what occurs in news stories when activists from the disability rights movement are used as sources—and when these activists' perspectives are found on the opinion pages of the newspapers.

The same day Cimons' story ran, the *Los Angeles Times*'s opinion page carried a column by disabled Californian Bill Bolte, who wrote eloquently about problems he encountered in the toilets of the California state Capitol—pointing out the all-too-common problem of restrooms that are allegedly "accessible" but which do not meet code and which are, in fact, not usable by people in wheelchairs.

Bolte pointed out that "the Capitol toilets are still unusable by many disabled people, decades after regulations requiring access." But commentary like Bolte's happens still too infrequently.

From *The Disability Rag* (Winter 1990)

4

Disability Rights as Civil Rights: The Struggle for Recognition

Joseph P. Shapiro

When disability rights lobbyists in Washington set out to pass the Americans with Disabilities Act (ADA), they made a highly orthodox strategy decision: there would be no attempt to explain the sweeping antidiscrimination legislation to the press. As the lead ADA lobbyist, Patrisha Wright of the Disability Rights Education and Defense Fund put it, "We would have been forced to spend half our time trying to teach reporters what's wrong with their stereotypes of people with disabilities" (interview with author).

To avoid the press in a lobbying campaign on a bill as major and potentially controversial as the ADA is a rarity—even a heresy. Public relations is a multibillion-dollar-a-year business in this country, supporting some 173,000 flacks nationwide.[1] Virtually every corporation and every cause—from General Motors to the Tube Council of North America (the folks who make the plastic squeezable tubes for toothpaste)—depends on the press to raise awareness of its issues.

Yet the media were of little use to the disability rights movement as it sought passage of the ADA. The reason is that journalists have been too slow to understand the new civil rights consciousness of disabled Americans. As a number of writers have shown, press coverage of people with disabilities has tended to fall into one of two stereotypes: the sad, unlucky disabled person, in need of pity and charity, or the plucky, courageous disabled person, celebrated for overcoming a disability and performing seemingly superhuman feats, whether it is holding a job or scaling a mountain. One is the image of Tiny Tim; the other that of the "supercrip." In these stories, disabled people are grist for feature stories that usually focus on one person and his or her struggles to overcome a "handicap." The overcoming is not connected to facing a societal barrier; the individual is not seen as taking part in any larger civil rights or social movement of people with disabilities.[2]

The stereotypes of Tiny Tim or supercrip have slowed the progress of disabled people toward full inclusion in American life. To be seen as a patient or in need of charity is to be thought incapable of the same life as others. To be lauded for superachievement is to suggest that a disabled person can turn pity into respect only at the point of having accomplished some extraordinary feat. Sociologist Erving Goffman noted that people with such "spoiled identity"—he draws on the common outcast status of racial minorities, drug addicts, people with disabilities, and others—find themselves labeled abnormal and therefore disqualified from social acceptance.[3]

Journalists were of little relevance to ADA lobbyists because the press has been one of the last institutions to catch on to disabled people's new rejection of old stereotypes. Politicians were among the first to catch on. They quickly came to see a potentially powerful voting bloc of activist constituents. Not needing to make its case through the filter of the media, the ADA lobby went directly to the politicians in a highly effective grass-roots campaign. Every member of Congress received a personal visit from a constituent— either an individual with a disability or a family member—with a compelling story to tell about disability discrimination. Most important, however, is that since disability hits nearly one in six people and cuts across class and racial lines, many key members of Congress understood the yearning for disability rights. Some key members had disabilities themselves; Senate minority leader Robert Dole lost use of his right arm as a result of a World War II injury and Congressman Tony Coehlo has epilepsy. The bill's original Senate sponsor, Connecticut Republican Lowell Weicker, has a son with Down syndrome. Iowa Democrat Tom Harkin, who took the lead when Weicker was defeated for reelection, has a deaf brother and a nephew who is a quadriplegic. Senator Edward Kennedy, who led key negotiations with the White House, has a sister with retardation and a son who lost part of his leg to cancer. Former president George Bush, whose support for the bill was crucial, also understood disability. His son Neil has dyslexia, and the Bushes were told he would never be able to attend college (he did), and son Marvin has had a colostomy.

The best way to describe news coverage of the ADA was that there was very little of it. The few stories published presented a mixed picture. The *New York Times* early on ran an alarmist lead story on the front page predicting "a wave of lawsuits" and reflecting business fears about the burdens of the bill.[4] A follow-up editorial asked whether Congress was offering a "blank check for the disabled."[5] The *Times,* the *Washington Post,* and other newspapers printed just a handful of stories on the bill as it moved through Congress and, but for a few exceptions, ignored the broader disability rights movement. Given the highly publicized struggle to pass the Civil Rights

Act of 1964—and the fact that the ADA was the most extensive civil rights bill since—the relatively little scrutiny of the ADA once again made clear that the disability rights movement has been a quiet, grass-roots rebellion. Yet even without the aid of a knowledgeable press, the ADA passed. It moved swiftly and with relatively little controversy through Congress and was signed into law on July 26, 1990, in a ceremony at the White House.

There is, however, a danger in being a stealth movement. With the ADA in place, disabled people are now in a tricky spot. They have new civil rights protections, but society has little understanding of those protections or of why disabled people need them. As disabled people begin asserting these newly won rights, moving from the halls of power in Washington, D.C., to the public, there will be clashes and misunderstanding. The disability rights movement will come increasingly to be played out in streets, schools, workplace—and the press.

There are already signs of a backlash and of a press that still lacks the mind-set or the history to understand the new thinking of disabled people. As the employment title of the ADA went into effect, there were two bills in Congress either to limit the ADA or abolish it outright. Luckily, they failed. And when disabled people reasonably demand the rights granted to them by the ADA and other civil rights laws, they are depicted in the press as a selfish minority with dubious claims. Typical was the press coverage of New York City's plan to set up public, outdoor toilets. The city's original proposal did not include any that were accessible for wheelchair users. The ADA, as well as New York City law, was clear that such public accommodations must be accessible. But city officials complained that a toilet big enough for a wheelchair user would take up too much space on a street corner. Besides, officials argued, larger toilets would attract junkies looking for a place to shoot up and homeless people needing shelter to sleep. Most stories about the toilets presented them as a clever and welcome idea, with the complaints of wheelchair users of secondary importance.[6] One newspaper editorial chided the disability community, saying the issue was one of "weighing civil rights against common sense."[7]

To disabled people, the failure to make the toilets accessible was as outrageous as if the city had built toilets just for men or put signs on them that said "Whites Only." Yet press coverage of the controversy painted the dissenters as demanding a narrow right that would benefit just a small number of wheelchair users over a common good that would benefit the vast majority of New Yorkers. The opposition to separate toilets imperiled the entire project.

The 1964 Civil Rights Act passed after years of press coverage of events that stirred the conscience of a guilty nation to its history of separatism and racism. The law was preceded by images of courageous Freedom Riders, marches, bus boycotts, lynchings, church bombings, peaceful protesters mauled by police dogs on the streets of Birmingham, and Martin Luther

King, Jr., electrifying a crowd delivering his "I Have a Dream" speech on the steps of the Lincoln Memorial. The disability rights movement is not powered by such compelling imagery. But if the news coverage of the toilets holds true, disabled people may be burdened by an image of being selfish pests, even if they are asserting rights they already own.

In the black civil rights movement, people put their lives on the line to assert their moral claim to laws that guaranteed their inclusion in society. When public attitudes about race changed, African-Americans won civil rights protections. Disabled Americans got their civil rights protection before the same kind of sea-change in public understanding. The hope behind the ADA is that integration in the workplace, restaurants, parks, and theaters will end others' impulse to offer pity or seek inspiration from disabled people and that fears and misconceptions about disabled people will fade.

Will integration make the media better understand the disability movement's claim to rights? There are signs that this is already happening. It is no longer easy to separate reporting between the progressive and the traditional (see chapter 3). More reporting sees disability as a rights issue, not just a feature story. In preparing to write this chapter, I asked the library at *U.S. News and World Report*, where I work, for the newspaper clippings that had been filed under "Handicapped—General" in 1991. This was the file that would include all general interest stories in 1991 about disability. (I did not include an almost equally large file, "Handicapped—Regulations," which contained press coverage of the implementation of the ADA.)

Clogston in Chapter 3 defines traditional articles as showing a disabled person as a medical or economic defective, the result of a disability, and progressive articles as viewing a disabled person as limited by society, not a physical or mental limitation. He found that 60 percent of articles were traditional and only 13.2 percent progressive. My random survey found the inverse proportion. Of fifty-eight articles from thirteen newspapers, I classified thirty-nine falling in the progressive model (67 percent), ten were traditional (17 percent), and nine defied classification (16 percent). Of the last nine were three that I classified as "backlash" stories, which focused on supposed negative aspects of implementing the ADA.

Something is changing. Reporters are responding to two great consciousness-raising events of the disability rights movement: the Gallaudet student protest in 1988 and the fight for the ADA and its subsequent implementation from 1989 to 1992. At Gallaudet University in Washington, D.C.—a venerable institution that serves the hearing impaired—students took to the streets to protest the naming of a new president who, like the previous presidents in the 124-year history of the institution, had normal hearing. The student strike shut down the university, and after two weeks they won their crusade to have a hearing-impaired president installed. Even before those two events, a 1985 Harris survey found that 74 percent of disabled Americans say they share a "common identity" with other disabled people and 45 percent argue they are "a minority group in the same sense as are blacks and Hispanics."[8] One can assume that these numbers would be significantly higher today in the wake of Gallaudet and the ADA. The change in reporting on disability reflects it.

Reporting is largely a reactive exercise, writing about events and how others present themselves. A journalist holds up a mirror to society. As more disabled people see their issues as ones of rights, so will reporters. This conclusion is confirmed in a study that looked at stories about hearing-impaired people in the *Washington Post* and the *New York Times*. Sixty-two percent of stories before the Gallaudet student protest "reflected the traditional disability models." But "in the two years after the protest, the number of stories reflecting the traditional forms of presentation fell to 40 percent." (The author noted that on the whole, there was little press coverage of Deaf people, except for the spurt of stories in 1988 dealing specifically with Gallaudet. Otherwise, the number of stories in years following Gallaudet was roughly the same as the number in the preceding two years.)[9]

My own experience is telling. I wrote my first story on the disability rights movement in February 1988 but could not get it published. It was not until the following month, when Gallaudet students protested, that the story found a home in the Health section of the *Washington Post*.[10] The inclusion of a story on the disability rights movement—a cause that rejects the traditional view that disability is a health issue—was ironic. But stranger was the fact that my story carried the subheadline "Second Opinion." Editors wanted to make clear that the idea of the existence of a disability rights movement was the point of view of the author, and not something that could be treated as hard fact or a news story. Two years later, as the ADA moved to final passage, the *Post* would run its own story about the disability rights movement on the front page.[11]

As reporting increasingly describes the rights activism of disabled people, a peculiar hybrid has resulted: the "militant Tiny Tim" story, in which reporters tell a civil rights story but use the negative imagery of Tiny Tim and supercrips or dress up a traditional story with a little civil rights language.

Television seems slower than print journalism to give up the traditional disability images. Typical was a CBS Evening News "Eye on America" segment about a Massachusetts father and his son cycling across the country to gain attention for his son's cerebral palsy.[12] Anchor Connie Chung introduced the piece with talk of how the new ADA was forcing the removal of physical barriers and then noted, correctly and thoughtfully, "Still, Americans with disabilities have to fight to overcome other barriers in people's minds." The segment opened with a shot of the father pumping his bicycle across the California desert, pushing his son in a wheelchair-like seat attached to the front of the bike. "Dick Hoyt provides the arms and legs," says the correspondent. "Rick, the inspiration that will keep them going." There is talk about how Rick has "lived inside a body that never worked" and a soundbite from the father explaining, "I just think if people can see that Rick is being a productive human being with all the disabilities that he has that we're going to help out a lot of people."

The correspondent explained that she had reported on the Hoyts once before, and the point of this piece was to see "how much has changed for Rick and the disabled over the last six years. We found a family still fighting. People may say they admire Rick but it stops short of their pocketbooks. The Hoyt's trip was supposed to be financed through donations." The idea that they had to finance the cross-country trek largely out of their own pockets is the only part of the story that the reporter passes off as discrimination against disabled people. Never mind that Americans may understand better than CBS that disabled people do not need to superachieve to win respect anymore or that not funding a family's personal expedition is in no sense an act of discrimination.

A similar hybrid appeared in the *Washington Post*'s story about twenty-seven-year-old Jenny Langley, a quadriplegic who uses a ventilator as a result of an automobile accident. She was ready to leave an Atlanta rehabilitation center but needed accessible housing and personal assistance service or else faced being forced into an out-of-state nursing home. The dilemma facing Langley was a typical civil rights story of a society that fails to provide basic, humane needs of people who live with severe disabilities. The story, by freelance writer Remar Sutton, was done in a mawkish model, however. "First, you notice how pretty she is; then you think how nifty the bow tie around her neck is. And then you notice it's not a bow tie but the dressing around the hole in her throat," the reporter noted. Later he explained how Langley needed help with quad coughs, described as an undignified treatment in which someone pounds on her chest several times a day. "If you're Jenny, you say thank you every time it's done," Sutton wrote.[13]

The presentation seemed particularly jarring since the *Post* once again had been welcome territory for one of my stories, just six months earlier, on a similar case. Larry McAfee was another quadriplegic who used a ventilator. He too was from Atlanta and had been through the same rehabilitation center. McAfee had been treated brutally by Georgia's social service system, shuttled from one out-of-state nursing home to another and then placed in the intensive care unit of a grim Atlanta hospital when no Georgia nursing home would accept a man on a respirator. McAfee was capable of living on his own, with a personal assistant, and could work with a voice-activated computer. But not given those opportunities, McAfee went to court for the right to unhook his respirator and die. The court agreed, seeing a pitiful life not worth living. The story, in contrast, noted that the problem was a social service system pitifully lacking in providing basic support to let McAfee lead the productive life of his choice.[14] (Most other newspaper stories wrote about McAfee as a sad case who deserved to die.)

Since personal assistance service—necessary for Langley, McAfee, and others to live independently—is an important policy issue facing disabled people, it matters that reporters see forced institutionalization as a civil rights issue instead of being the story of an unfortunate person who should get the rare right to commit assisted suicide. The press would have done a better job had reporters come to Langley's and McAfee's stories with a knowledge of the new thinking of the disability rights movement.

Along with the hybrid stories is another new trend, the backlash story, which looks at claims for rights but finds them wanting. I found three in my random survey of 1991 stories. One was an August 25 story in the *Philadelphia Inquirer* reflecting the complaints of home builders that new barrier-free housing was not selling. "There are not as many disadvantaged persons who want barrier-free design elements as we were originally led to believe," complained a disgruntled builder, who also grumbled about the extra cost of making homes accessible. Nowhere in the article did the author note that universal design has benefits, that barrier-free houses in the suburbs may have little appeal to disabled people if local transportation is inaccessible, or that disabled people often lack the financial resources to buy a new house. Most egregious of all, the story never mentioned that the entire housing industry was in a slump. Instead, it blamed disabled people for not snapping up these new, expensive homes in the midst of a recession.[15]

A story in the *Baltimore Sun* played up the fears of restaurant owners and others confused about their obligations to make their businesses accessible.[16] The focus was on such concerns as the costs of providing access, the possibility of wheelchairs being in the way of waitresses or customers, or even of some diners being made uncomfortable by the sight of someone who was "different" at another table.

In the third story, the *Washington Post* argued that the local transit company's financial troubles "may deepen because of a new federal law requiring transit agencies to improve access to rail and bus systems by disabled people." Nowhere did the reporter mention why accessible transit is important to people with disabilities. Instead, he used an official's claim that the changes under ADA will cost $28 million a year for transit systems in urban areas of more than 1 million in population. This seems like a figure designed to scare. Even if a transit system made main bus and subway stations accessible and bought lifts for newly purchased buses, $28 million might be a one-time cost. Washington, D.C., the story failed to point out, already has a highly accessible subway, with elevators at each stop.[17]

There is one other way that disability activists can affect policy: with the heart-tugging pity approach that it decries. At least 10 percent of the 2,500 death row inmates have mental retardation. Five states have banned the death penalty for people with mental retardation, and similar legislation has been introduced in twenty-one more states. Georgia, in 1988 the first to introduce the ban, had been the scene of a particularly disturbing execution of Jerome Bowden, convicted in the brutal killing of a fifty-five-year-old woman. No physical or eyewitness evidence linked Bowden to the crime, but he signed a confession after a detective told him that signing it would help him out. Like many other people with retardation caught up in the criminal justice system, Bowden was eager to please authority figures and confused by the legal process swirling about him.[18] As advocates have noted, this is a problem of police using heavy-handed tactics to force confessions out of easily led people with retardation. But defense attorneys, death penalty foes, and others sometimes infantilize these people to make broader criticism of the death penalty. "Like children, mentally retarded defendants don't have the ability to really appreciate what they are up to," one North Carolina defense attorney was quoted saying in an investigative series.[19] But the series then devoted a sidebar to John Steinbeck's *Of Mice and Men*, trotting out the big and powerful Lennie whose retardation made him unable to distinguish between stroking a woman's hair and strangling her. This image may help states pass bans on executing people with retardation, but it will set back efforts to get neighborhoods to welcome group homes and businesses to accept workers with retardation.

The disability rights movement is not above taking advantage from time to time of the public's need to see disabled people as brave and courageous. The one lasting image of the fight for the ADA was members of American Disabled for Accessible Public Transportation (ADAPT) "crawl" up the steps of the West Front of the U.S. Capitol. In March 1990, a few dozen ADAPT demonstrators left their wheelchairs and climbed up the marble steps, carrying a "disability declaration of independence" to give to lawmakers inside the Capitol. Some disability activists, including *The Disability Rag* editor Mary Johnson, questioned this tugging on public sympathies. The cameras zoomed in on eight-year-old Jennifer Keelan. A disabled child's struggle played to every media reflex. But even if the crawl was a shameless play to old stereotypes, ADAPT knew what it was doing. The bizarre but arresting image of the crawl got the protest on the nightly news, albeit briefly. And more than one nondisabled person has told me that the sight of people crawling was the image that most moved them of the disability rights movement's fight for the ADA. Still, if activists play to these stereotypes, it becomes harder for the press to treat disability rights as purely a civil rights story.

It should not be too difficult to get reporters excited about disability stories. As Mary Johnson has noted, civil rights clashes are inviting stories for journalists. "Gripping personal sagas have been considered powerful writing," notes Johnson. "But issue stories can be more powerful. They can provide readers with information, they can involve people, they can change things."[20] This is rewarding territory for journalists, who have a natural affinity for writing about the story of one person or a group making a moral claim against prejudice.

NOTES

This chapter is adapted from Joseph P. Shapiro, "Disability Policy in the Media: A Stealth Civil Rights Movement Bypasses and Defies the Press and Conventional Wisdom," *Policy Studies Journal*, Winter, 1994.

1. Public Relations Society of America.

2. John S. Clogston, *Disability Coverage in Sixteen Newspapers* (Louisville, Ky.: Avocado Press, 1990); Douglas Biklen, "Framed: Journalism's Treatment of Disability," *Social Policy* 16 (1986):45–51; Irving Kenneth Zola, "Depictions of Disability: Metaphor, Message, and Medium in the Media: A Research and Political Agenda," *Social Science Journal* 22 (1985):5–17.

3. Erving Goffman, *Stigma: Notes on the Management of Spoiled Identity* (New York: Simon and Schuster, 1963).

4. Susan Rasky, "Bill Barring Bias against Disabled Holds Wide Impact," *New York Times*, August 14, 1989.

5. "Blank Check for the Disabled?" *New York Times*, September 6, 1988.

6. Celia Dugger, "In New York, Few Public Toilets and Many Rules," *New York Times*, May 21, 1991.

7. "Down the Toilet," *Wall Street Journal*, July 22, 1991.

8. Louis Harris and Associates, *The ICD Survey of Disabled Americans: Bringing Disabled Americans into the Mainstream* (New York City: International Center for the Disabled and National Council on the Handicapped, March 1986).

9. Beth Haller, "Paternalism and Protest: The Presentation of Deaf Persons in the *New York Times* and *Washington Post*" (paper presented to the meeting of the Association for Education in Journalism and Mass Communication, Montreal, August 1992).

10. Joseph P. Shapiro, "A New 'Common Identity' for the Disabled," *Washington Post*, March 29, 1988.

11. Sharon LaFraniere, "Doors Opening for the Disabled," *Washington Post*, May 25, 1990.

12. "CBS Evening News," July 9, 1992.

13. Remar Sutton, "Independence Days: One Woman's Fight to Surmount Paralysis," *Washington Post*, October 22, 1990.

14. Joseph P. Shapiro, "A Life Worse Than Death: Too Often, That's All America Offers the Disabled," *Washington Post*, April 15, 1990.

15. Kenneth Lelen, "Builder Finds Barrier-free Housing Doesn't Sell Well," *Philadelphia Inquirer*, August 25, 1991.

16. David Conn, "Equal Access for the Disabled: Business Owners Grapple with Cost, Uncertainty of Complying with New Law," *Baltimore Sun*, September 22, 1991.

17. Steven C. Fehr, "Metro to Find Law on Disabled Costly," *Washington Post*, September 27, 1991.

18. Robert Perske, *Unequal Justice? What Can Happen When Persons with Retardation or Other Developmental Disabilities Encounter the Criminal Justice System* (Nashville, Tenn.: Abingdon Press, 1991).

19. Karen McPherson and John Bennett, "Justice or Mercy? States Grapple with Executing Mentally Retarded," May 9, 1992.

20. Mary Johnson and Susan Elkins, eds., *Reporting on Disability: Approaches and Issues, a Sourcebook* (Louisville, Ky.: Advocado Press, 1989), p. 30.

The Americans with Disabilities Act: News Coverage ... and Commentary

A few days before newspapers around the country would carry stories about a historic signing of the Americans with Disabilities Act, a small Associated Press story appeared here and there in the dailies. The White House itself lacked accessible restrooms, it reported; disabled employees had to leave the White House grounds to find an accessible restroom. Children in wheelchairs who'd attended the annual Easter egg hunt had been forced to leave early because they couldn't use the restrooms provided.

The story came from a letter Rep. Mel Levine (D.-Calif.) had sent to President Bush just days before the signing of the ADA; Levine and activists behind the letter hoped in this way to point out the hypocrisy of the Bush Administration's "support" of the ADA.

But the piece went virtually unnoticed in the coverage that surrounded passage of the ADA.

The White House's refusal to let longtime disability rights champion Lowell Weicker, the former Senator, and other civil rights figures appear on the dais at the signing was reported by one of the few journalists in the nation to consider disability a "beat." His story got reported here and there—but was soon forgotten.

Perhaps the adulatory coverage of the signing—with no mention of such "controversy"—was only the kind of bandwagon coverage one should expect of things like bill signings. Still, when reporters choose to lead their stories not with that clear-cut example (provided, ironically, by the White House itself) of the kind of discrimination that had led activists to push this law through Congress, but with the tried-and-true staple that has attended reporting about things affecting "the disabled," one must pause to wonder how seriously journalists take the reporting of disability issues.

Here's how the *Philadelphia Inquirer*'s Washington reporter chose to lead his story: "In a ceremony attended by the deaf and blind, paraplegics and a woman dependent on a ventilator for every breath, President Bush yesterday signed into law a landmark civil rights bill for the disabled. 'Let the shameful wall of exclusion finally come tumbling down,' he said."

The *Philadelphia Inquirer*'s reporter, Gregory Spears, who in a recent [*The Disability*] *Rag* study was shown to have logged more stories "about" disability than any reporter for a major daily last fall, maybe didn't know about the White House's inaccessibility. Should he have? Should such "controversy" have intruded into a story on the signing of a law that is, essentially, about access?

The *Los Angeles Times*'s Don Shannon seemed to go Spears one better in conforming to the typical, how-amazing! school of disability reporting: "There was an empty wheelchair in the back row and somebody said the occupant must have gotten up and walked on the waves of emotions as about 2,000 disabled Americans cheered the signing of the Americans with Disabilities Act," he wrote in the opening sentence of his front-page story.

"Gotten up and walked . . . "?! Was reportage of the signing of the 1964 Civil Rights Act accompanied by stories suggesting that perhaps some Negroes had turned "white" with joy at the signing of their civil rights law? No doubt Shannon thought such a start a clever way to cover the signing of the antidiscrimination law.

The approaches used by Spears and Shannon remain typical—typical of the seeming lack of awareness, lack of context that continues to plague coverage of disability issues—even as we begin to see more "real" disability reporting.

How have journalism's opinion makers, those who shape the nation's media response to current events, viewed the Americans with Disabilities Act?

Few of the nation's syndicated columnists noted the passage of the ADA at all.

Charles Krauthammer, himself disabled, said nary a word. William Safire, Tom Wicker—nothing. Those who did mention it, like Paul Craig Roberts in the *Los Angeles Times*, did so merely to warn about its excesses. They saw it as another stage in the long road to hampering business; Roberts listed it among what he called "a burst of new regulatory legislation and aggressive enforcement of destructive laws already on the books" that he insisted would "add enormous costs to businesses that will cut into their profits."

Roberts's column was typical of the opinion pieces on the ADA. Liberal pundits have been notably silent about the ADA, seemingly not interested in weaving it into the fabric of diversity to which they give their attention—not believing, perhaps, that it even belongs there.

In the summer of the greatest rights push ever for people with disabilities, *Chicago Tribune* humorist Mike Royko chose to write about dwarf-tossing. That odious "sport" has over the years probably received nearly as much coverage as the Americans with Disabilities Act—most of it by humorists who think the issue little more than fodder for their laugh mills.

The venerable *New York Times* carried no opinion piece about the historic occasion. Yet in recent months the *Times* has run no fewer than five editorials exhorting passage of the Civil Rights Act of 1990. Why not the same support for disability rights?

Editorials on the ADA have mostly had a "canned" tone, as though the editorial writers had learned, perhaps from some disability group's fact sheet, what to say and were saying it. That in itself is a move forward and shouldn't be criticized. But one wonders how many of the editorial staff of these supportive papers have really taken the issue of disability rights to heart as they have civil rights or environmental issues. Giving disabled people a rights law is a good thing, say the supportive ones, but even they often throw in the worry of the business lobby: who knows what it will mean? The law is vague, editorials say, repeating the propaganda floated months earlier by the business community's fearmongers.

The *Arizona Republic* bites, hook, line and sinker:

Congressional critics of legislation requiring sweeping new civil rights protections and costly changes in public and private accommodations for disabled Americans argued that the bill, while well-intended, would mainly benefit the nation's huge litigation industry.

There is no more hyperbole ... no one ... has the least clue as to who might or might not be covered by the rubbery language of the law ... its multibillion-dollar cost to the economy ... the cost will be high.

The "nobody wants to be against the disabled, but ... " was typical of ADA editorials.

"Disabled people deserve a "chance" to get into the "mainstream," we read in some of the editorials. Have they taken that to heart, though? How many have hired disabled journalism graduates?

The timid "we support disability issues, but ... " tone has come through not only in editorials on the ADA but on the Fair Housing Act.

All the *Orange County Register* can say about proposed Fair Housing Amendment Act access guidelines is what by now passes for the standard, knee-jerk response to most of disability's changes in design.

"Humane? In theory, yes," the *Register* wimps, "but not necessarily in reality. It's the old saw again: Access (The ADA, employment requirements, captioned TV, you-name-it) will cost LOTS OF MONEY!"

Money seems to be all the *Arizona Republic* can think about.

One wonders when the understanding will come. Where are our backers who support rights and access for the right reason—not simply because they feel sorry for us? Where are the progressive journalists who see the disability rights as a rights movement that must be reported on, whether disability activists are pressing for coverage or not? Where are the liberal columnists who want the nation to understand the *justice* of disability rights?

Not too long ago, the *New York Times* produced a special supplement—reprints from twenty years of opinion pieces that had appeared on its Op-Ed page. In promoting the supplement, the *Times* noted that the pages had seen writers talking about the important issues of the past twenty years—and listed among them civil rights, the women's movement, and the environment. What didn't the *Times* list? Disability rights. Surprise?

Who in the media is trying to change the climate of opinion about disability? Who sees it as the human rights issue it is, and writes regularly about it? Where are our Ellen Goodmans, our Jesse Jacksons? We need them—now.

From *The Disability Rag* (Winter 1990)

Fat Prejudice? or Research Prejudice?

In a study to measure gradeschoolers' dislike of fat people, researchers asked children to select from drawings of an obese child and "children with various disabilities" who they would choose to be their friend. "The obese child always came in last," reports *Time* magazine.

What it didn't report: why did the study choose pictures of children with disabilities as controls? Was it to prove that, if the child selected the obese character, that would signal that fatness was *even worse* than being disabled? To form such a conclusion, wouldn't researchers have to believe that children intrinsically thought kids with disabilities were less desirable playmates than normal kids?

From *The Disability Rag* (September–October 1991)

5

Disability and the Media: The Ethics of the Matter

Deni Elliott

Advertising, news, and entertainment media have an important shared agenda: they all sell a dream of life-styles and beliefs. They give us heroes and villains. They tell us what is good and bad and what does not fit into the dream. According to the media, people with a disability do not.

The categories of stereotypes that media use to portray people with disabilities are damaging to perceptions of people with disabilities. So too is lack of presentation. For the most part, people with disabilities simply do not exist for the camera's eye.

The people with disabilities whom we meet through the media include a talented physicist who is described at the top of news stories written about his accomplishments as "a prisoner in his own body." The presentations include a man with a scarred face who is used to illustrate that driving when drunk can result in "a fate worse than death." And they include a teenaged girl who rates a feature story because she is managing to get through high school despite her blindness.

Disability could be presented as a usually unimportant consideration as media consumers work to achieve the dream world that media promote, but it does not happen that way. Rather, people with disabilities are presented as the stuff from which nightmares are made. They are offered as oddities and symbols of fear by which "normal" people can know their own worth.

People with disabilities are presented in ways that are just as offensive and destructive as the ways that women and minority groups were presented by media more than a quarter of a century ago.

News gives "aren't-you-glad-you're-not-him" stories. Advertising warns us not to "buy blind" and calls energy costs "crippling." Entertainment media specialize in inspirational "supercrip" stories.

The offensive presentation of people with disabilities is an ethical problem for media. Presentations that result in harm to individuals need to be justified, but it is not surprising that media managers would have a hard time understanding that people with disabilities are harmed by negative presentations when some of the major offenders are the public service groups with public service announcements.

These groups give us poster children. They warn that people who use drugs may end up disabled—a fate worse than death. In working on their own ethical problems concerning the presentation of people with disabilities, media managers must begin by understanding that their own sensitivity may, at times, be greater and more on target than those being exploited. This is not much different from the fact that for decades some minorities and women missed the realization that they were being exploited.

CATEGORIES OF EXPLOITATION

The Tin Cup Television Spot

What newsroom would turn down the opportunity to broadcast the need of a little girl who cannot read without a $10,000 visual aid? What newsroom would ignore the story of a ten-year-old boy collecting bottles and canvassing the neighborhood so that he can buy his mother an electric wheelchair? Not many would, but they all should. The need to plead for mobility or visual or hearing aids is not an episodic individual problem; it is a societal ill.

The individuals who attract media attention are not unique from those who lack such media savvy. They are only a few of many who have equal or greater need. When reporters focus on individual need as though it were an episodic problem, they miss a larger story and are necessarily unfair to those in need who fail to attract such attention.

There is no moral basis upon which a newsroom can decide that one person's need is greater than another's. Nothing but the capriciousness of the business explains how it is that last week's bone marrow transplant is news and that this week's is not. The decision to publicize one individual's need is economic: the slowness of the news day, how appealing the individual in need can appear to an audience, how well the fund raisers create media events. But the outcome, if it results in a lack of fair treatment, is unethical.

Additionally, journalists have a professional responsibility to see the big picture. Imagine what would have happened if news media had presented Rosa Parks as if she were an old black lady with an episodic complaint rather than a symbol for all African-Americans who were forced to give up their seats to white people. Instead, Rosa Parks exemplified a societal ill; news media correctly focused on the meaning of the event to the larger civil rights issue.

So it should be with media coverage of people in need. The individual's attempt to manipulate media attention raises a question that should not be missed by savvy reporters: What is going on when millions of dollars can be spent on a new bomber and people have to beg for mobility or visual or hearing aids?

Telethon Time

In recent years the media have worked well with promoters and public relations firms to raise money for various groups of individuals who have special needs: muscular dystrophy, Easter Seals, the March of Dimes, and others. Publicized group need, however, has two problems. First, the focus on the dependency of special groups of individuals directs attention away from the larger question of why people with disabilities should be dependent on private philanthropy to get what they need. Society makes a choice to allow every person equal access to police or fire services and to disallow equal access to medical care and to certain aids. That is the story that needs attention.

The second problem is the exploitation of individuals. The disability or illness is offered as the basis for negative comparison. The underlying message is, "Television viewer, look at this person who, because of a disability, is not capable of being 'normal' in the ways that matter to you. Disability means that the person affected cannot take care of his or her own needs. This person is dependent on you. Won't you help?"

It is not true that these individuals are dependent on philanthropy or that disability implies a loss of autonomy. It is society and the policy decisions that make the telethons necessary. A disease or disability of the week is no more sensible than a gardening need of the week or this week's hungry people. It may be an embarrassment that society does not care for all people in terms of their needs; we ought not to extend that embarrassment by allowing exploitation in addition.

"Help Me. I Can't Hear You." The headline screams the little girl's plight. The public service announcement is designed to attract givers. But the little girl's problem is not so much a lack of hearing as a societal lack that makes it a problem. People who lack hearing can do everything other people can do except hear. They grow and marry and parent successfully. They teach, act, dance, become doctors, lawyers, and college presidents. They may not become concert pianists, but neither do most hearing folks. The same can be said of any other disability. The disability is nothing more and nothing less than a characteristic of an individual that may present difficulty with a particular set of tasks. That disability is only one of many characteristics that any person has. When the disability is the focus, as it is with mass appeal fund-raising drives, the individual disappears behind the disability. The audience is encouraged to think of people with disabilities as dependent, unable to care for themselves. Why else would there be drives to raise money for them?

Such presentations perpetuate the view of people with disabilities as unable to function normally. Some people with disabilities are severely dependent, but most are not. Presentations of people with disabilities as dependent, particularly in the absence of positive presentations, imply that the dependent and needy are reflective of all people in that group.

The Supercrip

If the audience is accustomed to feeling sorry for and superior to people with disabilities, it is only natural that the "he's a credit to his disability" stories will follow. Some of these inspirational stories nest comfortably into the stories of subhumans; they are stories of people with disabilities who manage to perform what are hailed as spectacular tricks, like walking or earning a living.

"When I was 20, I Learned to Walk," proclaims a headline over a story about a young man who regained the use of his legs following a stroke and who finished a college degree. Becoming ambulatory was a personal challenge that is not necessarily connected to his ability to attend school successfully.

"My Deafness Doesn't Stop Me," reads the headline on a story about actress Stephanie Beacham. It is hard to imagine how her deafness could stop her unless her hearing problem is related to her mobility. What stopped this actress was a society that included hearing as a criterion for success.

Sometimes people with disabilities deserve news features or straight news stories because they merit notice for some special talent, such as athletic ability or scientific aptitude. However, the writers of such stories are sometimes too impressed by the disability to let achievement get in the way.

Physicist Stephen Hawking has yet to be mentioned in the media without discussion of his physical disabilities. Yet the effects of Lou Gehrig's disease have nothing to do with the scientist's work in theoretical physics. From initial write-ups I read on Hawking, I assumed that he fit the supercrip stories already described—that he was a run-of-the-mill scientist who was outstanding simply because he was also disabled. It was only through discussions with other physicists that I learned that Hawking is indeed among the brightest scientists of this century. The focus on his disability obscured his legitimate claim to fame. Hawking is no more impressive because he is a "crippled physicist" than Marie Curie was impressive because she was a "woman scientist" or James Earl Jones is impressive because he is a "black actor." The adjectives are descriptions of accidental traits that have no bearing on the importance of these people to society.

Fate Worse Than Death

When I tell a group of journalists that people with disabilities should be treated as "normal" by the media in the same way that women and people from all ethnic groups are treated as normal, someone usually interrupts to remind me that my analogy does not hold because there is nothing abnormal about being female or black, but that there is something abnormal about being disabled.

Being a woman is no longer generally considered a disability, but it was not long ago that a brilliant or athletic girl did not have the same opportunities as boys. If we create a world in which only the physically perfect can succeed, then being or becoming disabled can indeed be a fate worse than death.

Disability as a fate worse than death, and its accompanying metaphor of disability as punishment, serves as the basis for a horribly effective series of campaigns designed to discourage drug use and drunk driving. "Most of the damage caused by drunk driving can easily be fixed in a body shop," reads the headline on the public service announcement. Below a page full of prostheses, the tag line reads, "Don't drive drunk. Dying isn't the only thing that could happen to you." A man, sitting in a wheelchair, faces away from the camera. The headline, "Drugs Do More Than Kill," says it all.

No one would deny the effectiveness of these campaigns, but they are effective at the expense of people who have disabilities. Wheelchairs and protheses are liberating, not limiting, for the people who choose to use them. Users and others, however, are encouraged to think about the objects in a negative way when they are presented as something to be feared.

It is true that some people who have disabilities have them because of accidents or negligence, but most do not. Public service announcements like these imply that people who have disabilities deserve them. The implication is visual, not logical. Most people, if they stopped to think about it, would deny that the implication holds. But these types of persuasive techniques are emotional. They encourage feeling, not thought. And the negative feeling created by the campaign may surface the next time the consumer sees a person using a wheelchair instead of the next time the person reaches for a beer.

In addition, these public service announcements exploit one group of people to benefit another. The harm to the exploited group cannot be justified. Imagine the following pro-choice campaign: Pictures of dead, battered children lie across the billboard. The headline reads: "Now or Later?" A kicker reads: "Prevent Their Births or Expect Their Deaths." Children who are abused should not be exploited to encourage the termination of pregnancies, even if it is sometimes true that unwanted children are abused. People with disabilities should not be exploited to discourage drinking or drugs, even if it is sometimes true that people who drink or use drugs become disabled.

The fate-worse-than-death category of exploitation has spawned a set of metaphors that have taken on meanings of their own. When words with negative connotations are used in conjunction with words that denote disabilities, the denotations begin carrying negative connotations in other contexts. For example, we read in news stories and headlines that people are "confined" to bed or to a wheelchair. They are "imprisoned" by (heavy) braces or by their own bodies. These are words we use with people who are put in jail for wrongdoing. If we allow these words to be acceptable descriptions of people with disabilities, it should not be a surprise when words denoting disabilities are used in a negative fashion.

"Don't buy blind," the ad warns, and the consumer knows immediately that blind is a bad thing. "Cuts cripple services," says the newscaster, and the viewer knows that something bad has happened. The fact that the words are used metaphorically does not justify the offense to a group in society.

It is not likely that media would use terminology like "jew somebody out of it" as a way of describing getting an exceptionally good deal, although the phrase had vernacular use long after the reference was made concerning one ethnic group. How long has it been since you've seen a commercial-land father chide a sobbing boy by saying, "Stop acting like a girl!" The offense of women is taken seriously now. People with disabilities deserve the same consideration.

THE IMMORALITY OF THEM AND US

It is unethical to present people with disabilities in negative or exploitive ways because it is inaccurate and unfair to an oppressed societal group. The challenge of presenting people with disabilities in a normal or positive fashion gives media a new possibility for enlarging our understanding of what it means to be "normal."

The negative presentations of people with disabilities are not true of most people within that definable group. Providing accurate representations is a journalistic responsibility, but it holds to some extent for those working in advertising, public relations, and entertainment media as well. It is no more reasonable to expect "normal" presentations of people with disabilities in persuasive communication than it is to expect normal presentations of any other people. But people with disabilities should be represented as a normal part of society.

It is especially important to be sensitive to the need to present oppressed groups in a positive light. No more is being asked for people with disabilities than what was asked for women or ethnic groups. Principles of fairness and equity demand that no less be provided.

The interaction of various types of media creates a special power for media managers to change public perceptions. Journalists have a history of noticing and promoting oppressed groups in society. Through positive presentations, public relations, advertising, and entertainment, media reinforce the idea that *they*—the oppressed or isolated—are like *us* in all of the important ways.

In the past thirty years, criteria by which we measure success in the United States has grown broader than the designations of white and male. No longer do we hear young African-Americans say they wish they were white because so many more opportunities would be open for them. One can be female or a member of any ethnic group and be a success.

If our criteria were broadened a little more, as is the hope of the ADA, it would not be a tragedy for someone to use a wheelchair. It would not be professionally limiting for someone to lack vision or hearing.

Media can help by presenting people with disabilities as they now present women and minorities. Media can provide entry into society for people with disabilities by treating them as people.

Scaring the monkeys: Comments by Senator Lowell Weicker on the Introduction of the ADA Bill, April 1988

People with cerebral palsy are turned away from restaurants because proprietors say their appearance will upset other patrons. People who use wheelchairs are blocked by curbs, steps and narrow doorways from getting into many arenas, stadiums, theaters and other public buildings; many such facilities have no [provisions] for people with hearing or visual impairments.

It has been over 30 years since some zoos and parks were closed to keep blacks from visiting them at the peak of civil rights demonstrations and boycotts. Yet it was only last month that the *Washington Post* reported the story of a zookeeper who refused to admit children with Down's Syndrome because he feared they would upset the chimpanzees.

From *The Disability Rag* (July–August 1988)

6

Disability Issues and the American Society of Newspaper Editors: All of Us Are Disabled

Bill Breisky

Archbishop Desmond Tutu had been scheduled to address the Thursday luncheon at the 1990 convention of the American Society of Newspaper Editors (ASNE) in Washington, D.C., but a crisis in South Africa caused him to cancel his appearance at the last minute, and a substitute speaker had to be found. King Jordan, president of nearby Gallaudet University, the nationally acclaimed university for students who are deaf, was invited to fill in. Dr. Jordan accepted immediately, saying that while he was no Desmond Tutu, he would welcome the opportunity to challenge the editors of America's daily newspapers to help eliminate barriers that discriminate against people with disabilities.

King Jordan did more than that. His luncheon address illustrated his own thesis that people with disabilities must focus on what they can do, to counteract those who would focus on what they cannot do.

The introduction of Jordan by *Miami Herald* publisher David Lawrence, Jr., the incoming ASNE president, provided an unforgettable illustration of the power of the human spirit. Instead of making a trite statement about how King Jordan had "surmounted" deafness, Lawrence related a powerful story about how Jordan's life had been transformed—*salvaged* would not have been too strong a word—by his so-called disability.

"King Jordan," David Lawrence told his audience of editors that day,

grew up in a small community in suburban Philadelphia. Had he stayed in Glenwillard, Pennsylvania, a factory job probably would have been his life's work. An average student, he had no ambition for higher education. He was graduated from high school with a C average, and just one honor: You will find him in the yearbook under Class Clown. He joined the Navy for adventure, but ended up serving coffee in the Pentagon. In Washington, he loved to party, staying out all night with friends, laughing, telling stories. He would whip around the District of Columbia on a motorcycle, enjoying his freedom, and, frankly, not worrying about a lot. And then one night, while riding his motorcycle from a part-time job in downtown Washington, a car headed in the opposite direction turned across his path. King Jordan became a projectile. He flew over the hood and through the windshield, crushing his skull on the car's rearview mirror. A priest gave him last rites. The neurosurgeon at the hospital said, "If you are praying, pray that he dies."

In one instant, at age 21, "King Jordan had almost lost his life."

He had, indeed, lost his hearing, but, "In silence, King Jordan found clarity of purpose. He became convinced he could do anything anybody else could do, and more than most would do—except, of course, hear."

Jordan enrolled at Gallaudet. He married and started a family. He earned a doctorate in psychology at the University of Tennessee and returned to Gallaudet as a professor of psychology.

"He bolted through the system," Lawrence related, "with the speed and determination of a motorcycle rider—assistant professor, associate professor, full professor, psychology department chair . . . dean of the College of Arts and Sciences." And then, when the students closed down the campus and began chanting "Deaf president now!" after the board of trustees had selected a hearing person to run the university, King Jordan was invited to become the first deaf president of Gallaudet.

President Jordan was standing before the ASNE meeting with a message: "Deaf people can do anything. Deaf people can do anything but hear."

Many in his audience sat spellbound when Jordan told them, "I am deaf. So what? I cannot hear. So what? You do not have to remind me of that; I know that very well. But I can do many, many things. Focus on those things I can do." We did.

On the morning when Jordan was scheduled to speak, the ASNE microphone had been held by Loren Ghiglione, the society's departing president, who had, in order to help achieve a better respect for diversity in newsrooms and in communities, established an ASNE committee to focus on disabilities issues. Loren had introduced me, as chairman of that committee, and I in turn had introduced a remarkable National Public Radio reporter named John Hockenberry, who wheeled himself up to the mike and told us: "Diversity is worth doing. Diversity is what your newspapers are all about."

JOURNALIST IN A WHEELCHAIR

Hockenberry also empowered his audience to do some things most of us had not considered. He was speaking from first-hand experience when he said: "I can tell you that you can send someone in a wheelchair—who is a paraplegic, for instance—to cover the funeral of Ayatollah Khomeini. You can do it. You can send him to cover the intifada and the West Bank and Gaza. You can send him or her to Bucharest (to cover the violent overthrow of the Ceausescu regime), and you do not have to worry about your reporter becoming a hostage, dead meat, or losing his or her nerve, any more than you have to worry about that with any other journalist."

Hockenberry had covered those stories, and more, so he knew that a journalist in a wheelchair can be given such assignments. He cited references who could testify to the wisdom of putting a paraplegic journalist on such assignments—Juan Tamayo of the *Miami Herald*, Curtis Wilkie and Mary Curtis of the *Boston Globe*, Danny Williams of the *Los Angeles Times*, John Kifner and Joel Brinkley of the *New York Times*, Steve Franklin of the *Chicago Tribune*. "We worked side by side," he said. "There did not seem to be a problem."

And please, he implored us, don't get the idea that he covered those stories "despite his handicap." He has, in fact, employed "wheelchair tactics" that have given him an advantage over his competitors. The wheelchair has, indeed, "been an advantage, and it has illuminated more than it has suppressed or repressed or limited me."

I would like to think that King Jordan and John Hockenberry helped reprogram the minds of the ASNE editors who heard them that April morning in 1990. They taught us several important lessons—one of which is that talented people with disabilities afford us a largely untapped opportunity to bring true diversity to our newsrooms.

The ASNE membership's common understanding of disabilities issues took a few more steps forward the following spring, during the society's Boston convention, at an "earlybird" session on disabilities issues—despite the fact that few editors showed up. (The average newspaper editor, a few of us were persuaded that morning, is disabled in at least one respect: He or she is not quite able to summon enough energy at 7:45 a.m. to sit in a hotel conference room and listen to a program entitled, "Disabilities and the Newsroom.")

The four panelists that morning had a lot to say.

Harold Russell, who had his hands blown off in World War II and went on to win two Academy Awards for his role in the classic *The Best Years of Our Lives*, who chaired the President's Committee on Hiring People with Disabilities under presidents from Johnson to Reagan, and whose

Harold Russell Institute long has specialized in placing people with disabilities in industry and government, and who thus ought to know a thing or two about human potential, told us: "It's the guy who counts—not the disability."

Panelist Betsy Wilson, who lost her lower jaw to cancer in 1972 and went on to found the American branch of Let's Face It, a network for people with facial disfigurement, helped us begin to appreciate what it means to be judged by a visible disability.

Bill Torrey, a Voice of America reporter who had spent the previous year as a Gannett Foundation research fellow, demonstrated how technology can help newspapers improve access to news for people with visual impairments.

The panelist with the most pragmatic message at the earlybird session was Terry Sullivan, vice president for personnel of *USA Today*, who talked about newsroom applications of the American with Disabilities Act. Editors, she sought to persuade us, need to do a better job of reaching out to journalists with disabilities because the pool of young journalists entering the work force is shrinking. And she showed us how to overcome the biggest obstacle to mainstreaming workers with disabilities in newspapers—prejudice.

"In my experience," Sullivan said, "prejudice toward the disabled, like it or not, is based on an intense discomfort—I call it 'disease.' When one sees the disability as a disease, that is exactly how one reacts—with disease." Newsroom managers, she said, "are afraid that people with disabilities are going to cost them money, and professional reputation. We must get over that hurdle."

Then she showed us how to open the doors for journalists with disabilities—by conducting an educational program enabling all newsroom employees to confront biases and myths concerning disabilities and to remove attitudinal barriers of working with people with disabilities; by revising job descriptions to identify the essential functions of newsroom jobs; by calling local agencies that can help the newspaper recruit people with disabilities; and by consulting with services such as the Job Accommodation Network to learn about accommodation options.

HANDBOOK ON DISABILITY REPORTING

ASNE's real work is not accomplished at conventions, but by member-editors working on committees on a voluntary basis. And that certainly has been true of those who have worked on disabilities issues.

The first major project of the Disabilities Committee was a handbook titled "Reporting on People with Disabilities." Committee member Tom Grein, a Washington editor whose experience with polio taught him a few things about disabilities issues, volunteered to write the first draft.

That handbook—eventually printed as a pullout section for the *ASNE Bulletin* magazine—opened with a collection of reporting techniques, and focused on a long glossary ranging from AFFLICTED ("Connotes pain and suffering; most people with disabilities do not suffer chronic pain") to WHEELCHAIR ("Do not say that a person is 'confined to a wheelchair' or is 'wheelchair-bound.' . . . Wheelchairs help with mobility; they do not imprison people"). The handbook closed with a listing of reliable sources that reporters and editors might use in reporting about people with disabilities.

Grein's draft was circulated to members of our Disabilities Committee for comment. And I, in turn, showed my copy to two people.

Karen Jeffrey, who covers the human-services beat at the *Cape Cod Times*, which I edit, made me aware of an extraordinary oversight: Our handbook on disabilities dealt solely with physical disabilities. Thanks to reporter Jeffrey, and copy editor Nancy Ayotte, our handbook grew to include such terms as "bipolar disorder" "mania," "paranoid," and "schizophrenia"— and the ASNE definition of disability grew to embrace mental, as well as physical, impairment.

The second person was my eldest daughter. Karen Breisky and I sat side by side on the living room sofa over a period of evenings and debated definitions. Karen spoke from experience. At the age of 2, she had suffered a brain injury that left her temporarily sightless, speechless and immobile. By 1989, having defeated or come to terms with most of her disabilities, she had taken a string of psychology courses on her way toward earning an associate's degree at our Cape Cod Community College, had sat in on the first meeting of ASNE Disabilities Committee in Washington, and was more than up to snuff on the issues before us.

One of the glossary terms we polished together: "DISABLED: An adjective that describes a permanent or semipermanent condition that interferes with a person's ability to do something independently, such as walk, see, hear, learn or lift. Example: 'The amputation of his leg left him partially disabled.' Do not say simply, 'He is disabled'—because no one is totally disabled. And by all means do not use 'disabled' as a noun—such as 'The disabled will gather.' It can be argued that every human being is disabled in one or more ways." That statement, of course, is more than a simple definition; an attitude, even a philosophy of life.

A second major ASNE Disabilities Committee project was a survey of daily newspapers concerning their experiences in hiring people with disabilities, and in working with staffers who become disabled in one way or another. The initial draft of the survey was produced by John Reed, editor of the *Mail Tribune* in Medford, Oregon—and shaped and analyzed by Joseph Keefer, an associate professor of journalism at Pennsylvania State University.

The survey constituted ASNE's first effort to shed some light on newsrooms' records in employing people with disabilities. In November 1990, ASNE sent its survey questionnaire to 1,626 daily papers, seeking information on policies, practices and experiences. The questionnaire covered five categories of newsroom employees—reporters/writers, editors/ managers, copyeditors, photographers/artists, and support personnel/secretaries. The questions in the survey were simple and straightforward—but asking editors to provide accurate numbers of full-time and part-time employees with disabilities, over a five-year period, and to break the numbers down by job category and type of disability, was no simple task for many.

One in five of the papers surveyed responded—and of those, 111 reported having employed, full-time, at least one person with a disability at some point in the period 1986 through 1990. The results were analyzed and reported by Keefer and by Michael R. Smith, an assistant professor at Lycoming College in Pennsylvania.

"Of the 111 editors who reported that their newspaper had experience with an employee with a disability," Keefer and Smith wrote, "only nine were aware of such an employee who had performed unsatisfactorily. "The overwhelming majority of editors who had experience with an employee with a disability characterized the experience as a success, and many editors effusively praised employees with disabilities."

RESULTS OF THE SURVEY

Some specifics: Thirty-six percent of those who reported experience in employing a news staffer with a disability said they had needed to provide special equipment. Ninety-five percent said newspapers should encourage the hiring of such staffers. Only one in four respondents reported having been contacted by a representative of an organization that encourages hiring of people with disabilities. The survey's breakdown by job category and type of disability, among the 111 papers reporting such experience, may be seen in Table 2.

Few metro papers participated in the survey, probably because their staffs are large, memories are short, and their personnel offices simply had no records enabling them to provide accurate figures. Some of the small-town dailies that responded were particularly impressive, because on such dailies, every staffer—disabled or not—must be able to carry his or her

Table 2

Number of Persons with Disabilities Who Were Employed Full Time by Newspapers, 1986–1990, by Disability Category and Job Category

Disability Category	Job Category					Total
	Reporter	Manager	Copy Editor	Photographer	Support Staff	
Wheelchair Required	15	4	8	3	3	33
Walking Aids Required	16	11	15	1	4	47
Arm Use Restricted	12	4	1	1	2	20
Hearing Impaired	10	4	5	5	6	30
Vision Impaired	7	3	1	0	5	16
Mental Illness	3	3	0	1	3	10
Mental Retardation	0	0	0	0	3	3
Speech Impediment	6	2	4	3	3	18
Disfigurement	5	2	3	3	3	16
Other Disability	3	1	2	0	1	7
Total	75	34	39	17	33	198

Note: The total of 75 reporters represents 77 disabilities because two reporters have two disabilities each. Similarly, the total of 198 persons with disabilities represents 200 disabilities.

share of the load. Four Wisconsin papers afforded good models for the rest of us.

Mike Payton, managing editor of *The Evening Telegram* (circ. 16,000) in Superior, reported three staffers with disabilities, including "a veteran employee in our sports department lost both legs to diabetes and has been forced to use both crutches and a wheelchair while learning to walk again. He would have burned the building down if we had made a big thing of it. . . . "He doesn't want to hear the word disabled. 'I walk funny,' he says, 'but I'm not disabled.' "

Mark Baker, editor of the Chippewa *Herald-Telegram* (circ. 8,000), reported that two of his six reporters have disabilities—a sports writer with a hearing impairment, and a news reporter who is paralyzed from the waist down.

Should newspapers encourage the hiring of people with disabilities? The main thing, says Baker, is for newsroom managers to shed any preconceived notions that disabilities get in the way of good journalism. When a story breaks, the reporter in the wheelchair starts thinking right away about how to cover it well under deadline, says Baker—while his boss may be saying to himself, "I wonder if we should put Joe on that story." That editor's attitude, says Baker, is the real handicap.

Jeff Hovind, editor of the *Daily Citizen* (circ. 11,000) in Beaver Dam, reported two staffers with disabilities on a staff of 13—a reporter who is visually impaired and a photographer with a serious hearing impairment. "Both," Hovind reported, "are excellent workers." To accommodate their photographer's hearing problem, the *Citizen* rigged a safelight so they could call him out of the darkroom by flipping a switch. The vision-impaired reporter had to be driven to assignments—but he resolved that problem by engaging his girlfriend, now his wife, to do the driving.

The survey form submitted by Evan Sasman, managing editor of *The Daily Press* (circ. 9,000), in Ashland, concerned Sasman himself and two coworkers. "One employee with a prosthetic hand, hired as sports reporter in 1986, now is managing editor," he wrote. "One freelance reporter—a member of the Wisconsin Disabilities Council. New general manager with disfigured hand. We're all damn good!"

Sasman lost his right hand in a farming accident at the age of thirteen. Typing speed is no problem; he can type fifty to sixty words a minute, using his prosthesis to depress the space bar. Neither has special accommodation proved a problem. To the survey question concerning special equipment or other accommodations required for his staff, Sasman responds: "One pair of left-handed scissors."

Although the ASNE's Disabilities Committee has been dissolved, disabilities issues seem ensured of a permanent place on the ASNE agenda; they now fall in the portfolio of the Human Resources Committee. Edward Seaton, editor-publisher of the *Manhattan* (Kansas) *Mercury* and current committee chair, is seeking to focus on disabilities issues inside the newsroom—in particular, practical ways to accommodate newsroom staffers with disabilities. Virtually all physical disabilities—paraplegia, deafness, visual impairment, repetitive stress injury—can be accommodated with today's technology. Even a journalist with a spelling disability can be accommodated; a spell-checking capability is available with most newsroom computer systems.

The major disabilities that get in the way of solid, objective news reporting are, however, no easier to accommodate today than they ever were, nor should we want to accommodate them. Laziness, bias, easy assumptions—such newsroom disabilities cannot be overcome by technology or by modified work stations.

7

In the Workplace: The Reality

RARELY HAVE I HAD TO DUCK
James A. Fussell

I want you to imagine you are a city editor sneaking a peek at a frightening new job applicant. As you look at him, he jerks his head to the left, snaps it to the right, then slams it backward until, for a moment, he appears to be staring at the ceiling. Then he blinks his eyes, waggles his tongue and begins the same routine again.

Now I want you to imagine something even more frightening: hiring him.

Believe it or not, that's exactly what three editors have done with me.

I have Tourette syndrome, a neurological disorder caused by a chemical imbalance in the brain. Not something you'd choose to put on your résumé, I grant you, but hey, life is tough.

To their credit, editors wherever I have applied have taken the time to listen to me when I told them my odd physical movements did not affect my ability to gather news or spin a story.

If being a reporter for the *Kansas City Star* is interesting, being a reporter with Tourette syndrome is fascinating.

You do a lot of explaining—to the editors, co-workers, to sources and to strangers. You explain that Tourette syndrome is a medical condition that causes certain movements and that you are not nervous, weird or having an epilepsy attack.

I have to be honest, though. Tourette syndrome does limit what I can do. For instance, I wouldn't make a very good brain surgeon. But if you think my condition stops me from doing much else, you are mistaken. It doesn't stop me from being married to a sexy redhead. Or from having a house, a cocker spaniel, or a 1-year-old son who is already singing his ABCs.

And it doesn't stop me from being a reporter.

It is difficult for me to make it through some days with deadlines and stresses, but so what? Any job would be difficult for me, and I happen to like being a reporter.

At times I even think Tourette syndrome has made me a better reporter. It has made me sensitive, made me a good observer, made me confront prejudice and recognize unfairness.

Sometimes I do get frustrated, especially when shaking while gathering information in the field for a story on deadline.

"You're a reporter?" said one woman who obviously couldn't believe that the person shaking his head in front of her was a member of the working press. "You?"

"Yes ma'am," I said, exasperated. "I walk, talk, I've been known to write down whole sentences. I'm really fairly amazing, but I've only got 10 minutes, so can you answer my questions now so I can make my deadline?"

She did, I did, and everybody was happy. Later I told her about my disorder, and we had a good laugh.

I think most people would accept me if I could only sit down and talk to them one-on-one. But how do you tell a whole city about a strange malady that makes you shake and blink and, at times appear, stark-staring nuts?

I decided to write a piece about myself for our Sunday magazine. I received dozens of letters and more than 100 phone calls. Strangers came up to me on the street and introduced themselves. People called and thanked me for enlightening them about Tourette syndrome, or for helping them get diagnosed.

Still, not nearly enough people read that article. People mock me every day.

An editor on my paper once told me that, considering my symptoms, going into the stressful and public world of journalism was possibly the dumbest thing I could have done.

He was impressed, he said, that I could go out every day and meet new people while doing the strange things that I do.

I told him that as person with a disability, I face challenges, prejudice and people who would just as soon spit on me as look at me. But then so do reporters in general, I said, so what's the difference?

A *Wall Street Journal* editor once advised me not to say anything about my symptoms and to hide them if I could. I discarded his advice in favor of an old Slavic proverb: Tell the truth and duck. When it comes to my disability, I have always told the truth. Rarely have I had to duck.

The bottom line is that my co-workers and editors are great, not because they treat me in a special way, but because they treat me like anybody else.

They laugh at my jokes, they yell at me if I screw up and they don't make any exceptions for my disability. That's the only way I want it.

NOTE

Reprinted with permission from James A. Fussell and *ASNE Bulletin*, September 1990.

EDUCATING OTHERS NEVER REALLY ENDS
Ken Rains

The 90-day probation had passed quickly, and I was beginning to believe I actually had a job. No one seemed concerned about my handicap until a chance encounter in the restroom.

A colleague was waiting on me so he could wash his hands. We spoke a few words about the weather, and then he said he just had to ask me something and hoped it wouldn't offend me. I told him to go ahead.

"You seem to get along just fine, but . . . well . . . I've been wondering. How do you pick your nose? I couldn't live without picking my nose," he said.

I muttered something about using a cotton swab, and he replied that that sounded like a good idea. He fumbled for an apology for asking "such a crazy question," but I assured him it didn't upset me.

His question was unusual, but it wasn't crazy then and isn't now. Instead it reveals something about how too many people perceive the handicapped. They invariably see a problem and don't ponder about the solutions.

Fortunately, I live in a community and work in a newsroom that are people-oriented.

They know hiring the handicapped can mean giving an employee who not only will be competent but reliable and dedicated.

There are other spinoffs. Not only do the handicapped become self-supporting, but their presence enhances the awareness of co-workers and the community about people who are different in the way they look, talk, walk, think, work and go about their daily lives.

The handicapped, in turn, become more aware of the many possibilities for working and living in the mainstream of life. But it isn't something they can seek and obtain without carrying their share of responsibility.

They must be prepared, through education and training, to be competent employees.

But the process of learning, adapting to change and educating others about themselves never really ends. It is a continuing process even with the best of support from family, friends, employees, co-workers and community.

Stubborn determination helps, but it isn't enough. I remember a day when I was in a stubborn mood about doing everything for myself.

My father, after questioning my feelings, said: "You'll meet people every day who want to be nice to you. They'll go home and kick the dog, slap the wife and cuss the kids. You might be the only chance that day for them to feel good about themselves."

Thirty-three years ago a gasoline explosion resulted in burns over most of my body and seriously crippled my hands. There was a long recovery in an Army hospital, marriage, children and college.

Work on the Vincennes University *Trailblazer*, the *Indiana Daily Student* and a summer internship at the *Fort Wayne News Sentinel* provided some experience and encouragement. But the real test was getting a job.

I got the chance 21 years ago with the *Lafayette Journal and Courier*. I was pounding on a manual typewriter, fighting to beat deadlines for an afternoon newspaper.

I was determined to make a go of it, asking for no more or less than what was expected of others. But after a couple of months my nubs-for-fingers felt as if I had been punching bricks.

The solution was a portable electric typewriter that I had used in college, but I wondered what my city editor would do when he saw it. He walked over, watched me type and walked away. He returned after lunch, and I thought, "This is it. I'm going to have to ask for a special break. This could be the end."

It was—for the portable. He sent me out to buy whatever electric typewriter I wanted.

Since then, the newspaper has made the transition to computers. Computerization helped me and certainly has provided more opportunities for the handicapped to join the working world.

But I still see too few of us. In my 21 years as a reporter, I remember meeting only four other editors or reporters with apparent physical handicaps. That's hard to understand when there have been so many electronic and technological accomplishments that can benefit employers and the handicapped.

Unfortunately, there's no computer command that will make people think about the handicapped and all the possibilities for them. That's still up to employers and the handicapped themselves.

NOTE

Reprinted with permission from Ken Rains and the *ASNE Bulletin*, September 1990.

ALL THEY WANT IS TO BE TREATED LIKE EVERYONE ELSE
Tom Grein

It was the fall of 1953, about six months before they found a vaccine for polio. Four young children in our church in Bay City, Michigan already had died from it. They told us not to walk barefoot in the grass, swim in public pools or get chilled.

They found a prevention for polio before they even knew what caused it. Or how not to catch it. They didn't even know whether to isolate me in the hospital. They did, just because they didn't want to take a chance.

No matter. I caught it, and I have been physically disabled ever since, even though I never really thought of myself as being disabled, or handicapped, or even crippled. I've been labeled all of them, but as a kid, my friends called me lame. Sort of sounded like Tiny Tim, who was a hero of mine.

I missed the fifth and sixth grades altogether, a time I spent getting rehabilitated in a Sister Kenny polio hospital in Farmington, Michigan. I also missed most of the seventh grade, but after I got home they shipped me off to what they called the Bay County Orthopedic School.

It was a school for physically and mentally disabled kids, unwanted in the main school system because school administrators thought disabled students would never fit in with all the jocks and scholars. It took federal laws to change all of that.

There were three of us in the eighth grade. I just wanted to get on with life. There was Dick Jankowski, a fellow with a bad heart but a good soul, who had to sit all the time and wasn't supposed to play basketball even from a wheelchair.

He did, but we never told anyone.

And there was Everett Colley, a boy who walked around on his hands all the time because he didn't have any legs. His hands were huge, like feet, and they cracked from the hard use they got walking on concrete and hardwood floors.

He used to urinate on his hands because his father told him it would help heal the sores.

I wish I had been a journalist then.

Because my father was a schoolteacher, I got back in the regular system my freshman year, and I never thought much of it again until I was the editor of the *Fremont* (Nebraska) *Tribune*, a small Gannett daily outside of Omaha.

I had children of my own then, and one night my wife and I attended a school function, one of those Thanksgiving or Christmas musicals in which all the children get together on stage to sing songs, act out seasonal plays and make parents smile.

Across the gym floor came my son Will, a third-grader, hand-in-hand with a student who had Down syndrome. It was Will's task to help this youngster find his place and be by his side. They sang together, terribly out of key and out of step but very much in the companionship that two boys find together.

It was a touching moment, for they both relished their friendship. At least for this holiday season, their lives were undeniably intertwined.

Maybe it was then that I realized the supreme importance of integrating disabled people into schools, jobs and our newspapers. That night made me a better editor and a better person. Even though I had lived the life of being sent to "the school in the country," it took two small boys to remind me why it was all wrong.

As journalists, we try hard to see life the way it really is, with all its pimples, its joys, its unexplained and unfair sorrows. We often fail, simply because it's difficult to accept and explain those things that are so different from our own experiences.

Because of that we like to grab on to the story that tells the tale of the young man who walks across Canada on one leg, or the fellow who leaves his wheelchair to climb a mountain. After all, it's something we all could do with two good legs or one good heart.

It's our way of saying to our readers, "See, we do pay attention to the disabled."

But for millions of disabled people across the world, those spectacular stories are not necessary. All they want is to be treated like everyone else in our news coverage, to be sought out for quotes and opinions, not because they are disabled, but because they are people with jobs, families and futures.

Like the little boy with Down syndrome, all they want to do is to walk across the gym and sing a little song.

NOTE

Reprinted with permission from Tom Grein and the *ASNE Bulletin*, September 1990.

MY ADVANCEMENT WOULDN'T HAVE BEEN POSSIBLE
WITHOUT THE HELP OF MY COLLEAGUES
Joel Torczon

While many people with disabilities are struggling to enter the work force because of employers' fears about their impairments, I have been one of the luckier ones.

Having been employed for six years at the *Bakersfield Californian*, I was promoted to chief copy editor in October 1989 despite a severe-to-profound nerve deafness that requires me to wear hearing aids and rely on lip reading.

My advancement wouldn't have been possible without the understanding and help of my colleagues and supervisors.

They have taken or made phone calls for me. This continues today, although I now handle most calls through the California Relay Service, which sends calls through a telecommunications device for the deaf, or TDD. The TDD, which the *Californian* bought for me when I began employment, has been an invaluable tool for my work.

While I have difficulty understanding co-workers in groups, such as the editors' daily budget meetings, my colleagues have shown sensitivity by making sure I didn't miss anything through personal communication, written materials and computer messages.

My hearing impairment led me to copy editing because it involves less communication than reporting. My job primarily consists of editing stories, writing headlines, laying out pages and supervising a crew of seven copy editors.

Being a journalist wasn't my goal upon entering college. I majored in accounting at Hutchinson (Kansas) Community College and for a year at Kansas State University.

When it became apparent that accounting wasn't what I wanted to do for a career, I "listened" to my heart, which said to pursue journalism. The switch in majors meant that it took me a year longer to gain my bachelor's degree, but it was worth it. I also had gained the experience from working on the daily campus paper in various positions and from serving a year-long internship in the university's news office. But I still didn't feel ready to enter the workplace after graduation.

To resolve doubt about my future in journalism, I spoke with Bob Bentley, executive editor of the *Californian*, while visiting my family in the area. I was encouraged by the conversation and decided to return to Kansas State to earn a master's degree.

Just before I received my master's in 1984, Bentley called to see if I was still available for a vacant copy editor position. I readily accepted and began my journalism career. I started out with the least experience among eight copy editors but became the more experienced after several changes on the desk over five years.

At first I had reservations about being promoted to chief copy editor, not only because of my hearing impairment but because I was also working part-time as a temporary journalism adviser at Bakersfield College. The college job turned out to be a blessing. It helped me develop the leadership and communication skills necessary to be an effective copy-desk supervisor.

While I've been fortunate not to have encountered any outwardly negative attitudes toward my impairment, I am aware that many individuals with disabilities are being shunned by employers.

To combat this problem in Bakersfield, the Mayor's Committee for the Employment of Disabled Persons and Project Employment, a federally funded program directed by Chuck Wall, a blind business professor at Bakersfield College, has been educating employers about the benefits of hiring people with disabilities.

The advantages, according to a Project Employment brochure, are that disabled employees generally are more loyal, use less sick leave and are more reliable. With 70 percent of the 43 million disabled Americans being jobless, they make up the largest untapped, unemployed minority group in the nation, it says.

Project Employment is focusing attention on matching employers' job requirements with candidates' skills and abilities, rather than simply attempting to persuade an employer to hire a person with a disability.

I encourage newspaper employers to contact local agencies that work with disabled people to see if any prospective employees are available.

Those employers may be enlightened by a Project Employment motto: "Don't hire the handicap; hire the ability."

NOTE

Reprinted with permission from Joel Torczon and the *ASNE Bulletin*, September 1990.

SOME THOUGHTS ON "BALD, CRIPPLED MIDGETS"
David Lawrence, Jr.

John Wolin sits in the *Miami Herald's* afternoon news meeting, wiping a brow damp from the labor of walking, with cane, to the conference room. It's the first meeting for new executive editor Doug Clifton, and the assembled editors are on their best behavior. Wolin, grinning, starts off the presentation and introduces himself: "I'm the bald, crippled midget."

The remark evaporates the tension. Wolin's ability to joke about himself and others is something people who know him have prized for years. To the *Herald* family, John Wolin is one of the best: award-winning sports writer and assistant sports editor, husband to *TV Book* editor Glenda Wolin, father of seven-year-old heartthrob Lindsay and a damn good Girl Scout cookie salesperson.

By confronting his disability, and putting others at ease about it, Wolin has deftly turned his stature and his cane into non-issues. He is accepted, and is a great contributor to the *Herald*. Being accepted, being able to contribute are two things anyone with a disability seeks, whether a journalist on your staff or someone you are writing about.

Not patronizing. Not pity. Not coy avoidance.

Acceptance. Whether a person is blind or deaf, uses a wheelchair or deals with some other physical challenge, that person deserves equal treatment. It not only is common decency, but the law of the land.

Dennis Hollingsworth of Paris, Missouri, wants the midwestern papers he strings for to accept that he's a "pretty decent reporter" even though he's quadriplegic. Most of Donna Halvorsen's co-workers at the *Minneapolis Star Tribune* don't know that their award-winning courts reporter is equipped with hearing aid and amplified phone receiver.

ASNE's Disabilities Committee, headed by Bill Breisky of the *Hyannis* (Massachusetts) *Cape Cod Times*, took on the challenge of how to deal with disabilities on our own staffs and how to write sensitively about disabilities. Their work could not be more timely, paralleling 1990's Americans with Disabilities Act.

The act prohibits discrimination in employment decisions against qualified individuals with disabilities. It also requires guaranteed access for people in wheelchairs to public accommodations such as restaurants, stores, museums and theaters. The employment provisions will be phased in between 1992 and 1994, while the equal-access measures take effect January 26, 1992.

You'll find many questions answered in an 18-page document issued by the Justice Department's Office on the Americans with Disabilities Act. Write P.O. Box 66118, Washington, DC 20035-6118 (202-514-0301).

A word of advice from Breisky: "Consider the people first, not the disabilities, whether you're writing about them or hiring them."

Donna Halvorsen, Dennis Hollingsworth and John Wolin are entitled to that. So is everyone else.

NOTE

Reprinted with permission from David Lawrence, Jr., and the *ASNE Bulletin*, July–August 1991.

8

Is There a Future in Journalism for Those with a Disability?: The Other 80 Percent

Clark Edwards

It was one of those days that make you wish you had studied ditch digging rather than journalism in college. Vice-President Hubert Humphrey was campaigning for the presidency, and he campaigned hard. The day had begun at 4:30 A.M. in Minneapolis and had ended nearly a thousand miles and five cities later in Boston.

At each city, there was the routine: off-load all the television equipment, set it up, check it out, shoot the speech, get crowd reactions, do some interviews, knock it all down, pack the equipment and check it again, load it back on the plane, find a seat aboard the plane, check to be sure all of the crew members made it on the flight, make editing notes, scripting notes, fall asleep for a half-hour. When the pilot announced over the public address system the caution to place tray tables in the upright position, it was time for the routine again.

By the end of this particular day, I was ready for the day to end. My only consolation was that this was the first of an eleven-day campaign swing. Now there were only ten more days of the routine.

At nearly midnight we checked into the hotel in downtown Boston. By now, the three people in our crew were dragging more than carrying our gear to our rooms. As we passed down the hall, each person would disappear at a room number. I was at the end of the hall, the last room down.

While my aching bones were moving in slow motion, my mind was still able to run in a higher gear. I had the presence of mind to call room service and order breakfast and a wake-up call for 5:00 A.M. I dropped to the bed, removing jacket and shirt, reaching a somewhat numbed decision to crash, leaving the shower and shave for the morning. I unbuckled the harness holding my left-lower leg and let the "lumber" fall to the floor—slacks, sock, and shoe still in place.

The wake-up call and the knock at the door came within a few seconds of each other. The call had brought me to near consciousness, and the room service waiter's pounding made me sit up in bed. From that position I yelled, "Come on in."

The waiter opened the door and pushed his cart carrying my food into the room. The smell of fresh coffee was quickly connecting me to reality. The waiter, dressed in proper Bostonian hotel fashion, pushed the cart to the edge of the bed. I thought I detected a New World kind of British accent in his speech as he lifted the metal lids from the various plates and described the food on each. Without breaking the verbal rhythm of his presentation, he stunned me with a question. "Will the gentleman under the bed be having breakfast?" he asked, looking at some point on the far wall.

"Other gentleman?" I mumbled, my coordination between thinking and talking not yet up to speed.

"Yes. Will the other gentleman need breakfast?" he repeated.

I turned to the edge of the bed and looked down. I am sure I slept soundly but did not think I would have missed someone coming into the room during the night. By now, the phrase, "under the bed" had reached through my waking fog and was slowly being analyzed by a caffeine deprived brain. I peered over the edge of the bed and I saw my prosthesis, shoe, sock, and pant leg sticking out from under the bed covers that partially obscured it. I started to laugh and told the waiter, "No, that's part of me."

I reached down and pulled my leg from under the covers to reassure the waiter that there was not someone under the bed.

Still in very proper form, the waiter—only glancing at the leg—refixed his eyes on the far wall, spun in military fashion, and said, "Very good, sir," as he headed for the door.

I'm sure he did not wait long to relate this encounter to the rest of the hotel staff. I know I have since told the story many times. Each time I think of the incident, I try to think of great one-liners that I should have said. In any event, I am sure I provided that waiter with a bit of a lesson about dealing with the disabled.

I gathered up the crew. We carried our equipment to the lobby to catch the media bus for the airport. As we milled around, the same waiter passed through the lobby with another breakfast cart. He glanced at me. I nodded and smiled.

"All together again, are we?" he asked with a passing smile.

"Yeah," I said. "Running like a rebuilt."

STEREOTYPES WE MADE

I have often thought of this incident and have since reinterpreted the encounter and the waiter's staring at the wall. He was uncomfortable, unable to think of any other behavior. He knew I was part of a television news crew covering the presidential campaign. He had a set of expectations. When he confronted the reality of me and the "wooden leg," he suffered from a spontaneous paradigm shift.

It really was not his fault. He probably got his stereotypical image of television reporters from watching reporters promote themselves. Journalists working in all media sell themselves through promotional materials as being hard-charging, go-anywhere, do-anything kind of people. All three major networks promote their anchor people by showing the difficult places they have been to get their stories. Local promotions for newspapers use television promotional announcements and depict their reporters in the same way. Even if it were true that reporters needed the physical ability of a football wide receiver, reporters comprise only about 20 percent of those employed in journalism. What about the other 80 percent of the jobs where brain power, not arm or leg strength, is needed?

I am increasingly uncomfortable with journalistic promotional announcements—house ads—on television, radio, and in newspapers. My discomfort comes from the fact journalists are promoting journalism using a stereotype. For example, in Pittsburgh, a promotion announcement[1] presents a KDKA-TV anchor charging up a flight of stairs to an official-looking building in a scene reminiscent of a Rocky movie. Another promotional announcement for this same anchor was taped while she was riding an exercise bicycle. But she is already where she is going on the bicycle and it has nothing to do with her job. The stairs she is running up are indeed to city hall, but it is also obvious the building is closed for the day. There is also a radio promotional announcement—on television—showing a WTAE-AM radio reporter jumping from a news cruiser with walkie-talkie in hand and dodging through traffic toward a police car.[2] I have seen several newspaper ads in the past year that also equate physicality with journalism.

Physicality may be an easy image to focus on, and once it may have been a useful image. Now the stereotype is conveying a wrong message to disabled young people who might consider a future in journalism. This stereotype of journalism has had—and if continued will have—a major impact on disabled students looking for careers. The problem, over the years, has been that educational institutions that teach journalism have fallen into the trap of believing the stereotype. Most colleges and universities are ignoring the education for a potential 80 percent or more of the jobs in journalism for students who could enter the field without four-four speed in the forty-yard dash or perfect vision or hearing.

ROLE MODELS

There is a serious need to examine the number of newspaper, radio, or television journalism jobs that actually require this stair-dashing, running-gunning individual, as opposed to the intellectually able editorial writer or editor, the creative page designer, infographics-creating journalist, phone-beat reporter, television producer, radio or television anchor and the everyday city council or Congress-covering reporter.

Professionals and educators need to define better all the complex roles of journalism. Depiction of successful journalists doing their individual jobs, including those who use wheelchairs, or crutches, or canes, or technological-assisting devices, could encourage disabled young persons to look closely at journalism as a career path.

There are exceptional individuals in the media now who are role models. A Peabody Award–winning radio journalist for National Public Radio and the ABC network, John Hockenberry, uses a wheelchair to cover assignments around the globe. Kay Maddox, an information services editor for the *Atlanta Journal and Constitution* has spina bifida. Los Angeles television anchor Bree Walker has an inherited condition, ectrodactyly, which is a congenital deformity of the hands and feet. Liz Campbell, born blind, is a feature writer for the *Fort Worth Star-Telegram*. Bill Strothers uses a wheelchair and is the ombudsman for the *San Diego Union-Leader*. Emilio Milian, a Cuban-born journalist, news director, and talk show host at WQBA in Miami, lost both legs to an anti-Castro terrorist car bomb. Milian, now using a wheelchair, is still reporting and speaking out for the nonviolent overthrow of Fidel Castro. These are a few of the most visible disabled journalists. The problem is there are far too few disabled in all job categories in journalism in the nation, visible or not.

EMPLOYMENT

There are enough visible exceptions to the stereotype to dispense logically with old beliefs regarding what the disabled can do; however, old ideas do not fade away easily. In a 1992 survey of 323 responding newspapers, 111—approximately one-third—reported they employed people with disabilities in their newsrooms. The survey, conducted by the American Society of Newspaper Editors (ASNE), stated that most responding newspapers thought newsrooms should be open to all.[3] However, there are very few disabled who are working professional journalists. Annemarie Cooke and Neil Reisner, writing in the November 1991 *Washington Journalism Review*, note that "those disabled journalists with notable credits in newspapers, radio and television view their successes as aberrations."[4]

A third of the newspapers responding to the ASNE survey said they employ the disabled, but that does not correlate well with national unemployment figures for the disabled. Of the 43 million disabled in the United States, less than one-third of those eighteen-years or older are employed. These statistics demonstrate how much of an aberration those few who are successful are and how misleading some mail-in questionnaires are.

Chris Jennewein, the *Atlanta Journal and Constitution* director of information services, says, "In journalism, where you are manipulating information, physical disabilities don't have a bearing on the job—it's more intellectual than related to physical strength and agility. People with disabilities can more than pull their weight in the newsroom environment.... I wonder if disabled people bring a certain kind of wisdom others don't have by seeing the tougher side of life."[5]

Because the majority of the jobs in journalism require brains, not brawn, the classroom is the obvious place to begin to dispel the stereotype and resolve the aberration. But we will see very few disabled students in journalism classrooms if the disabled do not see role models in education and career paths within the industry. Some changes are required in the way we promote the profession and the way we recruit students into journalism education. Students are recruited into journalism to fill jobs in the news industry.

Of the typical jobs in a medium or small daily newspaper newsroom (see Figure 1), only in two areas might a person with a disability encounter physical difficulties: street reporters and photographers. However, even these positions can be (and are being) successfully filled by persons with disabilities. If a small newspaper has four photographers, one or perhaps two of them need to be able to deal with the mountaintop plane crash or the run-through-the-door drug bust photos. Most newspaper photographic assignments do not involve these physical demands. Chief photographers should also realize that a person with a disability who can overcome life's obstacles to become a photographer can overcome most of the occasional professional obstacles. The same is true of reporters. Every job and every disability has to be judged individually. It is hard to imagine that a person with a disability who has the mental toughness to become a reporter is not creative enough to overcome any obstacles to getting the facts for a story. Most of the other newsroom positions pose few potential physical obstacles, and any of these obstacles can usually be overcome with computer-based or technical-assistance devices. Much radio reporting is done using the telephone and two-way radio equipment. Audio recording equipment is small and operated easily. The 1973 Architectural Barriers Act removed most barriers and made virtually all public buildings accessible. Other than an inability to speak, what could prevent a disabled person from becoming a successful radio reporter?

Television reporting poses a few potential problems. Most of these difficulties deal with the fact that someone has to move some of the equipment, some of the time. Nevertheless, very few disabilities could prevent a person's dealing with the equipment. There are, in fact, few jobs in a television newsroom that a person with a disability could not successfully do.

The point that the few working disabled professionals have made is that it is time to discuss an individual's ability on the job. To get access to the newsroom, we must develop journalistic skills in the classroom.

Figure 1
A Typical Newsroom Organization

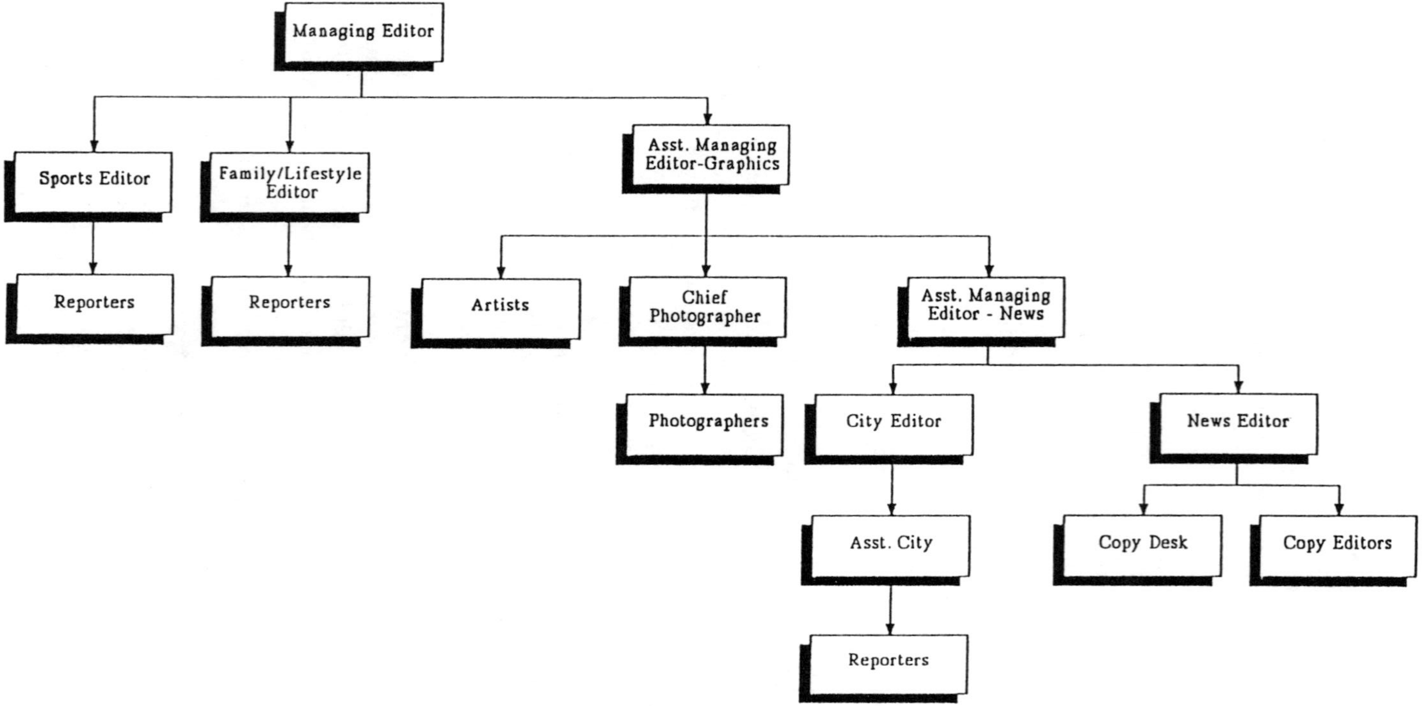

OPENING THE CLASSROOM

The moral, voluntary approach to integrating the disabled into journalism—or most other areas of human endeavor—has not worked, a situation that led to passage of the Americans with Disabilities Act (ADA) in 1990. The ADA is often called the civil rights act for the disabled.

Education is the foundation for employment access, and employment access is primary to social integration. David Broder of the *Washington Post* called the ADA "the most significant civil rights and social-policy legislation to become law in more than a decade."[6] Some of its congressional sponsors noted that it is the most sweeping piece of social legislation since the 1964 Civil Rights Acts—and the media missed the story. It was as though the media collectively were staring at the wall, wondering about the other gentleman under the bed.

Following the passage of the act, I checked newspapers and full-text databases for stories concerning the ADA and found little coverage. I expanded the search pattern to encompass the categories "disabled" and all "minorities." Coverage of the disabled amounted to 0.1 percent of the stories in eleven major daily newspapers in the two years after the law was passed.

Michael Smith, writing in the December 28, 1991, issue of *Editor and Publisher*, "Shop Talk at Thirty," urges newspapers to become the "engine to fuel change for the disabled." Smith notes the AEJMC's People with Disabilities Committee is "suggesting ways to teach the next generation of journalism students to use some creative alternatives to the standard 'supercrip' or 'sadcrip' stories so popular with reporters."[7]

Eldon Nelson, manager of awareness programs for the IBM National Support Center for Persons with Disabilities, notes that there are 43 million disabled in America. This means that "one in six Americans have some type of disability. Every year 750,000 more Americans join their ranks, most of them through accidents." In fact, Nelson often refers to himself as "temporarily able-bodied," to point out that the "disabled are not people just like you and me—they *are* you and me."[8]

Another national organization points out that a disabled person affects the lives of other individuals—family members and friends—making the real number of the "disability movement" closer to 120 million. It is no wonder that Congress finally noticed what Annemarie Cooke and Neil Reisner called the "last minority."[9]

ACCESS, INTEGRATION, EDUCATION

The purpose of the ADA is to facilitate the integration of the disabled into the mainstream of society by providing the disabled with access to opportunity. The law, signed by President George Bush on January 26, 1990, contained a two-year transition period to enable institutions, business, and education to get their facilities and programs into compliance with thousands of pages of specifications. The transition period ended January 1, 1992.

Because the law defines denial of access as discrimination, the full force of the U.S. Justice Department and other federal agencies can be brought to bear. Class action suits are often based on patterns of past policies and procedures. Past patterns of institutional behavior, for example, have become the legal basis for many racial discrimination lawsuits since 1964 and one of the primary tools in gender-pay inequality legal actions.

A body of specific precedent law has not emerged yet, but the Justice Department Civil Rights Division has suggested that discrimination by race, gender, or disability will be treated all the same way. In the *Chronicle of Higher Education* issue of January 8, 1992, the "Washington Update" section reported that the Education Department's Office for Civil Rights was complaining "of a high case load because of an increasing number of complaints about discrimination in education programs. The bulk of the cases involve allegations of discrimination against the handicapped."[10]

At a December 1992 meeting of journalism and mass communication educational administrators, I raised a question about the wording in the proposed revisions of accreditation standard 12, which deals with "recruiting, advising, retaining and preparing minority students and minority and women faculty members for their intended career paths." The proposal is filled with language referring to women and ethnic or racial minorities. My question about whether the language dealt with the need to include the disabled in order to comply with the 1990 federal law was brushed aside with the response, "It's something to *think* about."

There are several problematic considerations for members of the academy to think about. One deals with faculty employment, specifically whether colleges or schools are including the specific wording "disabled are encouraged to apply" in their advertising search for faculty. A review of the *Chronicle of Higher Education* and *AEJMC News* found that only one, the University of Tulsa, had included such language in its faculty search announcements as of January 1992. Other journalism/communication positions being advertised at that time, however, specifically encouraged racial minorities and women to apply. Will this type of information be used as evidence of a pattern of discrimination against the disabled? Legal experts say it might.

Chicago Sun-Times book editor Henry Kisor has attempted the transition from the working professional world to the classroom. Kisor noted, "I've applied for professorships at various universities, and either never heard a word or didn't even get an initial interview once my deafness was revealed."[11] Similarly, *Buffalo* (N.Y.) *News* life-styles editor Susan LoTempio relates the story about a colleague's advising her not to go into the profession, suggesting she would not get a job in journalism because of her disability. LoTempio, who uses a wheelchair, is succeeding in her fourth news editorial position.

She and other panelists speaking to the December 1991 Conference on Covering the Disabled in America at St. Bonaventure University noted the difficulties they have had with journalism educators who are devoted to the old stereotype.[12] Many journalism educators still see the real-world journalist as the person who charges up flights of stairs pursuing an interview with a firefighter in a burning building or clamoring up the side of a mountain to a plane crash site for a picture or a story. They fail to recognize the fact that few journalists do either of these things in their lifetimes. Mary Johnson, editor of *The Disability Rag*, a magazine focusing on disability issues, said, "There are issues that affect the lives of people with disabilities that aren't being covered." Johnson also noted that features involving the disabled that do appear in the media emphasize—and thus perpetuate—the "heroic cripple" or the "pathetic cripple" stereotype. LoTempio believes that disabilities make editors uncomfortable, so newspapers are more willing to cover stories involving medical breakthroughs and "gee-whiz sympathy stories."

What constitutes news, what should or should not be covered, and how a story should be covered—the angle—are taught in journalism education. Stories concerning race—other than crime or similar societal exceptions— seldom appeared in the mainstream press or network television newscasts until the mid-1950s. Stories about female athletes—other than the "super-mom" or "supergirl" athlete—seldom appeared in or on the nation's major news outlets with any consistency or prominence until the 1980s.

The stories about the social extremes—superwomen or supercrips—were only momentarily fashionable, and it can be argued they fit the "uniqueness" criteria of news judgment and were good journalism. Perhaps. If these stories were good journalism, then they have been done enough and it is time to move disability stories and stories by disabled reporters into the mainstream of society. It is time stories about the disabled be judged by the same criteria as city council, airport commission, local political races, or school boards. Journalism educators should be teaching this normalized approach in the classroom.

Perhaps editors would be more comfortable—stare at blank spots on the wall less—if journalism educators and reporters were sensitized to the issues of the disabled. Educators need to train all journalists to be as sensitive to the nature of disability issues as they are currently to training journalism students to deal sensitively with race and gender issues.

There is no extensive research on disability issues available at the moment, other than a count of the "supercrip, sadcrip" stories. However, the Canadian Parliament's Standing Committee on the Status of Disabled Persons has examined disability reporting in the Canadian media. The first annual report by this committee, delivered in August 1988, noted "that coverage of disabled persons and of issues concerning disability was relatively slight. On average, there were fewer than one item per issue in most papers." And what coverage there was focused on "local services rather than on government policies and that disability-related issues are not high on the public policy agenda."[13]

The Canadian study's examination of the CBC and Global Television Network found that coverage tended to focus on "celebrity" aspects—that is, disabled persons who had become prominent or famous. It "usually failed to link disability issues with advocacy, interaction with government or the provision of services." Generally, the Canadian study found, the patterns of coverage left much to be desired. It concluded "that the mass media do not present the items of concern to disabled persons with great frequency or prominence. . . . In terms of subject matter, most coverage is pegged to events such as fund-raising and charitable activities, incidents involving disabled persons, and accomplishments of disabled athletes. Furthermore, editorials and commentaries on issues relevant to disability issues were almost completely absent."[14] I would expect a similar report on the American mass media would be as dismal—if not more so—concerning story content and story angle, a result of the way journalists are trained to deal with people with disabilities and disability issues.

Once disabled students are educated in journalism's craft and assume editorial decision-making positions in newsrooms, the approach to coverage will change. But it is also imperative that nondisabled students are trained to deal with disability issues.

Another consideration for journalism academics relates to the fact many universities spend a considerable amount of money, energy, and time recruiting ethnic minority students, including for journalism/communication programs. On the other hand, very little money, energy, or time has been spent in the past two years by any university specifically to recruit disabled students. This raises the question about how equally an entire class of people is considered.

The ADA was signed in 1990. Business, industry, education, and the government itself had until January 1992 to make physical changes to buildings and to make any other programmatic and policy changes needed to implement the law fully. The two-year transition period built into the ADA did not excuse anyone from getting their house in order.

Justice Department investigators say they will use a technique developed to implement the 1964 Civil Rights Act to enforce the ADA. That technique involves using statistical analysis of past performance and patterns of corporate or educational prior behavior.[15]

TOP-DOWN CHANGE OF HEART

Society and the profession of journalism will have to experience a change of heart before discrimination against the disabled comes to an end. That change should come from the top down. However, the view at the political top—the national political parties—is less than promising.

The February 1992 issue of *Advertising Age* magazine contains a small note dealing with the disclaimer policy requirements for political advertising on television. In December 1991, the Federal Communications Commission (FCC) had ruled that audio disclaimers must accompany all political advertising to accommodate the blind and visually impaired viewer. Two months later, the FCC had bowed to considerable pressure from the Republican and Democratic national parties and rescinded the December mandate. Political commercials need to carry only video disclaimers, and these disclaimers must be visible for only four seconds.[16] The complaints from the national parties are coming from the same politicians who passed the ADA.

The National Organization on Disability, a Washington-based nonprofit group, stated that the federal government's own figures indicate there are 43 million people with disabilities in the United States, and these 43 million people directly affect an additional 50 million family members.[17] The "disability movement," as James Brady, former presidential spokesman for Ronald Reagan, calls it, is large and emotional. Brady, who serves as vice-chairman of the National Organization on Disability, has helped launch a major informational campaign, Calling on America, with public service advertising aimed at raising awareness of issues affecting people with disabilities. Brady's group is trying to enlist 5,000 communities across the nation for their support at the local level. "I know from personal experience that we do not have equal access to fulfilling lives in our towns and cities because of society's attitudes, biases and physical and social barriers," Brady told the Washington National Press Club in August 1991. "We hope to turn on Americans to an urgent need. People make partnerships work. I urge their support in areas such as employment, education, recreation, worship, shopping and all aspects of community life which today are not fully accessible to people with disabilities. By participating more we can contribute more."[18]

Alan Reich, president of the National Organization on Disability, told the National Press Club, "Crucial laws like the Americans with Disabilities Act are a good start, but laws are not enough; you cannot legislate attitudinal changes and acceptance. A national change of heart requires action and commitment. That is already happening in hundreds of communities across the nation, and our campaign is designed to encourage thousands more to get involved."[19] This national change of heart forms the moral basis of the ADA. No one with a disability wants to force the issue; however, if both the spirit and letter of the new laws are ignored, expect direct confrontation.

PREJUDICE, BAGGAGE, AND GOOD LUCK

I was covering an extensive spring flood in Alabama in 1979. Because of the danger of dropping expensive, new cameras into the water, I had opted to assign all reporters, photographers, assignment editor, anchors, and myself to use the old CP-16 film cameras. I had decided we could cover the entire state in one day by sending everyone out alone with his or her own camera. We thus scattered to the wet countryside.

I found myself peering down a backcountry, two-lane highway that disappeared into a huge body of newly arrived water. I saw several people on a rooftop several hundred yards into the water and a person with a john-boat poling his way toward me and dry pavement. I jerked the CP-16 to my shoulder, rolling and zooming to record the wide, medium, close-up sequence of images that I knew I would need. The boat docked on the white center-line in the road, and I shot the two passengers disembarking.

The captain was a "good-old boy," typical of south Alabama. He was dressed in bib overalls. No shirt. No shoes. A slight tobacco stain was evident in his five-day-old beard. He grinned at the camera a lot. I asked him if I could ride out to the house on his way back for the others and get some pictures from that end to complete my story sequence. Still standing on the middle flat-board seat in the boat, he said, "Ya'lls welcome to come . . . but I'm real prejudiced agin' ya'lls extree baggage." He smiled, spit tobacco juice into the muddy water, and nodded to indicate to me that I should look down. In a New York second, I did a frantic Texas two-step without any subtle New Mexico nuances. While I was standing—rock-solid, still shooting pictures—a water moccasin had come up to me, hit my left leg, and had buried its fangs in the large heavy seam at the cuff of my Levis.

I panicked. I started hopping on my right foot, shaking, swinging, jerking, and stomping my left leg in an attempt to get rid of what looked like the biggest snake in history. I should have given the camera to the john-boat skipper so the event—no doubt my last story—could have been recorded. It would have made good action picture for my obituary. I could tell by his cackling he was enjoying the show.

I finally realized the south Alabama ballet wasn't getting the snake loose. I stopped my performance, stomped on the snake just behind its head with my right foot, and with my left leg delivered a blow into the air that could have produced a seventy-yard field goal. The snake both came apart and came loose of my trousers.

It took a few minutes and a few profanities before my professional demeanor returned. The john-boat driver climbed out of the boat, walked to me, going down on one knee to examine the snake's former attachment point. It was his turn to be surprised. "Ya'lls got a wooden leg!" he said several times. I didn't tell him I already knew that. He stood up and patted me on the back saying, "Ya'lls lucky to have that wooden leg. Yessir, you got you some good luck there."

We got into the little boat and started moving over the shallow, muddy floodwater toward the mostly submerged house. About midway in the trip, he told me his name was Trent McBee. I told him my name.

"Ya'lls understand what I meant back there? Me and them snakes just don't understand one another. That's why I'm prejudiced," he said.

I know the dialogue is correct, and I've got old Trent's words exactly. I forgot to turn the camera off and recorded a lot of strange, bouncing, jerking images but perfect audio. It all edited into a good story.

TOMORROW

In the context of the late 1970s in south Alabama, Trent McBee had said a lot in his few words. Put the meaning of those few phrases into today's context, and they have significant meaning for the future.

Disabled persons, by strength of will, courage, and ability, have repeatedly proved that there is little they cannot do if given the opportunity. Opportunity really comprises preparation and venue. Preparation comes from education. If the disabled are to be given an opportunity in journalism or any of the related fields of mass communication, educational institutions must accept them into their classrooms for training and professional development. If educated, prepared, disabled individuals are to gain access to a productive career, they have to have a place to work, a venue at which they can demonstrate what they can do. This means that nondiscriminatory employment practices must be followed by managers in the media.

Most of the prejudice against disabled journalists will fade with understanding. It will end when nondisabled media managers shed the stereotypical baggage that most now carry around and give disabled journalists an opportunity to fill positions in the other 80 percent—or more—of all journalistic jobs.

Journalism educators and journalism professionals need to face the challenge of the 1990 Americans with Disabilities Act. Journalism educators must integrate disabled students into their programs. Journalism professionals must integrate disabled journalists into the newsroom. Denying access to the classroom and the newsroom is discrimination—as illegal as denying access on the basis of race or gender.

Journalism, both education and the profession, was at the cutting edge of integration in the racial civil rights movement. Both are active and publicly expressive in the battle over gender equality. Both, however, seem reluctant and silent concerning the disability movement.

Perhaps it is the difference between identifying a "handicapped" person in a news story when in fact you are referring to a "disabled" person. *Handicap*, as the *AP Stylebook* notes, is the barrier, while *disabled* is the status of the individual. The difference also is one of understanding.

NOTES

1. This "promo" aired from March to June 1992.
2. This video promotion for WTAE Radio aired during September and October 1991.

3. See Thomas W. Grein and Bill Breisky, *Reporting on People With Disabilities.* American Society of Newspaper Editors, 1991.

4. Annemarie Cooke and Neil Reisner, "The Last Minority," *Washington Journalism Review*, 13:10, 14–18 December 1991.

5. Cooke and Reisner, p. 17.

6. David Broder, "Americans With Disabilities Act Signed," *Washington Post*, January 4, 1990.

7. Michael Smith, "Newspapers must be the engine to fuel change for the disabled," *Editor & Publisher*, December 28, 1991, p. 40.

8. Joseph Lazzard, "Computers for the Disabled," *Byte*, June 1992, p. 59.

9. See Cooke and Reisner.

10. P. A-38.

11. Cooke and Reisner, p. 16.

12. "Covering the Disabled in America," conference at St. Bonaventure University. Oleans, New York, October 18–19, 1991.

13. Patrick Boyer, M.P., "No News is Bad News," *First Report of the Standing Committee on the Status of Disabled Persons*, House of Commons, Ottawa, Canada, August 1988.

14. Ibid.

15. Scott Jaschik, "46 colleges found to have violated rights of the disabled, U.S. documents show," *Chronicle of Higher Education*, April 21, 1993. p. A-18.

16. "FCC changes disclaimer policy," *Advertising Age*, February 1992, p. 21.

17. Speech by John Brady, National Press Club, Washington, D.C., August 1991.

18. Clark Edwards, "The Americans With Disability Act," *News Computing Journal*, 7:3 (Fall 1991), pp. 1–9.

19. Alan Reich, speech to the National Press Club, Washington, D.C., August 11, 1991.

9

From Mailroom to Newsroom

Joe Coughlin

The response was polite enough—it just was not what I wanted to hear. "We'd like to use you on television," said the executive producer, "but we just can't. It's the immediacy of the medium. We wouldn't have time to explain that you have cerebral palsy."

I had always known that it would be difficult, but lifting myself over barriers and skirting obstacles had been part of my life since I was old enough to fall. Graduating in 1975 with a joint degree in broadcast journalism and political science from the University of Windsor, I had already learned that most institutional doors are meant to be opened by able-bodied people. I was about to be confronted with the most intractable barrier yet: an attitude.

"People would not be paying attention to what you were saying, Joe," he went on, sensing I had not understood the first time. "They'd be looking at your crutches and your crooked legs, and wondering what was wrong with you."

What *was* wrong with me—or with the multitude of talented women who had tried to break into television newsrooms? With them, male viewers would be held hostage to their hormones and mentally incapacitated by the mere sight of a female anchor. With me, my "withered legs" and crutches would ignite such curiosity that the viewers of Canada's premier news shows would drift off into speculative la-la land.

At least he was being honest. A few weeks earlier, I had been told that I was welcome to work for the Canadian Broadcasting Corporation (CBC, a government-funded network). However, for persons with my education and experience, entry-level meant working in the mailroom.

Yeah, right.

In the fifteen years since that conversation, I have anchored a national news show the night Iraq invaded Kuwait, hosted three seasons of a highly rated national weekly news and current affairs program targeted to people with disabilities, and watched the sun come up after numerous all-night shifts on "CBC Newsworld," Canada's twenty-four-hour news channel. I have seen talent blossom when affirmative action programs have delivered previously denied opportunities. I have shared the excitement of breaking new ground with individuals bursting with new ideas. And I have been dismayed when well-intentioned people, wanting the same ends, cannot agree on the means. But most of all, I have been patient—not by choice but by the reality imposed by generations of misconceptions and stereotypes, many perpetuated through media. At the same time, I have benefited by attempts to redress the imbalance. My belated start in television came in 1988 through co-hosting a thirteen-week special on disability issues.

Getting journalists with disabilities into mainstream media, though, is much more difficult, and until this happens, and journalists with disabilities become assignment editors, news editors, and anchors, many of the stereotyped attitudes and barriers will persist. Other groups in society face similar problems. Women, people of color, aboriginals, gays and lesbians: all have mounted campaigns to ease representatives into positions of influence, including media. Issues become mainstream when significant numbers of people with influence are affected.

By the very nature of disability, those affected face additional barriers, physical and attitudinal, in breaking into and advancing as journalists. And the situation is getting worse. In an era of media downsizing, those with seniority are the ones to retain their jobs; journalists with disabilities are not on this list.

For those lucky enough to land a first job, it is likely to be covering the disability beat, an assignment that brings many rewards (and a few heartaches too). The achievements of people with disabilities can become big stories in mainstream media. "What determination! An inspiration to all!" they suggest. But they also lend themselves to stereotyped coverage. As a journalist, I want to recognize these people's achievement but avoid stereotyping. Story selection is another contentious issue. Accusations of oversight are inevitable because of the diverse nature of disability itself; covering every constituency equally is impossible. Other issues to consider are the balance between an individual's rights and the responsibilities of society, and the role of humor in covering disability issues.

The rights of people with disabilities are discounted when society says it cannot afford the changes necessary to create a level playing field. Yet those rights are as important as those of any other minority. For me it was difficult to achieve objective journalistic balance when individuals with disabilities were denied access to education, transportation, and employment because of some fiscal restraint program. Often there was only one side to the story.

As for humor, I feel the same as John Callahan, a nationally-syndicated cartoonist who uses a wheelchair. We both see a humorous side to the dark aspects of a disability. Because of the news focus of television shows I have hosted, my sense of humor was edited or—even worse—discouraged. Some producers were not willing to take the risk of offending our audience. A true test of our integration occurs when people allow us to laugh at ourselves and join in the fun.

My first professional television interview was with a Canadian athlete who raised $25 million for spinal cord research by completing an around-the-world tour in a wheelchair. Rick Hansen's Man in Motion tour had taken him three years, preceded by three and one half years of training. An athlete before his car accident, he had become a world-class wheelchair athlete after it, several years before training for the tour. I was interviewing him for the premier episode of "Challenge Journal," the first television series in Canada to be hosted by people with disabilities. Its purpose was to portray people with disabilities in a positive light and reflect their need for integration. The series ran through the fall of 1988 and was aired throughout most of Ontario.

To date, most of the media coverage of the Man in Motion tour—and there had been plenty in Canada—had focused on the scale of Hansen's physical achievement, and it was no mean feat. But tending to get eclipsed were the issues facing the average person using a wheelchair. The slant was not unusual. Media coverage of people with disabilities commonly portrays them as either superhuman heroes, who should inspire us all, or helpless victims who deserve pity—if not something from our wallets.

Yet what Hansen accomplished for the disabled community was obviously important. An astute person himself, he was also surrounded by astute people whom he had trusted. The annual interest from the $25 million Man in Motion legacy fund—the principal of which is to be untouched—would be a major source of funding for research and would help Hansen shape the public agenda on disability issues throughout North America. It was these issues I wanted to discuss in the interview. I was thoroughly prepared and sure I could strike the right tone in my questioning.

Hansen's unpretentious manner quickly put me at ease, and he gave intelligent and thought-provoking answers to my questions. Critics within the community had suggested that Hansen had sold out to corporate interests by getting the backing of Nike and McDonald's. He answered these charges by pointing out that with the roughly $2 million annual interest from the Man in Motion legacy fund, his group had achieved virtual political independence. He also carefully downplayed his hero image in mainstream media. "What I did wheeling around the world is comparable to someone with a respirator getting up out of bed to go to work," Hansen said. "It takes the same amount of preparation." Since then, Hansen has successfully led a coalition in the establishment of National Access Awareness Week in Canada and was largely responsible for organizing the first international congress on disability, Independence 92, held in April 1992 in Vancouver, Canada.

If anyone in the community needed reminding how diverse a group people with disabilities are, Independence 92 served to focus the issue. In attendance was the People First movement, an international group for people with mental impairment. They vigorously protested throughout the congress that the level of discussion was too sophisticated for them. They were right. They were unfamiliar with the professional jargon, and the issues discussed are complex. By the nature of their disability, this group could not effectively participate in debate with the rest of the community.

My next major television contract was to be co-host of the Disability Network (DNET), a program produced, directed, written, edited, and hosted by men and women with disabilities. In addition to serving the information needs of the disabled community, the show was to serve as a springboard for launching staff into positions with mainstream shows. Funding for the program came from Canada's federal Department of Employment and Immigration and Metro Toronto through the Centre for Independent Living in Toronto; CBC provided a studio, office space, and four weeks of training.

The program's debut was March 31, 1990. It was quick and classy and had an edge to it. We started with an excerpt from the Academy Awards showing Daniel Day-Lewis accepting the Oscar as best actor in *My Left Foot* for his portrayal of Christy Brown, a writer with cerebral palsy. We wanted to know, Why did the parts of the younger and older Brown have to be played by able-bodied actors? Next was an interview with the head of the Canadian Human Rights Commission, Max Yalden, who commented on attitudes toward people with disabilities and decried the lack of progress made during the United Nations–designated Decade of the Disabled. "I have seen no leadership," he said, "only occasional flowery statements as to how important the decade is." We closed with a look at Toronto's inaccessible transit system.

After the first episode, CBC Newsworld, a twenty-four-hour all-news cable network, decided to carry the show across the country. Shortly after, CBC-owned and -operated stations and other affiliate stations started coming on board. Soon we were given access to CBC's extensive tape library. Then came satellite technology; viewers could now see both the interviewer on set and the person being interviewed. During the first thirteen weeks of the program, we went from being a local cable show to a technically polished national show. We typically opened with a quick newscast and then examined the issues in the lead story in more depth.

Covering all the possible issues of interest has been a challenge, and we have been accused of not covering the broad spectrum of the disability community. For example, people with hearing deficits have repeatedly criticized us for not producing enough stories tackling their concerns. They may be right. The issue is largely one of language—American Sign Language (ASL). Unless an interviewer knows it, getting the story can be difficult. Other barriers are that many stories begin with casual conversations—virtually impossible through an interpreter—and, people without hearing have developed their own culture. Without benefit of knowing the language, understanding and appreciating deaf culture is a barrier for many journalists.

These barriers admittedly represent the extreme. However, every group in the disabled community has a somewhat different agenda from other groups. There are now organizations representing people with virtually every disability known: multiple sclerosis, cerebral palsy, visual impairment, hearing impairment, learning disabilities, cognitive disabilities, mental impairment, and the others. Politically, then, the broad community is splintered.

The broader question raised is this: If people with disabilities have difficulty communicating among themselves, how can they hope to speak in unison to the mainstream media? In truth, the expectation is not a fair one. People with disabilities are no more monolithic than African-Americans, women, aboriginals, gays and lesbians, or any other group. But the reality is that given the choice, reporters and editors go for the simple story—the statement that in less than ten seconds or two lines sums up the aspirations of millions.

There is another related issue here, and it concerns organizing the community. When I interviewed John Owen, chief editor of CBC News, I asked him how women's issues, aboriginal issues, and the African-American experience became part of mainstream media agenda. "Well, they demonstrated," Owen replied. "They made a lot of noise." He suggested organized protests. "Do something that's going to attract our attention so that we can get a three-minute piece onto the national news—or at least get a thirty-second sound bite out of it."

Natives, African-Americans, and the other groups can climb on a bus and get somewhere. But for people with physical disability, going anywhere beyond the front door can mean having to book transportation four days in advance—if it is available at all. Organizing a rally, or even a meeting to plan a rally, can be tremendously difficult. By the very nature of disability, public protest is much more difficult to organize and mount than for others.

Other barriers are more subtle. For a public relations professional, often the first step toward generating a story is to take a journalist out for lunch in an effort to get to know the person. But people with disabilities are usually not familiar with business lunch culture; if they are, they can still be intimidated by the logistics of making sure they have access to or can use the restroom.

One of the hardest aspects of hosting DNET has been maintaining balanced coverage. Having a disability myself has been both a help and a hindrance. I am in touch with the issues, but living the life every day tends to make me identify very strongly with those whose struggles—and triumphs—we profile. Five stories we have covered illustrate this tension best.

The first is a story about access. York University, one of three universities in Toronto, was built in the early 1970s. Its design is incompatible with Toronto's winters (the buildings are far apart) and people with disabilities.

A fourth-year fine arts student at York contacted us, explaining that she could not attend her studio classes; no passenger elevator served that floor of the fine arts building. There was, however, a freight elevator, and she had persuaded the university administration to let her use it. But then the Ontario Ministry of Labour, which regulates elevator use in the province, grounded her for "safety" reasons.

The university spokesperson who came on the show at our request explained the institution was "just out of money." It did not have $300,000 for an elevator and building modifications, she said. We then inquired about the tens of millions the university had just committed to construct a new student center/shopping mall and an academic wing, when this student and three others could gain access only to the ground floor of a four-story building that was central to their studies. It quickly became apparent that the administration's defense simply was not credible. We were later accused by the university of being one-sided and biased. We did not represent their side of the story, they said; the shopping mall and new wing were more important than the elevator. In the end, the fine arts student gave up and continued her studies alone in a first floor classroom—to the shame of the university.

Another memorable interview was with Justin Dart, chair of the President's Committee for Employment for People with Disabilities, whose work was instrumental in the writing and unamended passage of the Americans with Disabilities Act (ADA) in May 1990. His message in our interview was that governments are paternalistic; they will not go to disenfranchised groups and give power to them. Rather, this power must be wrestled away.

One of the most satisfying stories we have covered was the fight of someone who almost single-handedly took on the Ontario government and won. When DNET started, Steve Macpherson was living in a hospital on a respirator. For five years, he had requested an apartment, maintaining that although he was quadriplegic, he could look after himself. The response was always the same: "You can't do that. What happens if you die?" The second year of the program we were pleased to interview Macpherson in his own apartment, enjoying the privacy and dignity he deserved.

Our most controversial show to date focused on vivisection—experimenting on animals for medical research. Often the people who benefit most from the animal experiments have disabilities. Therefore, their emotions tend to run deep over the vivisection issue. The subject of the show was Jim Kenyon, director of veterinary service of Toronto Hospital Corporation, metropolitan Toronto's largest hospital, whose research included practice in cutting and grafting of blood vessels on animals, before attempting the procedure with people. Kenyon had been receiving dogs from an animal pound in Oshawa, Ontario, a small town twenty-five miles east of Toronto. Animals not claimed within thirty days were sent, according to contract, to the hospital for research. Antivivisectionists within Oshawa's Humane Society, however, had succeeded in canceling the contract, and Kenyon offered to be interviewed on the subject. For balance, we contacted the Oshawa Humane Society, interviewed its spokesperson, and toured the pound. Its argument was that there were effective alternatives to practicing techniques on animals: the use of dummies or computer simulation.

Co-host Susanne Pettit and I had a difficult challenge in putting a balanced piece together. Susanne owed her life to testing that had been carried out in that research center. Born with cystic fibrosis, she was helped by antibiotics to outlive all predictions for anyone with this condition. But in early 1991, her lungs seemed about to give up. For months, she had been hooked up to an oxygen machine off-camera and had been assessed as a candidate for a lung transplant. One day on set, she collapsed. Miraculously, four weeks later, Susanne was given two new lungs, one of the first double-lung transplants the Toronto Hospital Corporation had attempted, and it worked. Six months later, Susanne returned to the show, strong and healthy. Her body seems to have accepted the new lungs without rejection, and she has continued her work.

Without the experimental surgery at the research center, the operation would have probably failed, but there is no doubt that animals suffered as a result. Approximately 3,000 dogs, whose lungs are similar to humans, were operated on for the surgeons to gain enough confidence in the technique to try it on people. The dogs' pain was minimized through anesthesia, but no surgery is entirely painless.

Certainly Susanne's sympathy was with the hospital, and so was mine. Another procedure practiced at the research center is infant tracheotomy. Cerebral palsy, which I was born with, is frequently caused when the umbilical cord becomes wrapped around the baby's neck at delivery. If an incision is quickly made into the windpipe, the infant can breathe, and damage is minimized or avoided. Doctors at the center practice and perfect this emergency surgery using cats, which are about the same size as a newborn infant.

The tour of Kenyon's center was complemented by sound, rational arguments. In contrast, the Humane Society spokesperson at the Oshawa pound attempted to sway the audience's emotions, offering no arguments concerning the value of human life versus that of animals.

The hardest interview I have ever done was with a young man with severe cerebral palsy who had been sexually assaulted. With help from the Victims of Violence group, he had started an affiliated chapter in Ottawa, Disabled Victims of Violence. During the interview he talked about his work and the attack that had precipitated it. There is a true need for this organization. Reported cases of attacks on people with disabilities have doubled in the past five years; sexual assaults on people with disabilities are twice the national average of those without disabilities.

At the time of the assault, John (not his real name) had called a local referral service for attendant care. A man employed by a private company providing these services was assigned to help him. He helped John get up, prepared meals, helped feed him, and looked after bathing and toileting him. One night this man sexually assaulted John. A friend whom John took into his confidence encouraged John to report the matter to the police. He did, but the outcome was not what he expected. John's speech, although coherent, is somewhat difficult to understand because of his cerebral palsy. Communication should not have been a barrier in working with the police, but it was. Second, the police were not familiar with the issue of sexual assault against people with disabilities. And third, the justice system has generally not been aggressive in prosecuting these crimes, largely because they are so frequent. When the referral service learned of John's complaint, they threatened to cut his services if he pursued the matter further. After being victimized through a system intended to help him, John was thus subject to extortion. But John did pursue it further. The provincial government launched an inquiry, and it came to the light that the attendant had a criminal record of sexual abuse and that the agency apparently had not bothered to check his background. The province revoked the offender's nursing license, but the damage had already been done. The police never pressed criminal charges against the caregiver or the referring agency. It was difficult to interview John and not react.

To a certain degree, covering each of these stories—and simply working on the show—has been a form of advocacy. We have been fair but have not pulled any punches, either. We have given "comfort to the afflicted, and afflicted the comfortable," as a nineteenth-century humorist advised the media. For the most part, though, we have been preaching to the converted. The vast majority of the viewers of DNET are already aware of the key issues of concern to people with disabilities. Going into the next season, I ask myself, "What *have* we achieved?"

First, we have done consciousness raising. The show has been written about in media journals and in the country's dailies. The single largest piece of coverage, however, was a bit of a windfall. Within the first eight weeks of broadcast, DNET won the Into the Mainstream Award from the Alliance of Canadian Television and Radio Artists (ACTRA), a prize given to media groups for the positive portrayal of persons with disabilities and other minorities. Actually, it was not the award that put us in the limelight; it was our inability to receive it. On the day of the ceremony, two of our staff who use wheelchairs discovered they could not enter the premises; stairs led up to the building, and no ramp could be found. Both the ceremony and dignitaries had to be moved outside. It must have been the first time people with disabilities had attended, because apparently no one had checked for access.

The mainstream media had a field day. Toronto's six and eleven o'clock news covered the story, and it made the front page of the city's largest paper. ACTRA later apologized for the oversight, but in fact, we could not have made the point better ourselves.

Beyond the irony of this situation is a more serious, and unsettling, issue:

mainstream media organizations' minimal understanding of disability issues, which is reflected in their attitude toward journalists with disabilities.

First, there are the physical barriers. My first professional interviews with "Challenge Journal" in 1988 were in a station probably typical of most others. The studio was a flight of stairs down from the dressing rooms, restrooms, and make-up rooms. We taped thirteen shows in six days, switching costumes three times each day. I changed in the prop room on the studio level; on a number of occasions, I was standing half-dressed when someone walked in looking for supplies. Physical barriers like this one have prevented many aspiring journalists from even entering the field, let alone advancing.

The need for "door openers" like DNET is clear. As originally conceived, the show had two objectives: to reflect the needs and interests of people with disabilities and to launch staff into positions in mainstream media. The first has been achieved. The second has not. To date, none of the show's staff who have disabilities has obtained a comparable permanent position within CBC or elsewhere. However, two able-bodied people on the show have done so. In fact, opportunities for journalists with disabilities seem to be more limited than before. One problem is the economic recession. In December 1990 $110 million was slashed from the CBC's budget. Twelve hundred employees were laid off as shows were cut and stations closed. Doors that were opening slammed shut. During the summer, I had been anchoring CBC's local eleven o'clock news three nights of five during the week and the all-night show for Newsworld on the weekend. Susanne was working as a producer for a popular CBC afternoon news and current affairs show. But when the cuts came in December 1990, this work dried up for both of us. In 1991, neither of us had work outside DNET. Susanne was able to do a few months work in the spring of 1992 on the entertainment beat for "CBC at Six." I have not been called back by CBC Newsworld; there are too many unemployed journalists from other programs who have more seniority. Further, the trend in television broadcasting is to give the anchor jobs to veteran correspondents with years of experience.

There seem to be two issues: What is an appropriate entry level for journalists with disabilities? How should news organizations approach affirmative action, especially in tough economic conditions?

Most journalists with disabilities would have difficulty with the job of field reporter. It is a grueling pace for anyone, let alone someone with limited mobility. And there are other barriers. Reporters push, shove, and do not observe niceties. Many news conferences are held in inaccessible locations. Foreign correspondents' job description includes diving from bombs and ducking bullets. There is certainly a strong argument that field experience is helpful as an editor, assignment editor, or anchor, but is it *really* necessary? No. It is possible to build the necessary skills through programs like DNET; it has been a vital proving ground for me and others.

Things didn't always go as expected, just as in mainstream news shows.

On the day the Americans with Disabilities Act (ADA) was signed into law in the United States in late May 1990, I convinced CBC to give me an hour on three satellite hook-ups for that evening. Going live to tape, this would form the basis for that week's show. Standing by in Washington, D.C., was Jay Rochlin, the executive director of the President's Committee for Employment for People with Disabilities. Linked up in Ottawa, we had a key member of the House of Commons Standing Committee of the Status of Disabled Persons. In our studio in Winnipeg, the capital of the province of Manitoba, we had invited spokespersons from two Canadian disability rights groups.

Then the vagaries of Canadian politics threatened to torpedo the whole show: the government's most senior cabinet member from Quebec announced that evening he was leaving the party to form the Bloc Québeçois, whose aim is to achieve sovereignty for the province. The CBC's evening national current affairs show had priority. One hour before we were scheduled to begin taping, we lost our Ottawa link. But we still had Washington and Winnipeg, so we went ahead anyway. Rochlin was informative, and the spokesperson from the Canadian Disability Rights Council elaborated on its work in promoting similar legislation to cover public transportation.

As we were taping, the satellite from Winnipeg crashed. Luckily, our technical staff had the presence of mind to redial, and we were quickly relinked. At the stroke of the hour, the satellites shut off.

I was soaked with perspiration and exhausted but elated. Although other networks announced the package, we scooped them on in-depth coverage; CBS's backgrounder was several days later. It was good journalism by any standard. Perhaps "reasonable accommodation" in broadcast journalism means having the opportunity to sweat and struggle with that which we can do, without being first asked to do that which we cannot.

The question of affirmative action in hiring and firing is a tough one; there is no doubt that white able-bodied male journalists are penalized, especially in a recession. Do they deserve to pay the penalty for generations of exclusionary hiring? Should female journalists be asked to step backward to aid a minority? I don't know. But if journalists with disabilities are ever to get into mainstream media, seniority rights alone cannot determine layoffs. Legislation in Canada and the United States is continuing to strengthen the rights of people with disabilities to participate fully in mainstream activity, including journalism. Perhaps it is the only way change will come. I am hopeful that the next generation of television journalists will reflect the broad spectrum of society, including people with disabilities. And I look to the spirit of human progress for assurance that those who would work in the newsroom are no more asked to start in the mailroom.

10

Assistive Technology and Software: Liberating All of Us

Michael R. Smith

Private Investigator Spencer entered his New York office to find his friend Hawk with his lizard-skin boots propped up on the desk. Hawk peered over the top of his book as Spencer asked him about the title.

"Book by Stephen Hawking," Hawk said, "bout the universe."

This scene from Robert B. Parker's novel *Playmates* helps illustrate the complex nature of Hawk, a street-smart partner to an incorrigible private eye. By showing Hawk reading a thought-provoking book by a guy with a similar name, the writer makes the savvy reader realize that people cannot be easily categorized. The use of the book becomes even more noteworthy if the reader is aware of the genius of Hawking, a brilliant British physicist and a man who has the degenerative nerve condition commonly known as Lou Gehrig's disease.

The high visibility of Hawking, who is the subject of a major motion picture as perhaps the greatest scientific mind of this generation, has brought to the public's attention the power of technology to improve lives. Hawking cannot speak or walk and uses a voice synthesizer to communicate. This kind of technology, once available only to the wealthy, is becoming more affordable. Hawking often apologizes for the sound of his synthesizer—not because he is embarrassed to use it but because it has an American accent. Such technology is just one example of the ever-growing number of technical devices available to improve the quality of life for those who need them.

In 1991, *USA Today*'s Thomas Curley told an audience that the information age has to do with delivery systems, not content changes. "Around the corner are direct broadcast satellites, high-definition television, and enhanced-definition television, in which a computer or computer-like device is hooked to a television allowing the user to talk back or to play 'Wheel of Fortune' along with Vanna," he said.[1]

But although computers and technology are unleashing access never before imagined, many of those who need access the most are not necessarily going to receive it any sooner than anyone else. Many disabled people are not even aware of the new technologies that hold such potential for them. Nor do they know where to get information about special equipment or how to pay for it when they do locate it.

Rapid changes are taking place in technology, so anything published about these advances will shortly be out of date. In order to help readers stay current, I provide a strategy for finding information on technology and a list of organizations that provide counseling to people with disabilities. Such groups can provide the way to learn about customized solutions to individual problems. (Note: The addresses of the companies and organizations discussed in this chapter are found in Appendix 3.)

SOME CAUTION ABOUT TECHNOLOGY

Americans gravitate comfortably to science and technology, yet a considerable time lag occurs before a new product reaches wide acceptance. This observation is not lost on people with disabilities. A few years ago, the Technology-Related Assistance for Individuals with Disabilities Act of 1988 (Public Law 100-407) highlighted this problem: "Many individuals with disabilities do not have access to information on assistive technology devices and assistive technology services that such individuals need to function in society commensurate with their abilities."

Assistive technology helps people with disabilities to live more normal lives. Devices range from a specially adapted lift that helps a farmer into a tractor to computers, which may be to the disabled what the printing press was to the American Revolutionaries. Although technology promises much, the Office of Technology Assessment found that technology is not adequately utilized. Technology offers three benefits: facilitating and implementing of therapeutic regimens and educational activities, improving a person's physical abilities, and providing opportunities for greater participation in the mainstream of society.[2]

Sometimes those who need assistive devices the most are unaware of what is available to help them. The state of Massachusetts found in a survey that more than 75 percent of the people with disabilities said they needed more information on assistive devices. A majority also noted that they are dissatisfied with the information available on these devices and services.[3]

Technology is not the only solution for people with disabilities, but it has ample benefits. Consider *Newsday* reporter Susan Harrigan, a financial reporter with an M.B.A. and more than twenty years of reporting experience.

She has repetitive strain injury (RSI), ranked as the country's leading occupational illness. It typically occurs when a person repeats the same motion over and over, as in typing. People with this condition feel pain in hands, arms, necks, and shoulders.

The widespread use of computers in offices has led to occupation-related health problems such as cumulative trauma disorder, carpal tunnel syndrome, and muscle spasms. Constant typing is often blamed for these maladies, but by adjusting a typist's posture and the level of the keyboard or by providing better chairs and desks—known as ergonomic aids—some people may avoid these injuries.

When Harrigan realized she had RSI, she said her writing stopped for seventeen months, until she began using a voice-activated computer similar to the kind of system Hawking uses. She is using the DragonDictate system developed by the Newton, Massachusetts–based Dragon Systems. It allows users to dictate information that appears as words on a computer screen. "I see the Dragon as the Model T of voice-activated computers, and I like to think I'm helping to refine it," she said. "I love the thought of doing that. But as Americans we put so much faith in technology, and I want to caution people that so far the technology that has crippled so many of us hasn't really rescued us, either. It's far better to try to prevent RSI in the first place" (interview with author, 1992).

Voice recognition systems are proving useful to news writers, people with disabilities, and many others. According to Andrew Meshulam of Dragon Systems, lawyers are frequent users because of the dictation function of the $9,000 DragonDictate or the $3,500 IBM VoiceType programs. Dragon-Dictate has a 30,000-word vocabulary and is considered easy to learn to operate. The system works with an IBM personal computer and allows a person to dictate between thirty-five and forty words per minute without spelling errors using ordinary speech patterns; some users can dictate faster. The use of macros can significantly increase productivity in all professions, including the media, which now recognize its value around the nation.

SUCCESS STORIES WITH TECHNOLOGY

Dave Gerwig and Muscular Distrophy

For many people with disabilities, the standard keyboard is the mainstay for word processing. That is the case with Dave Gerwig, age forty-four, who has had muscular dystrophy since he was thirteen years old. He began writing for the *Palladium-Item* in Richmond, Indiana, in 1970 and retired from the newspaper on disability nineteen years later. "We had a tremendous relationship," Gerwig said of his newspaper. "They did everything to help me" (interview with author, 1992).

Although Gerwig is not now paid for contributing to the newspaper, since his retirement he has written a column on baseball during the off-season. Using a personal computer and a modem, Gerwig has written about the Cincinnati Reds baseball team, the woes of Pete Rose, and the increasing abusive behavior of fans at sporting events—all from his bedroom in Richmond, Indiana. The computer is mounted on a four-foot-high stand with wheels. When Gerwig is ready to write, his wife, Kathie, or his nurse helps get him into a typing position.

Gerwig has limited motion in his arms and legs and uses a respirator. His motorized wheelchair is outfitted with a place for the respirator to allow him to travel. (Some wheelchair users have to elevate a desk to work, and many use concrete blocks and two-by-four boards, but AbleOffice at the Center for Rehabilitation Technology, Georgia Institute of Technology, Atlanta, offers a modular workstation.) "We travel when we can, out of state, too, and we go to movies or dinner," he said. "I read a lot—a couple of hours a day. We do more family activities than work." The Gerwigs have two children, eight-year-old Jefferson and two-year-old Rachel, and Kathie operates a day care center.

According to Tom Stolle of the news services department at the *Item*, Gerwig's column is popular. Gerwig and Stolle worked together in sports and on the copy desk in the years before Gerwig's retirement. "We wrote excellent headlines," Stolle said (interview with author, 1992). During the years the men worked together, the *Item* won Best Newspaper of the Year twice, and the sports section gained additional awards.

In 1970 when baseball greats Johnny Bench and Tony Perez were competing for the most home runs on the Reds, Gerwig wrote the following headline after Perez was given a day off: "Perez Takes Seat on Bench. Bench Takes Lead on Perez." When Lou Holtz, known for his quick wit, took over as coach of Notre Dame football, Gerwig wrote: "Irish Hope to Win One for the Quipper."

"I tried to be a positive force in the newspaper," Gerwig said. "I spoke up and did the best job that I could and was never one to do the job and just go home."

Gerwig said his newspaper, a Gannett property, "constantly went out of the way to make things easier," including adjusting furniture and the restroom. In his mind, that newspaper will not have a problem implementing the Americans with Disabilities Act (ADA).

John DeMott

Despite the assistive equipment available, many people with disabilities do the best that they can without modifying ordinary equipment. Journalism educator John DeMott, a former editor with the *Kansas City Star*, uses an ordinary personal computer.

"My right arm is deformed," he says, adding he has use of his thumb on that arm and this helps him hit the space bar. "My problem is typing speed; I'm operating at half speed" (interview with author, 1992). Personal computers such as those produced by IBM and Apple have features that allow operators with reduced arm or hand mobility to capitalize letters using a sequence of keystrokes. DeMott is interested in ways to help increase his typing speed. "I've learned to accept this as a drag on productivity because it takes me twice as long to type as my associates," he said.

DeMott is also interested in technology that will help students with disabilities work better. He knows a student, a fine writer who has difficulty speaking but can spell a question using a device on the armrest of her wheelchair. This approach may be cumbersome, but it is a benefit to a person who wants to participate.

Dan Cooper

Dan Cooper, age fifty-seven, of State College, Pennsylvania is not shy about adopting new technologies. A businessman who left two successful careers to return to college, Cooper is surrounded by computers and gadgets.

"I knew I had a problem, but I wasn't diagnosed as having a learning disability until 1983," he said. "I didn't think I could write at all, but computers have helped" (interview with author, 1992). Cooper has a special type of learning disability known as dysgraphia, an inability to write. Computer software programs help him with writing by fixing his spelling and grammar.

Computers are helping many people with writing skills, including Jay Brill, president of the National Network of Learning Disabled Adults, who said, "My dysgraphia ... prevents me from writing more than a few words at a time." Brill says his computer has helped him concentrate on writing and not mistakes.[4]

While working in his businesses, Cooper avoided all writing and proved to himself that "writing is over-valued as a way of doing business. I had to depend on my memory." His memory remains excellent and permits him to maintain a B average in his American studies program at Pennsylvania State University. He uses a computer datebook primarily for the thesaurus, a laptop computer, a facsimile machine, and an Apple computer. Recently he joined Prodigy on-line service for the messaging capability.

"I have a problem with spelling so I hesitate to get into writing conversations, but I'm going to give it a try," he said. He once used CompuServe, a nationwide electronic conference and information service, and joined Prodigy Services Company in the spring of 1992. Prodigy is a joint venture between IBM and Sears, Roebuck, with about 500,000 members.

Another way for people with disabilities to find information is to use computers and modems to search databases. This access is one more way a person with a disability can accomplish tasks and be connected to a community and the rest of the world. Many are available at libraries, and some services are affordable for the individual user. Computer users can tap into databases from personal computers and conduct searches using keywords. Subscribers usually pay a flat fee plus an hourly rate.

Vu/Text, one of the services, has grown from a four-newspaper data bank in 1981 to one of the largest U.S. newspaper data banks offering information on companies, products, and people. Most files are available within twenty-four to forty-eight hours of publications. The system now offers seventy-two U.S. daily newspapers. Another service is Data Times in Oklahoma, with a collection of more than 640 periodicals.

CompuServe, American Online, GEnie, and other information services have dedicated forums on disability issues, and users can communicate with each other electronically.

"Computers aren't the total answer for people with disabilities," Cooper said. "The spelling function is good, but it won't help if you're using the wrong word. Computers are frustrating, but they are better than nothing."

Scottie Reed

Eight-year-old Scottie Reed of Muncy, Pennsylvania, has a different approach to communicating. He uses a laptop device, Light Talker, manufactured by Prentke-Romich, that allows him to combine a series of symbols to form a sentence. He wears a small light attached to a headband, and when he wants to form a sentence, he aims the light at the icons on the computer. Thousands of words and phrases may be retrieved from Light Talker. The device also has a spelling option that allows a user to generate new vocabulary. The speech synthesizer will speak the phrase in ten different voices.

Reed has had cerebral palsy since he was three. He remembers talking before his disability, but he now relies on the Light Talker to help him express some of his more complicated thoughts.

"He's a very intelligent little boy," his mother, Sheila, says, but even with the Light Talker, getting a message across can be frustrating. "He sometimes can't make the Light Talker say what he wants it to say" (interview with author, 1992). Nevertheless, she notes, "It's given my son a voice when he needs one."

Marlene Craven

For Marlene Craven, forty-five, of suburban Philadelphia, movement is a problem. Since a blockage in her spinal cord caused paralysis of her legs in 1986, Craven has used a wheelchair. In 1990, however, she obtained a manual, stand-up wheelchair developed in France and distributed by M.D.F. Technologies in Pittsburgh. The chair uses self-contained pressure cylinders that allow a user to activate a lever and stand using his or her own energy and motion. Craven had tried another chair but found its design was not right for her, and it irritated her knees. She initially thought the first Lifestand folding wheelchair she saw was too bulky, but it gave her a sense of independence that she thought she had lost. Lifestand's width and height measure the same as most standard wheelchairs, and it also can be used as a wheelchair, a feature that sometimes is overlooked because users concentrate on the chair's standing feature.

"I was able to get ice cream from the freezer by myself," she said (interview with author, 1992). Later her son, Marcus, told her: "Now we can have a family hug."

A graduate in human services from Beaver College, Craven hopes to attend graduate school in Washington, D.C., and participate in a special training program on the ADA. She says technology has helped her achieve goals such as higher education. "The body compensates and technology provides the tools for independence," she said.

WHERE TO BEGIN: A LOCAL SEARCH FOR HELP WITH TECHNOLOGY

Because people with disabilities may have difficulty using retail stores— if for no other reason than barriers such as stairs—a need exists to alert these consumers about products that may be helpful, particularly adaptive devices that are not widely available. Each state has agencies for people with disabilities, and some may provide assistance in purchasing equipment. State and local agencies are a good place to start inquiries.

In central Pennsylvania, radio personality Lou Kolb, a man blind since birth, received assistance in purchasing a computer printer that allows his radio station to produce braille music lists and other information he needs to work on air. "More and more, I am a believer in what technology can do; today it is much easier to generate braille," Kolb said (interview with author, 1992). The station uses a computer to produce music lists, but it has a printer for the sighted staff and a braille printer for Kolb.

Although the text is the same, sometimes errors occur. Once Kolb used some dated copy and announced sunny skies when rain was pelting the area. However, those mistakes are rare, and after two decades in the studio, Kolb has earned a reputation that helped him land a job in one of the most competitive radio markets in the nation.

While on the air, Kolb has a talking clock that says the correct time with the push of a button. At home, he uses a talking calculator and relaxes by talking on a ham radio. Recently, the Pennsylvania Department of Labor and Industry used Kolb's mellow voice to narrate a videotape concerning the Americans with Disabilities Act.

Kolb is hopeful about additional breakthroughs in speech output devices.

"What I'd like to see is speech output that is as common as screen output," he said.

PRENTKE ROMICH

With more than twenty-five years' experience, the Wooster, Ohio–based Prentke Romich Company has been a leader in assistive technology. "It is our contention that the proper application of technology, and not technology itself, leads to achievement," says a company publication. The company, considered a world leader in the areas of augmentative and alternative communication, computer access, and environmental controls, supplies a number of products beyond computers, such as control systems that will allow a person who is nonambulatory to turn on a light, change a television channel, and accomplish other tasks. Its Hospital/Home Environmental Control System, for instance, uses a backlighted display that allows a person to activate an electrical appliance through a sip-puff switch or another switch. Some of the systems cost more than $3,000, but one unit can empower a person to operate more than 250 electrical appliances without rewiring.

The company has developed a number of communication aids to assist people with limited communication ability. Thousands of words and phrases can be stored in portable lap-size devices. The aids cost more than $5,000, but they enable children as young as two years old to communicate. Because of the dazzling number of changes that occur in this field, Prentke Romich allows its customers to try out a product before making a final decision, and it provides training on some communication aids.

JOB ACCOMMODATION NETWORK

One of the best sources of free information for people with disabilities is the Job Accommodation Network, a federally funded information and referral service in business since 1984. The information is available by calling a toll-free number: (800) 526-7234. The telephone counselors are friendly and knowledgeable about assistive technology that can help a person accomplish a particular task.

The counselors also provide information on adapting environments to work, rest, or play. Their approach is to customize a solution for a person with a disability and offer suggestions on restructuring a job or using a piece of equipment. Typically, a counselor listens to a person's request, provides some initial information, and follows up the telephone conversation with literature on a product that may be suitable. Included in the mailing is a questionnaire that asks the recipient to evaluate the product or the service should he or she use it. Products or services that do not receive passing marks are not recommended by the network to future callers.

Because an abundance of material is available on products and services, a counselor will not necessarily tell a caller that one brand is the best. Just as no one color or one size is the best, no one product is the best; however, some solutions are more appropriate for some people than others. Winnowing the hundreds of possibilities to some manageable suggestions is the goal of the Job Accommodation Network.

USEFUL ORGANIZATIONS AND SOURCES

Begun in 1992, the Technology Information Project (TIP) of Seaside Education Associates, Lincoln, Massachusetts, provides information on assistive technology along with referrals. According to director Paula Sotnik, the project's goal "is to increase awareness of the uses and benefits of assistive technology and encourage people to seek more information from appropriate local sources." Part of the group's work is to get information to Cambodian, Latino, and Portuguese communities while being "sensitive to cultural values and attitudes toward disabilities."

Implementation of the ADA has some employers concerned that compliance with this law will be costly, but TIP says reasonable accommodations will cost less than $50. According to a 1990 Job Accommodation Network National Study, 19 percent of the accommodations will cost between $500 and $1,000 and 12 percent will cost between $1,000 to $5,000. TIP notes that inexpensive accommodations can include simple solutions, such as providing a raised-edge lip on desk's edges to keep materials from falling on the floor or attaching a cord to tools for easy access. An example of low technology is a plastic door knob lever that sells for less than $15 and allows people who have difficulty turning a knob to open round door knobs. Produced by Lindustries of Weston, Massachusetts, the device is easy to use.

TIP provides information on funding sources for assistive technology, including governmental sources such as Medicaid, Veterans Administration medical centers and the Social Security Administration's Plan for Achieving Self Support. It provides vendors' names for products, including low-technology solutions such as reachers, devices to help people grasp objects ordinarily out of their reach. TIP also circulates a free videotape on its program.

The Education Resources and Information Center (ERIC) is a prime source of information for assistive technology and software databases. Information that was once provided by the Center for Special Education Technology is now available from the ERIC database. ERIC may be accessed through 700 locations, including most major university libraries and some public libraries.

ERIC's *Directory of Assistive Technology Data Source* lists a number of useful organizations in an at-a-glance format. Each entry includes the full name, address, telephone number, services, and a brief description of the mission of that organization. Many of the organizations in that guide are mentioned in this chapter. Information on locations of ERIC information at various libraries may be obtained by calling (800) USE-ERIC.

ABLEDATA, considered one of the largest information sources in the United States for products for people with disabilities, lists thousands of products and provides up to eight pages of free information. ABLEDATA provides custom searches of products. ABLEDATA can be reached at (800) 344-5405.

An organization that provides information on technology for the blind and visually impaired is the National Federation of the Blind. This organization also has NFBNet, a computer bulletin board, at (410) 752-5011, and it operates the National Federation of the Blind in Computer Science. Questions may be directed to: Curtis Chong, National Federation of the Blind in Computer Science, (612) 521-3202.

Directory of Software Data Sources contains a list of vendors and organizations concerned with software. For instance, it lists a preview guide of software from the International Society for Technology in Education (ISTE), which reviews software and sells the *Software Preview Guide,* an evaluation of software for educators, for about $10. To order the guide, the telephone number is (800) 336-5191.

The Alliance for Technology Access, a coalition of people with disabilities, professional organizations, and community groups and the developers of computer equipment and other technology, began in 1987 and focuses on computer solutions for people with disabilities. The various offices are electronically linked to each other and other national databases and electronic bulletin boards to share information. A number of states have resource centers that are members of the alliance that help people find an appropriate computer or adapt a computer to a special need.

IBM is working with the Alliance of Technology Access and its forty-six resource centers with loans of educational software and equipment to help them serve the needs of students with disabilities. "The Alliance for Technology Access Centers are committed to transforming the tools of technology into open doors to education, to employment, and to a new level of personal fulfillment for these students," notes an IBM publication on outstanding organizations for people with disabilities. "The Alliance Centers combine resources of teachers, professionals and parents to provide training, hands-on consultation, and software demonstrations. Because of its strong involvement with local communities, the centers have an active volunteer base." Federally funded, Alliance for Technology works with school districts to provide technological solutions to people with disabilities.

JONI AND FRIENDS

An organization that provides help for people with disabilities and people associated with churches is Joni and Friends. Founded by Joni Eareckson

Tada, who was injured in a diving accident, Joni and Friends provides spiritual counseling to people with disabilities and their families. The organization features regular radio broadcasts and retreats and attempts to link people with disabilities and their families to churches.

"Disabled people are often handicapped by society's attitude which communicates, 'I can't,' " said Tada, a quadriplegic. "Technology has made it possible for us to be able to say, 'I can,' but it takes the right tools. For me, that has meant the ability to drive, to use a computer, to write, and, with a mechanical easel, to paint. Thankfully, my church got involved in helping me find and afford technological assistance such as this and it's how the church can help others who are disabled as well." Call (818) 707-5664.

Another organization that provides information is Closing the Gap, (612) 248-3294. According to Maryann Harty, advertising and exhibit manager, the name refers to the organization's commitment to "close the gap between the able and the non–able bodied." Organized in 1982, Closing the Gap publishes a newspaper on developments in technology (cost, about $30) and conducts workshops. One newspaper issue each year includes a resource guide that features the latest in computer technology for people with disabilities. In addition, Closing the Gap conducts an annual conference each October in Minneapolis that features nearly 200 presentations on practical matters of interest to people with disabilities. The cost for registration in 1992 was approximately $200.

Information on rehabilitation technology also may be obtained from RESNA. It was formerly known as the Rehabilitation and Engineering Society of North America but is now an interdisciplinary association for the advancement of rehabilitative and assistive technology. RESNA, (202) 857-1199, is an information exchange organization, according to John Greene, publications coordinator. It offers publications that cost from $2 to about $60, including a 500-page resource guide published in 1990 that lists various technology and where to obtain information. In addition, each June RESNA hosts a conference for researchers, vendors, and consumers to examine the latest developments in aids to people with disabilities. Registration is about $200.

On the policy front, the World Institute on Disability (WID), (510) 763-4100, is concerned with issues "that are central to the goals of integration and independence for persons with disabilities." According to Susan Brown of WID, "We say accessibility should be built into all technology." Twice a year, WID conducts panels on issues that are crucial to people with disabilities. This organization is not an information service, although it publishes reports on research, policy analysis, model program development, technical assistance, and public education. For computer users who have telephone modems, WID launched WIDNet late in 1992, an internationally comprehensive communications link between people with disabilities and organizations such as government services, communities and service agencies.

INFORMATION AND REFERRAL

The Trace Research and Development Center, (608) 262-6966, is another source of information. Formed in 1971, the Trace Center's initial mission was to help people communicate who are nonspeaking and who have other severe disabilities. More recently, the mission added research in communication and people with disabilities and the use of computers, communication aids, and home environmental controls. A primary goal is to make this technology accessible to everyone.

The Trace Center draws on a number of fields in its pursuit of solutions. Headquartered in the Waisman Center and the Department of Industrial Engineering at the University of Wisconsin–Madison, the center relies on more than twenty specialists with backgrounds in electrical engineering, computer science, industrial engineering, speech pathology, biomedical engineering, psychology, communicative disorders, and occupational therapy. It conducts its own research on computer software and products, including sophisticated analysis such as the "comparison of factors in tactile shape discrimination, and studies of the cognitive factors in the use of computer interfaces," says a mission statement. Designing computers and software with people with disabilities in mind is part of the center's work, along with product development and standards. Training also is available from Trace Center workshops for parents and professionals working with disabled people.

Among the center's most valuable contributions is the dissemination of information from its vast database of products, services, and publications. It also publishes an annual directory, *The Trace Resource Book*, which lists products and resource information on assistive technology for consumers and professionals. Useful appendixes guide users to additional sources of information. User friendly, the book includes color-coded cross reference indexes. All of these services and devices have the goal of helping people live the highest quality lives possible. Jerry Weaver is an example.

JERRY WEAVER

Jerry Weaver spent the day before Halloween 1990 in his Palm City, Florida, home teaching his nephew Marky how to dribble a basketball. Satisfied with his supper of hot dogs, Jerry took his all-terrain vehicle to meet his friends for the evening. That is when he had an accident that left him a quadriplegic at twenty years of age. Gone were the days of fashioning trucks into convertibles and low riders. As he spent months in therapy, his dream of becoming an accountant looked bleak. "He was pretty discouraged," his mother, Peggy, recalls (interview with author, 1992).

Slowly Jerry began using assistive technology to compensate for the loss of the use of his arms and hands. He tried using a mouth stick to type on a computer and found that technology moderately rewarding but time-consuming. Then a therapist suggested that Jerry try an IBM product still under development, VoiceType voice recognition, which allows a user to control applications and to input text by speaking. It adapts to the speaker's voice and includes more than 7,000 words and up to 2,000 user-specified words and commands.

"It looked hopeless that he could do anything in the real world," notes John Roberts, planning and marketing manager for the IBM Special Needs Systems in Boca Raton, Florida. VoiceType, however, helped Jerry see new possibilities of productiveness. "He tried VoiceType and he enjoyed it," remembers Jerry's father, Mel.

Jerry began working with IBM to test VoiceType. He learned to avoid extraneous noises to keep gibberish off the screen. He also learned how to produce 4,000-word term papers for his college classes at Indian River Community College in Stewart, Florida. According to Roberts, the mouth stick took Jerry hours to write a paragraph. "With VoiceType, Jerry had something that he felt he could use in a business environment," Roberts said.

Jerry agrees. "Without this technology, I definitely would not have gone back to school," he says. "I type five letters a week to friends and I spend ten to twenty hours a week on the system. I definitely type more than ever."

Jerry is considering his own term paper writing service. With a grade point average of better than a B, Weaver says VoiceType has helped him set a new goal: work in bioengineering in the design of prostheses.

TRACE AND IBM

The Trace Center develops new technology that is distributed by vendors. IBM, for instance, carries AccessDOS, a Trace product (a set of programs) that allows the user of a DOS machine to extend the keyboard on an IBM personal computer. It contains seven functions, including StickyKeys, a keyboard feature that allows users to press keys consecutively to achieve the result that occurs when both keys typically are pressed simultaneously. This feature is handy when a user wants to capitalize a letter, but cannot press more than one key at a time.

The same package allows the user to use the keys on the numeric keypad to move the cursor around the screen, to duplicate the function of a computer mouse. Repeat keys can be used when a typist wants to avoid repeating a character but finds that movement difficult. Toggle keys are used to alert a computer user with a beep that the Caps Lock, Num Lock, or Scroll Lock keys are on. ShowSounds can be used to make the screen blink or display a musical note when the computer makes a sound. This product, available at no charge in 1992 from IBM, (800) 426-7282, is just one of eight that IBM featured for people with disabilities in its Independence Series in 1992.

Prices for various products, such as a telephone communication device that allows a personal computer user to see a telephone conversation on a computer screen, are about $600 and a speech recognition program is about $3,200.

IBM continues to be a leader in devising solutions for people with disabilities. Although it stopped providing information and referral services in late 1992, it still provides in-depth information on its eight products for people with disabilities. The best approach for contacting IBM is to call for information at (800) 555-1212 and request the toll-free number for additional referrals.

Among the services IBM provides is the IBM Disabilities Assistance Network, a $4.5-million loan of computer systems and software to federally funded disabilities support centers. This program loans computer equipment and software to agencies and nonprofit organizations in more than thirty states. For people with disabilities who are interested in purchasing computers for rehabilitative and therapeutic purposes, IBM offers up to 50 percent discounts on its IBM Personal System/2 computer products. The National Easter Seal Society, (800) 221-6827, may be able to provide information on discount pricing and the eligibility procedure.

IBM also has two programs to train people with disabilities: Computer Programmer Training for Severely Disabled Persons (CPT) and Personal Computer Based Skills Training for Disabled Persons.

In 1972 IBM began CPT at the suggestion of an employee with a disability. The corporation learned that computer programming was a job in information processing with which people with disabilities could excel. Closely related to CPT is PST, a training program that IBM says "broadens the training opportunities available to persons with disabilities and provides opportunities for students who could not qualify for or complete the computer programmer training." People who have participated in the program include those with quadriplegia, paraplegia, partial or total vision loss, partial or total hearing loss, muscular dystrophy, cerebral palsy, ataxia, post-polio impairment, closed head injury, diabetes, heart transplant, hypertension, back injury, arthritis, Hodgkin's disease, emotional disorders, Charcot-Marie disease, epilepsy, blood disorders, neurofibromatosis, and renal failure. According to IBM, it has placed more than 3,000 graduates. Information on these programs may be obtained by calling, (301) 240-0111.

Community service organizations associated with IBM can help people with disabilities by demonstrating and providing guidance in choosing a computer configuration, suggesting appropriate adaptive devices, helping with the ordering process, providing hardware setup assistance, and offering telephone support after initial orientation. A list of participating community service organizations may be found in IBM's *Technologies for Persons with Disabilities—an Introduction.*

THE APPLE SOLUTION

Apple Computer has developed the Worldwide Disability Solutions Group that offers computer solutions for Macintosh computers. It provides hundreds of questions and answers on a floppy disc, Macintosh Disability Resources, available free by calling the Worldwide Disability Solutions Group, (800) 776-2333.

The best part of the Macintosh Disability Resources disc, says Apple's Gary Moulton, is that it includes an animated explanation of a number of features that are built into Apple Macintosh computers. The disc contains information on general motor ability, hearing and speech, learning, and vision. Each section presents a list of the most frequently asked questions for that disability classification and provides answers. Another section lists hardware, software, publications, and built-in features of the Apple Macintosh that may be of interest to people with disabilities. For instance, a user who selects hardware and requests information on doors will learn that Resource Doors "is a system of hardware and software that enables individuals with a disability to use the Macintosh. Complete computer control is made possible via single/multiple switch scanning, spinning cursor control, expanded keyboards (e.g., Unicorn Model II) and point and click keyboards (e.g., Headmaster)."

The program uses little pictures that help guide searches. For example, a small picture of a dog is next to the command "search." By pressing that box using a pointer connected to a mouse device, a user can locate a particular type of product, information resource, or telephone number. The program can print a personalized letter to a resource requesting additional information using a print command.

In addition to the MDR disc, Apple provides telephone counseling and responds to as many as 500 telephone calls each week. Callers may use the (408) 974-7910 number, the voice TDD (408) 974-7911 number, or the toll-free telephone number mentioned earlier.

"Our mission is to demonstrate to Apple as well as to the disabled community around the world how technology can fundamentally change what it means to be disabled," says an Apple mission statement. Apple tells more about its goals with technology and people with disabilities in its free publication, *Toward Independence*, which describes Apple's attempt to make its personal computer. Among the features that are available in the Macintosh utility programs are the following:

Control Panel: The Control Panel allows users to adjust some of the functions of the Macintosh, including changing speaker volume, customizing the keyboard's operation, and enlarging images on the screen.

CloseView: CloseView allows users with visual impairments to enlarge the information on the screen with an electronic magnifying lens. Information on the screen may be magnified up to sixteen times the standard size. "In addition, because some people have difficulty seeing black images on a white background, CloseView allows users to invert the screen images to white on black," notes *Toward Independence*.

MacroMaker: Instead of a user's pressing a series of keys, MacroMaker can be used to record the sequence so that a user needs to press only one key to activate a program. This program is helpful for people whose disabilities make pressing a computer key difficult.

System Beep: This is a sound feature that beeps when the computer wants the user's attention. The speaker volume can be adjusted to zero or no beep sound at all. When no sound is indicated, the Macintosh will blink its menu bar to allow a user to see what may not have been heard.

Repeat Key: Some people who want to type find that their fingers have a tendency to press a key more than once, although the intent is to type a single letter. The Macintosh allows a user to turn off the key repeat function to avoid typing a series of letters.

Easy Access: Users who use a head stick or a mouth stick cannot hold down two or more keys at the same time; the Sticky Keys feature of Easy Access lets the user type one key at a time with the computer responding as if the keys were pressed simultaneously. This feature works like the IBM keyboard with a similar function that uses the numeric keypad on the right side of the keyboard.

The Macintosh can be fitted with adaptive devices that provide additional help for people who own an Apple product but need an additional piece of equipment to make the system work. The following is a partial list of some popular equipment:

Optacon II/in Touch: The Optacon II/in Touch provides help to people with vision problems. It uses a small camera that passes across the screen and transmits a replica of what it views to a small bed of vibrating pins. The user places a fingertip on the pins to determine the shape of the images on the screen and reads the image by touch.

Voice Navigator II: Voice Navigator II uses speech recognition to translate the user's spoken words into computer commands. For instance, a user who wants to quit a word processing program, says "quit" into a microphone, and the machine responds. OutSpoken software is another program that allows visually impaired users to transform the visual elements on the Macintosh screen into audible information.

Headmaster: Small movements of the head can be combined with Headmaster, a device that allows a user to sip or puff into a plastic tube to control the clicking of the mouse.

OTHER TECHNOLOGY

A number of organizations and manufacturers other than IBM and Apple also provide an abundance of tools for mobility, education, and augmentative and alternative communication. The list provided in this chapter is a primer to the vast world of technologies. It is a place to start.

For many, the point is not that technology can liberate people with disabilities to accomplish tasks. The real issue is accessibility and the need for visionaries to build accessibility into all products for all consumers. The technology issue is more aptly a policy issue—the policy of making advances available for all. Affordability will be a major consideration as products are researched and developed. Educators, manufacturers, elected officials, and others will be challenged to maintain the momentum gained in breakthroughs in the 1990s—not just in technology but in all the areas of concern to people with disabilities. Like a new language that may be shared by all who want to communicate, technology may offer another tool to unite many voices in separate causes.

NOTES

1. Thomas Curley, "Back to the Future: Communications in the 21st Century," Sixteenth Annual Ruhl Lecture, University of Oregon School of Journalism, 1991.

2. R. B. Parette, "The Importance of Technology in the Education and Training in Mental Retardation," *Education and Training in Mental Retardation* 26 (1991): 165–78.

3. S. Blackstone et al., *Technology with Low Incident Populations: Promoting Access to Education and Learning* (Reston, Va.: Enter for Special Education Technology, 1989).

4. B. Meng, "With a Little Help from My Mac," *MacWorld* (September 1990): 181–88.

BIBLIOGRAPHY

Blackstone, S., et al. *Technology with Low Incident Populations: Promoting Access to Education and Learning.* Reston, Va.: Enter for Special Education Technology, 1989.

Brill, J. "Statures of Liberty." *MacWorld* (September 1990): 188.

Cain, E. J., Jr., and Taber, F. M. *Educating Disabled People for the 21st Century.* Boston: Little, Brown, 1987.

Curley, Thomas. "Back to the Future: Communications in the 21st Century." Sixteenth Annual Ruhl Lecture, University of Oregon, School of Journalism, 1991.

Hembree, D., and Sandoval, R. "RSI Has Become the Nation's Leading Illness." *Columbia Journalism Review* (July–August 1991): 41–46.

Johnson, M. "Journalists with Disabilities Have Access to a Growing Array of Helpful Devices." *ASNE Bulletin* (July–August 1992): 12–15.

Meng, B. "With a Little Help from My Mac." *MacWorld* (September 1990): 181–88.

Parette, R. B. "The Importance of Technology in Education and Training of Persons with Mental Retardation." *Education and Training in Mental Retardation* 26 (1991): 165–78.

Parker, R. B. *Playmates*. New York: Putnam, 1989.

Rogers, E. M. *Diffusion of Innovations*. New York: Free Press, 1962.

U.S. Congress. House. Committee on Labor and Human Resources, Assistive Technology for Persons with Disabilities, Hearings. 100th Cong., 2d sess., May 19, 20, 1988.

VanBiervliet, A., and Parette, P. *Technology Access for Arkansas*. Little Rock: Arkansas University, 1989.

Freedom

Computer scientist Mark Dahmke in the September 1982 issue of *Byte Magazine* estimated that there are as many as 600,000 nonretarded, nonvocal people in this country who could communicate with voice synthesizers—perhaps 100,000 of them in institutions—most diagnosed as retarded.

From *The Disability Rag* (June 1985)

A Bit Pushy

An editorial in a Dublin newspaper last September [1986] criticized as "unseemly" Ireland Prime Minister Garret FitzGerald's habit of pushing his wife's wheelchair in public.

FitzGerald, who felt it was "a deeply offensive political criticism," retaliated by cancelling a news conference *Munster Express* Editor Joe Walsh wanted to attend.

But Walsh was unrepentant. "I think it is most unbecoming of him to push his wife's wheelchair," he insisted. "He should engage a nurse to do it."

From *The Disability Rag* (January–February 1987)

11

How Deaf Students Won Their Case at Gallaudet University— By Taking to the Streets

Lillie S. Ransom

On March 6, 1988, students at Gallaudet University in Washington, D.C., closed the campus down for six days. Americans watched shocked at scenes more reminiscent of protests at Latin American universities than anything in the nation's capital.

The Gallaudet student protest cry of "Deaf President Now!" (DPN) was publicized throughout the world on television, radio, and in the print media during the spring of 1988. The protest was an important event in the lives of members of the deaf community in the United States and abroad.

On March 6, 1988, the Gallaudet board of trustees had announced the appointment of Elizabeth Ann Zinser as the new university president. The two other finalists were deaf men: I. King Jordan and Harvey Corson. Members of the Gallaudet community expected that after 124 years, the university would have a deaf president, and students were shocked and angry when they learned that once again the board had selected a hearing person for the position. It was particularly insulting that Dr. Zinser did not know sign language and had no experience in the deaf community.

Students made four demands of the university administration when they closed the campus that week: (1) resignation of Dr. Zinser and Jane Basset-Spilman, chair of the board of trustees; (2) appointment of a deaf president for the university; (3) appointment of deaf individuals to fill vacancies on the board, until the majority of board members were deaf; and (4) no retaliations for students, staff, and faculty involved in the protest. One week after students closed the campus, the board of trustees agreed to each of these demands. Students received an outpouring of support from politicians and from deaf and hearing individuals throughout the country and abroad. The media played a crucial role in publicizing DPN. Did they also influence audience perceptions of the protest by emphasizing some aspects of the protest and playing down others?

Television, like other forms of media, participates in constructing meanings for its viewers. Television viewers and reporters have meaning systems. Often audience and reporter meaning systems are the same, but sometimes they are not. There are at least three perspectives from which one could examine meaning: the meaning system of the news reporter or producer, the meaning system of the audience member(s), and the interplay of these systems or the cultural meaning system.

There are a number of strategies for the analysis of meaning in TV news stories. Research can focus on both trying to delimit the possible range of meanings available to an idealized or implied viewer within the audiovisual discourse; alternatively the meanings of the programmes can be probed from a broader cultural perspective. In both cases attention is paid to the manner in which a sense is encoded and communicated by the news stories, and the overall programmed format.[1]

Here I limit the focus to the analysis of possible meanings encoded by television producers. I do not attempt to analyze audience reception or handling of these meanings. Yet the network coverage of DPN was encoded with particular meanings, and alternative meanings were overlooked or downplayed.

NETWORK COVERAGE OF THE PROTESTS

I secured videotapes from the Vanderbilt News Archives for ABC, CBS, and NBC coverage of DPN for the week of March 6, 1988, and transcribed and reviewed the footage numerous times to determine key words, phrases, and themes in the news stories. I found that the themes of self-determination and overcoming oppression play themselves out in television news over and over again. Examples are easy to find; news stories about Bosnia, the former Soviet republics, the Israeli-Arab peace talks, and the African National Congress and South African government negotiations or conflicts, are just a few of them. On any evening, a television viewer will see one or two stories about social upheavals and protests between disenfranchised groups and authoritarian groups. In general, these news stories are about groups or individuals battling for the right to determine for themselves who will govern and how they will govern. The DPN news stories also fit this frame. The story is about the struggle of discourses between two cultures.

The main distinction between the hearing and deaf cultures is in how each views deafness. The typical hearing person views deafness as a disability. To most hearing people, deaf people are lacking something. Their view of deafness includes the notion that deaf people need to compensate for or be compensated for their lack of hearing. This is the pathological view of deafness. On the other hand, members of the deaf community view deafness as a characteristic that bonds people to a way of life. This way of life centers around visual communication, not aural communication. "There is a different center, a different point from which one deviates. In this case *deaf* not *hearing*, is taken as the central point of reference."[2]

American Sign Language is the preferred mode of communication for most deaf Americans with the deaf cultural view. Deaf culture is transmitted in schools for the deaf and deaf organizations since these are still the primary places deaf people meet and interact with one another. "The tension between Deaf people's views of themselves and the way the hearing world views them finds its way into their stories."[3]

One might expect to find telling differences between the way the hearing media talked about DPN and the way students at Gallaudet talked about it. The Gallaudet University board of trustees had a meaning system that dictated that the best-qualified candidate would be selected without regard to deafness or hearing status. Gallaudet University students had a meaning system that said the best-qualified candidate would have to be someone who is also deaf. The stage was set for opposition and dramatic tension. Following are sample transcripts from ABC, CBS, and NBC. The transcripts include a description of what was visually on the screen, too.

TRANSCRIPTS OF THE COVERAGE

ABC News Transcript[4]

Length 1:50

Date: 3/8/88

Peter Jennings: There was an unusual protest today at an unusual university. Most of the students at Gallaudet University in Washington stayed away from classes today to protest the selection of a *new* university president. All of the students at Gallaudet are hearing impaired. The new president is *not* nor does she know sign language. As ABC's Karen Stone reports, the students and many faculty members are angry.

Visuals: Talking head—center—close shot of Peter Jennings. Computers and monitors in the background.

Karen Stone ... (VOSOT [voice over and sound on tape]): Even though Gallaudet University was officially open today many students boycotted classes vowing not to give up their fight for a deaf president.

Visuals: Cut to campus shot of two students holding hands. Students are making vigorous motions up and down; they turn to face the crowd of moving students, who remain seated as they clap.

Tim Rarus, protester: We want to tell people off campus, other people, to let them know it would be better if we have a deaf president. A deaf president that understands us.

Visuals: Cut to interviewee responding in sign language. Student is male and standing with campus buildings in the background. He is wearing a white t-shirt and has braces on his teeth.

Unidentified male voice: How long will you go on with this?

Tim Rarus: Until we get a deaf president.

Visuals: Camera cuts to another male protester; he wears glasses and signs something. The person standing behind his left shoulder signs, index finger to ear and mouth, two fists across the forehead, and two open hands come down across the face, neck, and chest [this means Deaf President Now]. Fast cut to another group of protesters. Female student in the forefront signing and mouthing "Deaf President Now." Gallaudet buildings appear farther in the background this time. Man with yellow hat points to the message on the hat.
Cut to an indoor scene with more animated students. Ringleader here seems to be female student with yellow and black sweater or sweatshirt on. She is gesturing something that looks like "out," "out."

Karen Stone (VO [voice over]): The students who closed down the university yesterday are angry that in its 124-year history the world's only liberal arts college for the hearing impaired has never had a hearing impaired president. Students and deaf organizations are particularly incensed by the Board of Trustees Chairman Jane Basset-Spilman who defended the selection of the president who doesn't know sign language saying, "deaf people are not ready to function in a hearing world." The anger was felt far beyond the Gallaudet campus.

Visuals: A long shot . . . this time of board chair Basset-Spilman at a podium. Freeze frame/inset of Spilman's pained expression with this subtitle: "Deaf people are not ready to function in the hearing world."

Marlee Matlin: I'm really angry and upset about what's happened. Obviously deaf people were completely ignored by those individuals who work at the university level.

Visuals: Medium shot of Marlee Matlin with glasses; she is signing with a great deal of animation and determination.

Karen Stone (VO): The center of the controversy Dr. Elizabeth Ann Zinser, who'll be Gallaudet's first woman president, promises to learn sign language and vows to take office.

Visuals: Cut to Zinser and interpreter seated across a desk. Zinser looks calm and confident. Paneled background suggests an office environment.

Elizabeth Ann Zinser: I'm engaging in a relationship with the campus community that in a year from now, I think will be a very warm one and a very productive one.

Karen Stone (stand-up): Students, though, say they may risk arrests with more demonstrations and blockades until a deaf president is named. Karen Stone, ABC News.

Visuals: Stand-up in front of brick sign GALLAUDET UNIVERSITY. *Chyron for reporter and station. Students rather far in the background milling around. Cut back to Peter Jennings in the newsroom as he goes to a break.*

CBS News Transcript[5]

Length 2:20

Date 3/10/88

Dan Rather: What started as a student protest at the nation's only liberal arts college for the deaf is commanding national attention tonight. Lem Tucker reports.

Visuals: Talking head, medium shot. Rather to the left and a graphic of the Gallaudet University emblem on the right of the screen. World map is the background for this set.

Lem Tucker (VOSOT): Again today it was a stalemate at Gallaudet University. The school is shut down and the students say it can stay that way until they get a president who is like them—deaf. Protests began Sunday when the Board of Trustees named this woman Elizabeth Zinser as the next president. Zinser is *not* deaf and doesn't even know how to sign so she can communicate with the students.

Visuals: Cut to protesting students behind police ropes. Posters . . . "Success and Honor," buses passing by. Cut to a man hoisted up above the crowd while he reads a statement in sign language. Student mouthing and signing "Deaf President Now."

Cut to indoor shot of a bulletin board with papers that seem to be press releases announcing Dr. Zinser's appointment. Students set the papers on fire. Cut to Zinser and Spilman whispering to one another on the podium. Zinser addresses the students and cameras in a controlled fashion.

Howard Busby, administrator: I don't think one of those ten Board members who voted for Dr. Zinser can sign their way out of a paper bag much less understand deaf culture.

Visuals: Busby and interpreter in the left portion of the screen talking to an off-camera reporter. The video is shot outside, as indicated by a tree (without flowers or leaves yet) in the right portion of the screen. Station identifies Busby with a chyron.

Lem Tucker (VO): Anger over Zinser's appointment has forged a coalition of students, faculty, and some administrators who are demanding that *she* and the chairman of the Board of Trustees, who like most of the Board is not deaf, resign.

Visuals: Cut to five students outside; they are burning Zinser in effigy. Quick cut to clapping, cheering students. Woman smiles for camera and points to message on her t-shirt. "Deaf Prexy Now!" She turns around for the camera and on her back is another message, "Zinser 'n' Spilman Out!"

Unidentified protester: Can you imagine serving Italian food in a Chinese restaurant? That's the same thing as having a hearing president here after 124 years. C'mon, it's time for a change.

Lem Tucker (VO): Students say the appointment sends them the wrong message.

Visuals: Close shot of woman responding to off-camera reporter. Can see partial right profile of voice interpreter; her ear, chin, and right cheek are visible.

Unidentified protester: We need to look up to a deaf role model and that'll help us to lead our own lives.

Visuals: Cut to five students seated outside. Two are dressed alike. Four sign something in unison. Cut to a young deaf girl with glasses, denim jacket, and white or light-colored top under the jacket. Others standing patiently in the background.

Lem Tucker (stand up): The students say they have a good chance of winning this battle because what started out as their very important but local issue has now become one of national concern.

Visuals: Stand-up of Tucker across the street from the campus and protesting students.

Postal worker: This is where the American Postal Worker's Union stands: (signs "Deaf president now").

Visuals: Older gentleman with navy blue cap standing on steps. Talks and then signs slowly. Camera pulls out to incorporate his last movement. Some type of speaker or amplifier is sitting on the steps behind the man.

Lem Tucker (VO): That is the signing for "Deaf President Now." And others are picking up that call especially in Congress which provides most of Gallaudet's annual operating budget.

Visuals: Cut to Congress. Empty seats; people appear to be packing up. Cut to Congressman Barney Frank (D–Massachusetts) in an office with royal blue background, who is responding to question. Scene changes again to Gallaudet campus. Student leader standing on steps signing to a crowd.

Barney Frank: It is reinforcing prejudice when this institution ought to be combatting it.

Lem Tucker (VO): And disabled people across the country are watching with special interest.

Evan Kemp, EEOC [Equal Employment Opportunity Commission] commissioner: As long as any group in our society ... disabled group is controlled by able-bodied do-gooders we're all at threat.

Visuals: Interview in office with Evan Kemp certificates on the wall.

Lem Tucker: That threat is mobilizing others around the country. At Rochester Institute for the Deaf they rallied in support of Gallaudet tonight before boarding buses to join in a march tomorrow to Capitol Hill. Lem Tucker, CBS News, Washington.

Visuals: Posters—"Deaf Artists of America," "NTID Bound for Gally," "Gallymania." Close shots of cheering students.

NBC News Transcript[6]

Length: 45

Date 3/7/88 (first to broadcast story)

Tom Brokaw: There were no classes today at the world's only liberal arts college for the deaf. Gallaudet University in Washington, D.C. It was shut down by students protesting the selection of a new school president who is *not* hearing impaired.

Visuals: Talking head—center—close shot of Tom Brokaw. Monitors and computers in the background.

VOSOT: Hundreds of students sealed off the entrances to the school's campus. Their leaders say the protest will continue until the school's Board of Directors agrees to hire a deaf person as president and a majority of the Board's seats are held by deaf people. The protesters marched from the campus to the White House and the Capitol. The school never has had a deaf president in its 124 year old history.

Visuals: Cut to people standing behind gate with posters; traffic is going by. A chyron across the top left corner of the screen says "Washington, D.C." Cut to scene on campus with one person leading a group of swaying persons in a cheer in front of a dark brick building with many individual windows and a light brick building with several long windows up and down the length of the building. Cut to student adamantly signing to attentive group of students. This group seems smaller because of tighter shot. Camera pulls out and reveals that the group is on Capitol Hill. Back to long shot of Tom Brokaw and "NBC Nightly News" chyron. Cut to a break.

LIKE OTHER CIVIL RIGHTS PROTESTS

Network stories about the DPN protests used a great deal of natural sound, which included deaf students jeering, cheering, and shouting. This use of natural sound gave the audience a taste of what deaf people sound like when they vocalize. Viewers saw repeated crowd shots of students. Most saw and heard Zinser and Spilman standing in very controlled poses behind podiums making announcements, speeches, and declarations. Both women relied on interpreters.

The students, on the other hand, were standing on chairs (or whatever would elevate them enough to be seen by fellow protesters), flailing hands and arms, and vocalizing. There were shots of students carrying a "We Still Have a Dream" banner and shots of the Washington Monument and Reflection pool. These have become visual symbols that represent the earlier civil rights struggles of Dr. Martin Luther King, Jr., and the March on Washington.

The media helped the "deaf-inition" prevail. Except for the consistent use of the phrase *hearing impaired* to describe the kind of president students wanted—this term implies the pathological view of deafness—anchors and reporters showed viewers sights and sounds to reflect how deaf people have been historically alienated. The reporters interviewed deaf students and protesting faculty members rather than relying on the board chair's or the newly appointed president's statements. Both would have been the authoritative sources most likely quoted in the past. The phrase "Deaf people can do anything except hear" was repeated throughout the week of newscasts,

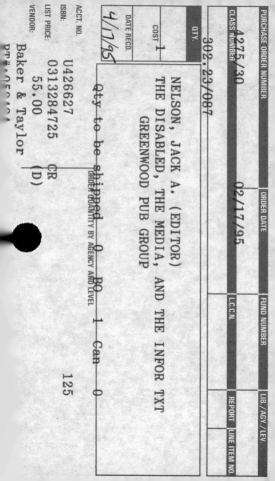

and the Gallaudet board members were cast as insensitive and unhearing. ABC News staff voted student leader Greg Hlibok Person of the Week when the protests ended and a deaf person was appointed president.

The networks were favorable to the protesters in their coverage. Here are several alternative ways the networks could have made meaning out of the events at Gallaudet University that week:

- The new president does not know sign language! Why?
- Student protests challenge academic freedom of board.
- Gallaudet students challenge law and order at campus.
- What do Gallaudet parents, employees, neighbors think about the crowds?
- Gallaudet University presidential finalists. Who are they?
- Jane Basset-Spilman from the Basset furniture family is asked to leave.
- I. King Jordan does a flip-flop.
- Is the new deaf president deaf enough?
- Who are the interpreters? What is their role in this?

Each of these slants would have led to different meanings for the DPN story. In the formal transmission model of communication, each was equally valid information for the public.

A MINORITY GROUP

Deaf people see themselves as members of a minority group rather than as disabled people. The networks helped deaf people communicate this. By elaborating on the students' feelings, by not focusing on I. King Jordan's initial support for the board's right to appoint a president and his public change of stance later, and by not stressing the monied background of the board chair, or any of the other angles just listed, the networks kept the public focused on the students. Minority discourse has usually been articulated in mainstream discourse when and if the actors stage events that disrupt the normal flow.[7] Granted, there were no dogs and fire hoses in this civil rights protest; in fact, there were few, if any, ethnic minorities involved in the protest. Viewers saw a sea of white, privileged faces instead of the brown and black faces from the 1960s. Nevertheless, the parallels were clear.

This demonstration was an unprecedented event in the history of the United States. Viewers saw and heard deaf people stand up and demand to be heard. Deaf people told the Gallaudet board of trustees, and later the rest of the world, through the mass media, that it was time for a change. They were no longer willing to wait until hearing people thought they were ready to lead their own institution and their own lives. Another parallel to the civil rights movement is striking: I. King Jordan is married to a hearing woman and both speaks and signs. He is like the mulatto of the early twentieth century for African-Americans. The mulatto sometimes passed for white and sometimes received privileges (such as education and office jobs) that were denied darker-skinned African-Americans. This type of person was often cast as the "tragic mulatto" in literature. The mulatto did not comfortably fit into either black or white society. Many, however, chose to align themselves with African-American causes and resisted the psychological and emotional compromises that a racist society might engender. Did Jordan's duality make him more acceptable to the hearing majority? Like the mulatto, his status is somewhat ambiguous because he has as much in common with the hearing majority as he does with the deaf minority. So far, Jordan seems to have used his duality to his advantage.

A CONTROLLED PROTEST

During the protests, Gallaudet students were angry but controlled. They challenged law and order and took matters into their own hands. No one was arrested for marching without a permit and blocking entrances with cars. All of these factors came together to make an event that the networks and newspapers deemed newsworthy:

The *Washington Post* (wittingly or unwittingly) maintained the symbolic visibility of DPN in its own advertisements for itself. For several months after the protest their advertisements showed a picture of and edition of the newspaper with the headline "Gallaudet U. Selects First Deaf President." Again, the means are ignored and the results highlighted.[8]

Sharon Barnartt and John B. Christiansen, faculty at Gallaudet University, argue that even four years later, the DPN protest maintains symbolic visibility on a national level. They temper their observation, however, by noting that DPN seems to have had more impact nationally than on campus:

It is possible that the most profound national impact the DPN protest had was on the passage of the Americans with Disabilities Act (ADA). One person we interviewed, who was influential in writing and lobbying for the ADA, feels that the publicity surrounding DPN gave King Jordan so much extra credibility that his subsequent testimony at several ADA hearings had a significant impact.[9]

Even deaf individuals who view themselves as members of a cultural minority understand the advantages of joining forces with disabled individuals and organizations to gain greater access to a society insensitive to disabled people. During DPN, network reporters communicated the frustrations of students, faculty, and staff at the world's largest liberal arts college for the deaf. They allowed viewers to see and hear deaf people stand up for themselves. In the limited time allotted to television news stories, the reporters grasped the notion that hearing people have historically oppressed deaf people. Viewers saw more footage of reporters interviewing protesters than interviewing the board chair or the newly appointed president. By highlighting these sources and downplaying the usual authoritative sources, network reporters were advocates for the deaf students in the protest.

Deaf people, individuals with other disabilities, and reporters for the national media still have hurdles to overcome. However, if the openness demonstrated by reporters during coverage of DPN is cultivated and maintained, we might soon see the day when reporters and students in journalism schools do not view disability as an oddity newsworthy in and of itself.

NOTES

1. Peter Dahlgren, "What's the Meaning of This? Viewers' Plural Sense-making of TV News," *Media Culture and Society* 10 (1988):288.

2. Carol Padden and Tom Humphries, *Deaf in America: Voices from a Culture* (Cambridge: Harvard University Press, 1988), p. 41.

3. Ibid.

4. Transcript from "ABC News World News Tonight with Peter Jennings." Reprinted by permission. Copyright ABC News 1988. Visual descriptions are the author's.

5. CBS Transcript: Copyright CBS Inc. 1988. All rights reserved. Originally broadcast over the CBS Television Network on "CBS Evening News with Dan Rather." Reprinted with permission. Visual descriptions are author's.

6. Transcript of NBC News Broadcast, March 7, 1988. Copyright 1988 by NBC News. Reprinted with permission. Visual descriptions are author's.

7. John J. O'Connor, "TV and Civil Rights: The Media Still Is the Message," *Perspectives: The Civil Rights Quarterly* 14 (Summer 1982): 39.

8. Sharon N. Barnartt and John B. Christiansen, "Symbolic Visibility: The Deaf President Now Protest Four Years Later" (paper presented to the Society for Disability Studies Annual Meeting, Rockville, Maryland, June 1992), pp. 13–14.

9. Ibid., pp. 9–10.

12

The Visually Handicapped Person and Technology

John M. Crandell and Lee W. Robinson

Approximately 2.5 million Americans have serious eye problems that result in a burden of living and working in a world in which sight is very important.[1] Modern technology can relieve many of those burdens if it is applied appropriately. The process of applying technology to the problems of persons with significant vision loss is not simple, however, and few generalizations can be applied to this group of people.

Persons with visual impairments represent a microcosm of the larger population but with a significant overlay of additional characteristics that set them apart from any other group. They are, as a group, older than the general population, with over half of those who are legally blind above the age of sixty.[2] They are, as a class, well below the average in socioeconomic status. Roughly two-thirds of those with vision loss who have no other disabilities and who are otherwise labor-force-eligible are unemployed, a rate that is about ten times the rate for the sighted labor force.[3] Nationally, this group is less well educated, more prone to serious depression, socially isolated, receives some form of government-financed public assistance, and is limited in access to information and transportation facilities.[4] There are, however, many exceptions to these generalizations. Those who have impaired vision are far from being homogeneous.

The prevalence of these characteristics varies greatly within subgroups based on such factors as ability to travel independently, age at which vision loss occurred, cause of vision loss, marital status, place of residence, group affiliations, and level and kind of education.[5] These similarities to and differences from the general population make the application of technology extremely difficult. Each individual's special and unique needs must be considered in finding solutions. Nevertheless, with available and easily attainable new technology, this group of people can be assisted to participate more fully in the mainstream of American life.

PRESENT TECHNOLOGY

A young woman who edits a technology-oriented magazine for the visually handicapped and who is blind herself also does freelance reporting for her local newspaper. She was sent by her newspaper on assignment to cover the signing of the Americans with Disabilities Act by President Bush in 1990. She took with her a portable computer equipped with a speech synthesizer and a modem. She took notes at the signing ceremony with the computer and then returned to her hotel room, where she prepared her story. When she finished, she connected the modem to the telephone and called the newspaper. The story was received and published as efficiently as any other reporter could have done.[6]

This is an accurate account of an actual event and illustrates an effective use of technology that allows a person without sight to function in a sighted world. The portable computer allows the person with vision loss to work in settings such as hotel rooms, automobiles, and trains. The voice synthesizer allows the reading of what has been written, as well as editing and monitoring what is being typed. Modems allow distant communications, either with "chat mode" or by sending files, with the synthesizer indicating with sounds that the transmission is taking place. This example of successful use of computer technology should not be generalized too far, however, because there are some limitations.

First, the speech produced by a voice synthesizer is sometimes difficult to understand. Someone has suggested that it sounds like a native Japanese with sinus trouble speaking English with a Boston accent. Sometimes the speech will not work with a program, especially if it is graphics based, as with a mouse. Even if a program works, often there is far more information presented than the user can assimilate, especially long strings of numbers or punctuation signs.

Next, many terminal programs do not work well with speech output.[7] Many have highly decorated screen layouts that may be attractive to the eye but represent so much "garbage" in sound. Even some of the programs that give a choice between a text-based and a mouse-based operating system do not give enough useful information with speech to allow quick analysis and response. For example, if a set of choices is placed on the screen without highlighting, everything is read, and the person without sight must remember often-abbreviated file names, which must be typed back into the computer. Graphics-based programs are simple and friendly—for those who can see. But even when text labels are presented along with the icon, the icons are difficult to locate and may change their position on the screen. A wise cartoon cat (Mr. Jinx) has referred to a mouse as "miserable meeces," and he then observed, "I hate meeces to pieces!" This is how many persons with vision impairments feel about the mouse, though some with retained vision have found it helpful.

In general, programs that work best with speech are those with a filtering system that allows only wanted information to be spoken, that are menu driven with highlighted choices that require only the press of the enter key to be selected, and that do not use graphics that move about on the screen, such as moving windows. Some of the problems described are being met. A Canadian group, SynthaVoice, for example, has produced Windows Bridge, a software package reported to work well with some high-end speech synthesizers.[8] Some synthesizers are being developed with clearer speech and at a much lower price than were formerly available; examples are RC Systems' Doubletalk and GW Micro's Sounding Board and Vocal-Eyes.[9] Many programs have very poor documentation and lack enough information to allow operation from verbal text alone. For example, they use a series of photos or line drawings to show a sequence, but the text is not comparable. In still other programs, the documentation is so complex and detailed that it is all but impossible to follow from either a recorded version or from a computer text file with speech.

A retired college professor who is blind composes songs, but until recently she had to hire a sighted musician to write the music down on paper for submission to a publisher. Now, using a music synthesizer with appropriate software, she is able to compose her music, edit it while listening to it, and then have it printed as a final document, all without sighted assistance.[10]

Although musical composition is a specialized skill, it illustrates how special technology can be employed to meet specific needs. Spelling and grammar checkers allow sightless secretaries to produce high-quality documents from dictation or recordings. Fax documents can be sent or received with a computer that uses converter programs to change from graphic to text files. The same equipment allows a blind user to scan documents with an optical character recognition device or optical scanner, thus allowing reading of correspondence, browsing through a catalog, or reviewing a shipping slip.[11]

CD-ROM computer disk drives place information at the almost immediate disposal of a person who is visually handicapped. Dictionaries, encyclopedias, zip code directories, quotations and so forth, available at a moderate cost, allow access to information that has been largely limited to persons with eyesight.[12] Extending this capability a bit further, it is now possible to have audiovisual materials made available for visually impaired teachers or students and with great flexibility in which aspects of the materials are needed and used at a particular time. The major difficulty with this technology is limited availability of the equipment and programs at a reasonable cost.

Databases and bulletin boards also provide specialized information for the blind. The 4-Sights Network specializes in information of special interest to the visually impaired community.[13] Legal databases allow blind lawyers a means for quickly and efficiently preparing court briefs or keeping up with the latest Supreme Court decisions. The scriptures on disk, a CD-ROM disk or a database allow clergy to find passages. Similarly, travelers can access airline or train schedules for trip planning, and some banks allow on-line access to one's account for tracking and monitoring personal and business financial transactions.

Speech synthesizers allow those without useful vision to access these services through a computer. For those with limited but useful sight, enlarged character sets, with a variety of fonts, allow screen access. Some types of screen output can also be accessed with either a braille-out printer or a line of braille electronic characters.[14] In the screen enlargements, it is difficult to see formats of materials, and braille output is expensive and not readily available. Yet these adaptations meet the needs of some individuals.

MOBILITY

The ability to travel independently, safely, gracefully, and efficiently is a major necessity if those with vision loss are to be able to participate fully on the modern cultural and economic playing field. Technology that facilitates travel would be helpful. Both obstacle detectors and orientation aids are needed. The devices already described for detecting obstacles in one's path are deficient in two areas: detecting drop-offs and overhead obstructions. Although the laser cane is designed to detect both of these, the necessity of swinging the cane, the unreliability of the electronics, and the method of giving the traveler a signal need improvement. Perhaps a head-held device with a wide-angle sonar could detect wires, branches, ladders, and other overhead obstructions. Miniaturized circuits could make this system light and inconspicuous. If the detect signal could be activated only when an obstruction is imminent, this would allow normal use of hearing, or a stimulator of the skin could be employed as the danger signal.

Identifying drop-offs, such as stairs, curbs, sidewalk edges, excavations, gutters, and ditches, is more difficult. If the traveler is moving rapidly, a drop-off detected too near at hand might not allow for stopping in time to avoid problems. If the detector is activated too soon, the angle of the signal might be "fooled" by only slight declines. The higher the signal generator is placed, the better. Perhaps a head-held signal generator would be best, with the warning generated only when the surface declines.

ORIENTATION

Orientation poses greater problems. Whereas sighted persons use either of two means for orienting themselves—specific landmarks with right or left from that point or an internalized compass—the visually impaired must rely on an internal compass or very limited and short-range landmarks such as street intersections, fireplugs, driveways, and fixed sound sources. For a fairly long walk, this system could pose great stress on the memory. And even with an internalized compass, it is necessary to have occasional checkpoints. One possible solution is a form of radar or sonar that could provide information about some distant landmark, such as a telephone pole, a parked automobile, a tree, or a wall. Once the landmark has been detected, it would need to be locked onto. Then, as the traveler walks toward it, a signal could be generated that would indicate veering either to the right or the left. This approach would not require a signal generator at the destination, which would increase costs and significantly decrease the routes that could be selected. Range should be up to a maximum distance of about one hundred feet.

In other situations, it might be feasible to have a signal generator activated by a signal from a hand-held or fixed transmitter carried by the traveler that would cause the signal generator to give information about its identity—for example, the entrance of a store, the service desk in a department store, street intersections, buses or trains, or other landmarks. The message would contain only information essential for identifying the location. Since the signal generator would be activated only when the traveler activates it, power needs would be minimal.

With miniature circuits and small memory chips that could be recorded with speech, costs should not be prohibitive. Many businesses and city governments might be able to bear the cost of the generators for high-traffic-density areas. The effective range would not need to be great.

INDEPENDENT TRAVEL AIDS

A major problem for persons with visual impairments is being able to travel safely, comfortably, gracefully, and independently.[15] After World War I, dog guides were used, first in Germany and then in the United States and elsewhere as travel helpers. For those who can use dog guides, they are a useful travel aid, but it has been estimated that not more than 1 percent of the totally blind population can use dogs efficiently.[16] After World War II, Dr. Richard Hoover pioneered the use of the long cane as a travel aid. Used properly, the cane allows sightless travelers to determine the nature of the terrain over which travel is being attempted, to detect obstacles and drop-offs, to ensure a corridor the width of the body through which one can move, and to identify stairs and inclines. Overhead obstacles cannot be detected with the cane, however.

A significant travel factor for the blind is spatial orientation: knowing where one is located, the relation of that point with reference to where one wishes to travel, and an appropriate route between the two points.[17] Studies have indicated that the blind, on average, are less able to orient in space than are the sighted, but there are wide differences in this ability among both the blind and the sighted. There is also some indication that some individuals can develop this ability. Neither the dog guide nor the long cane provides travelers with the ability to identify streets, house numbers, or other signs. Most sighted individuals use these signs plus familiar landmarks as guides in negotiating a specific route, but this is not possible for the blind and severely visually limited.

The use of a sighted human guide obviates these problems but introduces other limitations, such as the convenience of traveling when one needs to travel. Also, it is inefficient for two people to go where only one needs to go, and it creates a dependent relationship. Several new travel aids have been developed, though all possess limitations. One of these is the laser cane. Three laser beams are emitted from the shank of a long cane: one beam goes up to head level, another goes straight ahead, and the third goes down. The first two emit a signal when the beam is broken by an object, and the last emits a warning when the signal is not interrupted by the travel surface, indicating a drop-off. The cane is also used to detect terrain characteristics, clear foot spaces, and inclines and declines.[18] The information obtained with this device is useful but still very limited, and the electronics are unreliable. The device assists only in obstacle avoidance, not in orientation.

Leslie Kay, professor of electrical engineering at the University of Canterberry in Christchurch, New Zealand, developed a sonar device in which a cone-shaped beam of high-frequency sound is emitted from a head-held source.[19] The sound reflects from surfaces in its path, and these reflected sounds are picked up, amplified, and transduced to hearing frequencies and fed into the ear of the user. The signal varies with the distance of the reflecting object, the direction of the object, and its surface texture. Since the range of this device is about twenty feet, it does little for spatial orientation, and it does not indicate drop-offs. The Sensoritoner and the Mowatt sensor operate on much the same principles, but the kinds of information are far more limited.[20] All three devices are very expensive and have reliability problems.

PRINT-MEDIA ACCESS

The Library of Congress increases its holding by about 1 million items each year. Of this number, approximately 47,000 are books.[21] With interlibrary loans, most of this information is potentially available to readers but not to blind readers. In 1991 there were 303 titles published in braille, 105 on disks, and 1,645 on cassette tapes.

Many volunteer organizations produce other materials for the blind, but even with all this assistance, very little specialized information is available to the visually handicapped, and then only with great difficulty. (A notable exception to this generalization is Recordings for the Blind, which records materials on demand for blind and learning-disabled students and professionals.[22]) Journals, newspapers, pamphlets, and magazines contain even more information than do books, but this store of printed information is even less accessible to those with vision problems. At best, only information of a general interest is being made available. By the same token, the visually impaired typically do not have direct access to most reference materials. A single braille dictionary would require many feet of shelf space and numerous individual volumes and would still be nothing like the unabridged *Webster International* or the *Oxford English* dictionaries.

One long-standing method for gaining access to some of this printed information is to use sighted readers. This becomes expensive, is inefficient, varies considerably in quality, and makes the person with a visual impairment dependent on another person. Some modern computers are especially equipped with CD-ROM devices and represent another promising approach, but it will be many years before all new materials are published in this medium and before it will be online for access by blind readers.

Many databases developed recently contain and maintain current information. Accessing these databases requires a computer with terminal software, modems, time, and financial resources.

The optical scanner can be used to gain access to text materials.[23] In fact, this may become the primary source in the future for reading access, especially as more and more books are transferred to computer disk files using this medium. Means will need to be developed for improving the ability of speech synthesizers to distinguish sounds for two words with the same spelling but differing in meaning (e.g., *read* as both the present tense and past tense). An obstacle to the realization of this potential means for reading, however, is copyright protection. If books are published in electronic forms and if they can be printed from this form to paper, some method for charging a fee for use will need to be developed, even for public libraries.[24]

There is reason to believe that libraries of the future will show little similarity to those of the present. Reading materials will be available through computer monitors and keyboards, but not all will be available in the form of bound volumes. It may well be that users will not have to go to the library in order to use its collections. A home-based computer may take the place of the terminals in the library. This is possible to a small degree even now. If users gain access to the collection through electronic means, there will need to be an access charge, or tax dollars will be needed to compensate materials suppliers. (In public libraries today, the term *free* does not apply to the costs of buildings, salaries for librarians, and for collections, and this will continue to be true for library facilities of the future.) The "new" library will be far friendlier to a visually impaired person than libraries are now. Most likely the "Library for the Blind and Physically Handicapped" will remain a separate entity, but with unlimited access to regular libraries' collections and limiting access to its own patrons, as at the present.

At the present, many volunteers are used in the production of recorded reading materials and braille. A number of organizations exist for that purpose, including some prisons that offer recording facilities to inmates who read books needed by the print handicapped. Similarly, others sponsor braille transcribers who translate print materials into a touch medium. If all materials eventually are available through electronic storage and if means are found to allow the blind to gain access to these materials, such services may no longer be needed. Even when braille materials are needed, programs exist that translate print into braille.[25] This braille output can be used to emboss braille pages, either at the library or by the individual user with a personal embosser or through electronic braille displays.

INFORMATION: LIBRARY OF CONGRESS PROGRAMS

The Library of Congress has been funded for many decades to provide library services to the blind and physically handicapped through a number of regional and state libraries.[26] These facilities provide braille, large-print, and recorded materials by mail to their patrons through "Free-Matter for the Blind and Handicapped" mailing privileges. The number of titles is very restricted, though, and cater to general interests rather than individual needs. This program pioneered in the development of long-play records, which were the standard means for recording music before the introduction of recording tapes and compact disk recordings. Over the years, long-playing, heavy records were replaced with lighter-weight records, vinyl discs, open-reel tapes, and cassettes, recorded on four tracks at half speed. This track pattern is such that the tapes will not play on a standard reproducer.

Some patrons of these special libraries have found it difficult to use the reproduction equipment needed to gain access to the recorded materials. New machines only require readers to insert the tape and push a single button in order to read the materials recorded on all four tracks.

RADIO-READING SERVICES

Most states operate Radio-Reading Services that enable the print handicapped to gain access to newspapers, magazines, and other time-dependent materials.[27] Typically these reading services operate on a side carrier of an FM radio station, and local newspapers and current periodicals are read. Even with four to eight hours a day devoted to these materials, only selected parts can be read, and weekend reading is often limited to the Sunday supplements. Some services also read grocery advertisements.

Specially tuned radios are required to pick up the broadcasts of the Radio-Reading Services, which are provided on loan to the users. Some states, including Arizona, have found it necessary to use a different medium for distribution, choosing to use selected channels on cable networks for dissemination. Special transducing equipment is required.

NEEDED AIDS—COMPUTERS

Although the technology described here is having a major impact in the lives of visually impaired persons, there are problem areas that can profit from the basic technology that already exists for other systems.

An alternative to the use of a mouse is a screen that responds to touch for access. This technology exists and is available for some applications. It is not yet functional for those without useful vision, however, because just touching the screen could activate a program that is not wanted and because the icons are accessible by sight alone. If a nonreactive material could be placed over the screen with "windows" over the icons with braille labels below them, the sightless person could activate the desired programs by touch.

Another screen access need is for graphics interactions that do not require a mouse—a friendly tool for those with sight but decidedly unfriendly for those with significant vision loss. Programs need to be accessible with the keyboard as well as with the mouse, but even with keyboard access, much is lost, and many programs are too complicated to use in this way. Berkely Systems's Outspoken program uses the internal synthesizer of the Macintosh to produce speech and screen review.[28] This program is useful for someone already versed in the Macintosh environment before losing sight but far less useful if one must learn both the Macintosh and Outspoken systems simultaneously.

Many programs that employ graphics could be made useful to the visually handicapped if it were possible to bypass or eliminate some of the decorative screens. These screens usually contain a logo or a menu that adds little to the program itself. Another partial solution to screen access of graphic screens with keyboard equivalents would be better manuals. For example, the QuickLink II fax-modem program is accessible with keystrokes, but the documentation is extremely confusing on how this is to be accomplished.[29] If the program developer would have someone go through the process of using the program as the user will have to and then write the instructions, it would most likely be far more useful. WordPerfect Corporation does this, and it has been successful in assisting those without sight learn to use its programs.[30] An alternative technology could be developed that uses a tactile-graphics approach. Currently only one or two lines of braille are available as output, and this is insufficient for graphics. It would be possible to include a full-page braille display, but the cost would be prohibitive. The braille cells or characters are produced using vibrating picoelectric fibers, which are complicated and expensive to produce. If a new system for producing braille dots could be developed using either a mechanical transducer or less-costly electronic elements, a full page of output could be provided. This would not only provide better refreshable braille but could also be used to present graphs, diagrams, charts, and tables, which require users now to hold too much information in mind before the "gestalt" can be achieved. Several prototypical devices have been developed, but none has reached the marketplace.

TECHNOLOGY ACCESS

A significant difficulty in the use of high-tech solutions to the problems of the disabled is the costs involved. Appliances are often provided for clients of state-federal rehabilitation programs when they lead to greater employability.[31] Still other organizations provide low-interest loans that can be used to finance equipment purchases.[32] The Vocational Rehabilitation Amendments of 1989 specifically authorized the purchase of specialized equipment for the disabled clients of programs funded and guided by that program. These purchases need not be limited to currently active clients, so long as employability is fostered.[33] Public laws 100-407 Technology-Related Assistance for Individuals with Disabilities Act (TRAIDA) has mandated the setting up of demonstration sites for technology for the disabled and requires that any high-tech materials or equipment purchased by federal funds be accessible to the disabled. The demonstration sites are designed to allow disabled persons to try out various types of equipment before selections and purchases are made. These laws are designed to increase awareness of technology that is available to this broad group of persons and will make purchase plans more necessary.

The Americans with Disabilities Act requires that opportunities be made available to the disabled for greater participation in normal life activities.[34] If the law's intent is to be realized, specialized and off-the-shelf technology will have to be utilized. Prospective employers, service providers, merchants, and governmental agencies will be required to pay for changes to comply with the law, and it is incumbent upon the disabled individuals who will benefit from this law that they use its provisions for the good of the entire society to justify the expenses of the law's implementation. How can this be done? Individuals who are disabled have expenses in maintaining life. The resources for their support must come from family and friends, from government funds, provided by taxes, and from charitable organizations. If the disabled are enabled to work to any degree, the cost of their maintenance will be reduced, and in many cases these working disabled persons will be taxpayers rather than tax consumers. They can contribute in other ways to the betterment of society through sharing their work ethic with other dependent groups.

NOTES

1. C. Kirschner, *Data on Visual Impairment in the U.S.: A Resource Manual on Characteristics, Education, Employment and Service Delivery* (New York: American Foundation for the Blind, 1985).

2. Ibid.; J. M. Crandell, Jr., and R. K. Poplawski, *Executive Summary: Utah Statewide Needs Assessment of the Blind and Visually Handicapped* (Salt Lake City: Advisory Council for the Visually Handicapped, 1989).

3. Crandell and Poplawski, *Executive Summary*.

4. Kirschner, *Data*.

5. R. V. Bohman, "Employability Factors of the Visually Impaired in Utah" (Ph.D. dissertation, Brigham Young University, 1992); R. K. Poplawski, "Prevalence and Psychosocial Factors Influencing Depression among Adult Blind Residents of Utah" (Ph.D. dissertation, Brigham Young University, 1991).

6. D. Kendrick, "Main Menu," *Tactic* 6(3) (1991): 1–3. The technical journal is *Tactic* and is published quarterly by Clovernook Associates, Clovernook Printing House for the Blind, 7000 Hamilton Avenue, Cincinnati, OH 45231. It is available in both braille and large-type editions.

7. Described in Larry Skutchan, *Manual for the Automated Screen Access Program*, Microtalk, 337 South Peterson Avenue, Louisville, KY 40206.

8. Syntha Voice Computers, 125 Gailmont Drive, Hamilton, Canada.

9. RC Systems, 121 West Winesap Road, Bothell, WA 98021, (206) 672-6909; GW Micro, 310 Raquet Drive, Fort Wayne, IN 46825.

10. G. Napier, "Grace Note for Blind Composers," *Tactic* 7(4) (1991):38–45.

11. *TeleSensory*, P.O. Box 7455, North Bernardo Avenue, Mountain View, CA 94039-7455.

12. *Microsoft Bookshelf*. Microsoft Corp., P.O. Box 3011, Bothell, WA 98041.

13. 4-Sights Network, (313) 272-7111. 16625 Grand River Avenue, Detroit, MI 48227.

14. Enabling Technology, 3102 Southeast J Street, Stuart, FL 34997, (407) 283-4817.

15. W. H. Jacobsen and T. E. C. Smith, "Use of the Sonic Guide and Long Cane in Obtaining and Keeping Employment," *Journal of Visually Impaired and Blindness* 38(22) (1982); R. L. Welsh and B. B. Blaush, *Foundations of Orientation and Mobility* (New York: American Foundation for the Blind, 1980).

16. S. Finestone, *The Demand for Dog Guides and the Travel Adjustment of Blind Persons* (New York: Equity Press, 1960).

17. F. L. Crawford, "A Study to Determine How Independent Travel May Affect Employment and Earnings of Blind Workers" (Ph.D. dissertation, New York University, 1965).

18. Welsh and Blaush, *Foundations of Orientation*.

19. Ibid.

20. Ibid.

21. *Bowker Annual Library and Book Trade Almanac*, 37th ed. (1992), p. 503.

22. Recordings for the Blind, 20 Rozell Road, Princeton, NJ 08540.

23. Arkenstone, 1185 Bordeaux Drive, Suite D, Sunnyvale, CA 94089.

24. Utah State Library Board, minutes, August 1992. The comments were made by Bruce Griffin, chairman of the board.

25. Duxbury Systems, Inc., 435 King Street, P.O. Box 1504, Littleton, MA 01460, (508) 486-9766.

26. F. K. Cylke, *That All May Read: Library Service for Blind and Physically Handicapped People* (Washington, D.C.: Library of Congress, 1983).

27. Bill Pasco, P.O. Box 3663, Pittsburg, PA 15213; Steve Terry, 1850, Peabody Avenue, Memphis, TN 38104; David Judy, executive director, 589 Jordan Lane, Wethersfield, CT 96109.

28. Berkely Systems, Inc., 1700 Shattuck Avenue, Berkeley, CA 94709.

29. Reference to Quicklink II distributed by Logic Code Technology, Inc., 1817 DeHavilland Drive, Newbury Park, CA 91320.

30. The authors have worked with a programmer for Word Perfect. He explained the process that is followed in preparing manuals.

31. The Amendments to the Vocational Rehabilitation Act of 1986 attempted to get state agencies to be more active in assisting disabled persons through provision of appropriate technology, both current clients and those who are employed. See S. J. Mendelsohn, "Law Could Make 'Access Technology' More Accessible," *Tactic* 4(4) (1988):3–16.

32. American Foundation for the Blind, 15 West Sixteenth Street, New York, NY 10011, has a program for low-cost, low-interest loans for the purchase of the Kurzweil Personal Reader.

33. Mendelsohn, "Law Could Make 'Access Technology' More Accessible."

34. Americans with Disabilities Act, P.L. 101-336, 1990; Cylke, *That All May Read*.

Two for the Price of One

"Son, for the same price I'll get an actor with two eyes." Columbia Pictures's Harry Cohn to actor Peter Falk, who lost an eye in youth due to cancer. Falk retold the story of his meeting with Cohn—and the remark—in an article in the *New York Times*.

From *The Disability Rag* (March–April 1991)

Boycott Power?

ABC Television cancelled its comedy series "Good and Evil" after only 7 episodes when the show drew fire from the National Federation of Blind for its portrayal of George, a recurring blind character who, the NFB charged, "displays preposterous ineptitude and stupidity, which according to ABC spokesmen, are intended to be funny."

A letterwriting campaign and picketing at ABC affiliates nationwide were followed by NFB's announcement of a boycott of "Good and Evil" sponsor Unilever United States, Inc., corporate parent of Lipton, Mrs. Butterworth Syrup and Wisk detergent. A few days after the boycott was announced, Unilever announced it was pulling its sponsorship of the show, as did Playtex and Upjohn.

ABC said the decision to drop the show was based on ratings. The NFB claimed victory nonetheless.

From *The Disability Rag* (January–February 1992)

13

"My God! Another Little One?": Little Journalists' Contributions to the U.S. Media

Alf Pratte

When his son John led the new arrival through the big ranch house at Miramar to his father's office in 1908, chain newspaper owner E. W. Scripps was busy. He had just finished with several other visitors, all of whom, by coincidence, happened to be small men. Scripps was sitting on a davenport, wearing an old sweater and skullcap and smoking a cigar.

"Father," John intruded, "this is Roy W. Howard."

Scripps looked up, pushed his steel-rimmed glasses up on his forehead, and flicked cigar ashes on the carpet.

"My God!" he exclaimed. "Another little one?"

"Well, Mr. Scripps," Howard responded. "Perhaps another little one, but this time a good one."

Scripps frowned and then put out his hand. It was like a limp, cold mackerel when Howard grasped it. But the old man did not seem displeased. "One thing," he grumbled, "you'll never lick anyone's boots."[1]

This incident, told by Joe Alex Morris in his history of the United Press, is only one of a number of historical anecdotes or references that call attention to the socially learned emphases on global perceptions of the male body, including height or body build.[2] Numerous studies have indicated that tall men are judged to be more attractive than shorter men. Additionally, a person's height tends to affect the perceiver's evaluations of that person's traits or abilities, such as level of authority and status.[3] For example, *Chicago Tribune* publisher/editor Robert R. McCormick stood an imposing six feet four inches. Because of this, Caryl H. Sewell says, McCormick became accustomed to dominating others, and perhaps it was partially his body build that led him to assume superiority over them.[4]

Susan B. Kaiser notes that in several studies, subjects have been requested to estimate the physical heights of men when they had some previous information on the men's level of status in some regard. E. C. Lechelt found that male and female students rated or estimated the physical heights of men in different occupations as a function of the esteem or prestige they accorded to those occupations.[5] For instance, lawyers were estimated to be taller than plumbers or clerks. Male politicians have been found to be more successful in attracting individuals to them when they are taller.[6] A major exception to such prejudice has to do with gender. In contrast to desired tallness among males, tallness is a bodily trait that is deemed undesirable in females.[7]

One example of using height in a pejorative sense can be seen in the bitter comments President Franklin Delano Roosevelt used to make by referring to Arthur Krock in public as "Li'l Arthur" after the *New York Times* political writer wrote columns critical of the New Deal. One parable, repeated at press gatherings that did not include Krock, has the president telling other journalists:

Li'l Arthur—it runs, for that is what the President now calls him—once made a trip to Paris and wanted to see the sights. He asked for a guard of honor and was given the president of the republic and the commander in chief of the Army, for that is the way he likes to do things. By and by, they came to the Louvre Museum, and there they saw the Venus de Milo. "Ah!" exclaimed Li'l Arthur. "What grace, what classic beauty, what form divine! But"—approaching nearer—"alas, alas! She has halitosis."[8]

Historians and other journalists also use height as a method of description—usually negative—or as a metaphor in their writings. Retta Blaney recalls the lesson in accuracy she learned from a *Baltimore Sun* rewriteman who sent her back to police headquarters to find out if a suspect was a midget or a dwarf.[9] In his history of United Press, Morris repeatedly refers to Roy Howard as "slight," "very small of stature," or "small." In a defining anecdote to demonstrate how Howard pushed his staff, one associate murmurs, "We'll fix that little bastard one of these days." Other historians are equally as observant or biased. Journalist, economist, and philosopher Henry George is described "as an amiable man, only five feet six inches."[10] Tennessee editor Siliman Evans is described as "stubby little Siliman, who is as about as broad in the saddle as he is tall."[11] Journalist and government official George Creel, in a dispute he had as a police commissioner, is described as "rising to his full height of five feet, seven inches, exploded."[12] Marquis Childs describes the chief of the *Christian Science Monitor* bureau in Washington, D.C., as "five foot Roscoe Drummond, better known as Bulldog

Drummond." Historian Richard Kluger later describes Drummond as "a self-effacing little man who styled himself a 'liberal conservative.' "[13] Kluger extends the image even further with his pen portrait of political columnist Joseph Alsop as carrying "nearly 250 pounds on his short frame and found the simple act of crossing his legs as easy as a penguin would have."[14] Donald Robinson, in his pen portraits of *The 100 Most Important People*, describes Lord Beaverbrook, the five-foot six-inch, 146-pound Hearst of Britain, "whose squat build and round face, give him the look of an over-sized pixie."[15]

For some on the receiving end, such comments about appearance may serve as a handicap, not only because of the negative manner by which others perceive them but also because they add to a poor self-image. For others like Howard and dozens of other "pint-sized," "diminutive," "pixie-sized" reporters, editors, and publishers, such shortness may also serve as a clue to character, an added motivation to success, or push to power.

KEY TO CHARACTER

According to Frank E. Ford, retired chief editorial writer for Scripps Howard News Service, Roy Howard

measur[ed] a little under 5-feet, 7 inches, he certainly was no midget. But he was eternally conscious of his brief stature and was determined to be noticed. This resolve, amounting at times to an obsession, supplies the key to his character. His opinions on everything under the sun were explicit and firm. He was brutally, often profanely free with those opinions, was incapable of sham diplomacy, compensated for his meagre avoirdupois with a blistering vigor of attack. In the heat of anger or excitement his voice rose to a piercing tenor which, on a quiet day, could be heard for a block or more without benefit of mechanical amplification.[16]

Ford further argues that his lack of height contributed to the idiosyncratic wardrobe that became Howard's early trademark:

Spats and cane became routine accessories, along with checkered vests and carefully-patterned shorts with bow ties to match. As income came to permit, the shirts were tailor-made.[17]

Late in life, Howard explained that he had affected the gaudy attire because he was small and was determined to be noticed. As the years wore on, he tended to tone down the colors, and he discarded the cane and spats.

Howard is not alone among journalists whose height has served as one key to their character, as well as a means of identification. Other historians in *The Dictionary of Literary Biography* have called attention to the "short, bristly, German immigrant" cartoonist Thomas Nast; *Louisville Courier-Journal* editor Henry Watterson, who was "merely 5-feet tall," weighed less than

100 pounds, and had eye problems; the "short rolly-polly" William Allen White, famed editor of the *Emporia Gazette;* "short and stout" Harry Tammen of the notorious *Denver Post;* "little boy peep" Walter Winchell; and at least five "diminutive" or "pint-sized" presidents of the American Society of Newspaper Editors described in *The Bulletin of the American Society of Newspaper Editors*: founder Casper Yost, Basil "Stuffy" Walters, Vermont Royster, Eugene Patterson, and Richard Smyser. Other journalists whose height has not been as well highlighted include S. I. Newhouse, Lord Beaverbrook, Josephus Daniels, A. M. Rosenthal, Joel Chandler Harris, Walter Duranty, Max Lerner, Red Smith, Floyd Miller, and Stanley Walker. Notwithstanding their slight height, women such as Jane Grey Swisshelm, Dorothy Dix, Nelly Bly, and Ishbel Ross also made major accomplishments in journalism.

STATURE: A PRIMARY DRIVING FORCE

James William Crowl alludes to height as a primary driving force in a discussion of Louis Fischer and Walter Duranty, two foreign correspondents he describes in his book *Angels in Stalin's Paradise*. Duranty was regarded as the dean of the Moscow press corps because of his years of service, and for many Americans he was the most authoritative observer in Moscow. George Bernard Shaw called him the "king of the reporters," and Lewis Gannett, an editor for the *Nation* in the 1920s, noted that "Duranty, like Jack Reed, became a legendary character while still alive" and wrote "prose as strong as Hemingway's." Colleague Jimmy Abbe declared flatly, "His writings under a Moscow dateline have done more to influence American opinion in favor of the Soviet Union."[18]

Crowl argues that, along with Fischer, Duranty's work seems to have been "shaped in part by his feelings of inferiority." In particular, Malcolm Muggeridge saw the traits in Duranty and thought they stemmed from his diminutive size, the loss of one leg, and a childhood in which he had been educated with better-born classmates who treated him condescendingly.[19] One result, Crowl believes, was that Duranty became preoccupied with making himself known and respected even at the expense of betraying journalistic standards by inaccurate reporting of the post–World War I Russian situation.

This all-consuming personal ambition meant that he had few values or standards apart from himself. That made it easy, for instance, for him to completely reverse his views about the Soviet regime when the *New York Times* needed a Moscow correspondent who could get along with the Bolsheviks.[20]

In his *Chronicles of Wasted Time,* Muggeridge argues that Duranty's fascination with power stemmed from his sense of inadequacy and that the *Times*'s correspondent used Russia as a substitute for the physical strength he lacked in his own life: "It was the sheer power generated that appealed to him; and he was always remarking how big Russia was, how numerous Russians were." After listening to Duranty praise Stalin on one occasion, Muggeridge wrote:

I had the feeling . . . that in thus justifying Soviet brutality and ruthlessness, Duranty was getting his own back for being small, and losing a leg. . . . This is probably, in the end, the only real appeal of such regimes as Stalin's and later Hitler's; they compensate for weakness and inadequacy. . . . Duranty was a little browbeaten boy looking up admiringly at a big bully.[21]

POOR SELF-IMAGE

Another journalist whose self-image and personal relationships were harmed by his height and other disfigurements was Lafcadio Patrick Hearn, who in a playground accident was blinded in one eye, a disfigurement that affected his personal relationships. Despite his "gnome-like" body,[22] however, the talent of the literary writer was seen by John A. Cockerill of the *Cincinnati Enquirer*, who assigned him to write accounts of the city's lowlifes and their miseries. After leaving newspaper work, Hearn moved to the Orient, where he became internationally known for his books and collections of folk tales.

One of America's most famous publishers was also driven by an inferiority complex rooted in his lack of height. S. I. Newhouse, described by Richard H. Meeker as "the wealthiest, most mysterious and most successful newspaper publisher in American history," was also one of the smallest, at five feet two inches. His size affected his relations with an overbearing mother and contributed to a less-than-positive self-image, which helped motivate this child of poor Jewish immigrants to head an empire of newspapers, magazines, and broadcast holdings. According to Meeker, Newhouse was not born into a life of comfort or security:

He was the first child of recent Jewish immigrants. He was small for his age and was picked on by his classmates. But what made the most lasting mark on him was his family's seeming inability to capture the American dream. Years later, he was to confide in a friend that he thought he might never get over the shame he felt about his beginnings. At least one thing was certain, he added sharply. He would see to it that no member of his family would ever be poor again.[23]

Like so many other Jewish immigrant mothers in America, Meeker says, Rose Newhouse lavished attention on her tiny oldest boy: "Her doting became so extreme that some of her neighbors wondered if she might not be overdoing it, possibly to compensate for her husband's shortcomings."[24] "This little son of mine is no ordinary man," Rose Newhouse told her other children. Over and over again, she pressed on him her belief that if he used his brains and worked hard, he could do anything he wanted. His schoolmates were not as kind. His size came to rival his poverty as the butt of jokes in school, where he was the smallest in the class, a shrimp compared to even the shortest girls. Moreover, the numerous tough kids in the neighborhood were not about to leave him alone. Meeker records how Newhouse's small size influenced his relations with women and prevented him from joining the armed forces while the rest of his friends were going overseas in World War I:

At one time, a volunteer for the British Army had to be five feet eight inches tall, but so many soldiers were killed and then injured that the limit was lowered to five feet, three inches. Only one more inch, and Sam would qualify if similar revisions were made by the U.S. Armed Forces.[25]

Still another reference to Newhouse's lack of size is seen in Meeker's description following an interview between the small publisher and William Randolph Hearst, who was considering Newhouse as publisher for his *New York Journal*. The meeting took place in Hearst's magnificent Manhattan apartment just before Labor Day in 1938. Sitting in one of his finest antique chairs, a dachshund in his lap, Hearst peppered Newhouse with questions:

To signal that the interview was over, Hearst reached out and patted Newhouse on the knee. The great difference in the two men's sizes made the gesture a bit awkward, but Hearst appeared genuinely pleased with their conversation. "Young man," he said, "I wish I had met you earlier."[26]

Three other sons of Jewish immigrants refused to permit their lack of size to interfere with distinguished careers in the mass media: Max Lerner, Alfred Eisenstaedt, and A. M. Rosenthal. Lerner, an editorial director for *PM* and columnist for the *New York Post*, remembered the social distance between him and his classmates at Yale, as well as other disadvantages. "I was short and Jewish, and the beautiful girls didn't want anything to do with me."[27]

Eisenstaedt, one of the original staff photographers at *Life* magazine, compares himself to Napoleon when referring to his five-feet three-inch height. Other writers use the word *diminutive*. Charles Long says, "The chair seemed about to swallow him. He's only 5 feet 3 inches, and his presence otherwise doesn't belie that fact. That's [why he has been dubbed] the little man with the little camera."[28] C. Zoe Smith says, "His work has taken him all over the world, and his stature in photographic circles is far greater than his small five-foot-four inch frame." Once when photographing a bare-chested Ernest Hemingway, Eisenstaedt decided to stage his own macho act. He asked for a knife, rolled up his sleeve, flexed his arm muscle, and dropped the blade point on it. The knife bounced off the hard biceps, Eisenstaedt says, and Hemingway yelled to his wife, "Martha! Martha! It's little Papa!"[29]

As managing and then executive editor of the *New York Times*, Rosenthal has been described by both Gay Talese and Joseph Couzens as one of the most powerful men on one of the most powerful newspapers in the world. In his recent biography, Couzens says that Rosenthal helped save the *Times* during the serious economic crisis it faced in the 1970s, and helped to move the traditionally liberal newspaper into a more conservative, money-making mode. Joseph Goulden says his book *Fit to Print: A. M. Rosenthal and His Times* is about the power and insecurity of Abe Rosenthal and "how his talent and his persona combined to make him one of the more successful newspaper editors in America—and also one of the most detested."[30]

Although Rosenthal's height is not as much a factor in his life as it was with Newhouse and Duranty, Goulden noted its significance as a factor in initial impressions:

My first impression was one of surprise that the man is so small and frail, at close-hand. At a distance, he gives the impression of being a man of greater size. He was nervous; he had hoped to avoid this moment, but now he was face to face with someone on a mission he disliked.[31]

In the opening chapter focusing on how Rosenthal's character was formed, Goulden calls attention to Rosenthal's osteomyelitis, the death of his Jewish Russian immigrant father and other close family members, as well as his own physical frailities before Rosenthal began his drive to the top of the *Time*'s executive ladder. "A skinny kid," he described him, "barely 120 pounds on a five-seven frame." As the rather unflattering portrait of a power-driven man unfolds from dozens of interviews, Goulden concludes that about the nicest adjective he heard about Rosenthal's conduct over two years was *abrasive*, with *unfortunate* a close second:

Rosenthal is a shouter, a curser, a whiner; he keeps a "shitlist" in his head and he can hold grudges for years. He is a small man physically but his rages are so violent that he intimidates persons half again his size. . . .

Much of Abe's supposed bravery in shouting at other men lies in the fact that he can say two little words, "You're fired," one of his top deputies said. "Otherwise, they'd have carried him out on a stretcher with a busted jaw back in the 1960s."[32]

OTHER TINY MEN OF THE *TIMES*

Three other well-known members of the *New York Times* are said to have been both frustrated and driven by their height. Thomas A. Schwartz says the ambitions of the paper's founder and political aspirant Henry Raymond often exceeded his "diminutive size" and his ability to achieve them.[33] Gay Talese describes Adolph Ochs as both cautious and sentimental and as tough— "a short, dark-haired, blue-eyed little man, who when someone observed that he resembled Napoleon replied, 'Oh, I am very much taller than Napoleon,' and yet he was humble."[34] Describing the Ochs newspapers that would become "towering totems of nepotism," Talese says that members of the family referred to Adolph as their benefactor, "a little father figure even to his own father."[35] William L. Laurence, the paper's expert on the atom and journalism's only witness to the destruction at Nagasaki, was a "modest, shaggy-haired little man."[36]

Still another journalist troubled by his height, as well as other emotional problems, was Ernie Pyle, columnist for the Scripps newspapers in World War II. The only child of an Indiana farm family, Pyle was a frail boy who is described by historians and other writers from as small as five feet to five feet eight inches tall and never weighing more than 110 pounds.[37] Mary Ann Sentman says Pyle's understanding of ordinary people and those left out of the mainstream of life may have had its beginnings in his youth: "He was small as a child and did not participate in the sports and games of his schoolmates; he remained short and slight as an adult."[38] About his hometown experiences, Pyle later wrote:

I never felt completely at ease in Dana. I suppose it was an inferiority hanging over from childhood. I was a farm boy, and town kids can make you feel awfully backward when you're young and a farm boy. I never got over it. I should have, of course.[39]

An Associated Press story reporting Pyle's death on April 18, 1945, described him as "the wiry little columnist beloved by G.I.'s throughout the world."[40] In addition to his short stature, Mary Mander says, Pyle was plagued by bouts of severe depression:

He often felt lonesome, bored, and fed up. Landings, which he dreaded, were preceded by a last minute sense of fatalism. Others besides Pyle had similar feelings, but Pyle's depressions were not caused solely by the war, or difficulties of reporting it. His private life was in shambles. His wife was an alcoholic and frequently required hospitalization. On several occasions she tried to kill herself, the last time being a particularly gruesome attempt. They were divorced and remarried by proxy when he was in Africa. When Pyle wrote his friend Paige Cavanaugh, "If you think of anything to live for, please let me know," his words reflected his personal agony as much as it reflected anything else.[41]

One of the few war-related anecdotes that demonstrates the occasional good fortune of the small journalist is told by Joe Alex Morris. In recounting the efforts of reporters to get to and from news spots throughout the Pacific, Morris notes the efforts of UPI reporter Frank Hewlett and the AP's Dean Schedler to get off Bataan to Mindanao, where they could hitch a ride to Australia. When the two reporters went to an airstrip at one o'clock in the morning on April 12, they discovered that one of the planes had already gone, in disregard of General Wainwright's orders. There were two pilots preparing to leave in the second plane. "We can only take one of you," they informed the reporters. "In fact, we are in such bad shape that we can only take whichever of you is smallest." They looked at the two reporters. There was not much doubt which one was the smaller—Schedler. The taller and heavier Hewlett trudged alone back to headquarters.[42]

COMPENSATING FOR SIZE

Most small journalists have seen beyond their height. Hugh Swinton Legare, co-founder and editor of the *Southern Review*, had his growth stunted by smallpox as a child; only the upper portions of his body grew. Although his physical condition deprived him of some childhood activities and he became sensitive and sulked, he seldom spoke about his body size to others. Perhaps because of his physical condition and desire to excel, Edward Tucker says Legare developed a love of books and intellectual distinction.[43]

Red Smith became one of the most famous sports writers of all time although his short stature and near-sightedness prevented him from participating in athletics. Despite this fame as one of America's best-known sports writers, Smith's early childhood days were not filled with sports activities or sports heroes, although he took advantage of nearby outdoor resources, hiking in the woods, swimming, skiing, skating, and fishing:

In neighborhood games he wanted to be umpire because neither team wanted him; he was the smallest kid in the crowd, as well as being slow, uncoordinated and near sighted. Fishing by himself was his only sport, or actually, his relaxation.[44]

"I never played golf, and when I was young enough to play tennis, any girl could beat me," Smith recalls. Never the athletic type, he once tried out for the track team coached by Knute Rockne but placed last in the only race he ever entered. Biographer Ira Berkow says being little never seemed to gnaw at Smith's ego. Instead, he spent much of his time daydreaming and developing a writing style that later won him the Pulitzer Prize for commentary.

SMALL WOMEN

A number of women have not let their height interfere with their rise in American journalism. Abolitionist editor Jane Grey Swisshelm, lovelorn columnist Dorothy Dix, and foreign correspondent Rheta Childe Dorr were all about five feet tall. *New York World* stunt journalist Nellie Bly, who brought attention to women reporters in America, was five feet three inches. Scotland-born Ishbel Ross, who wrote one of the first major biographies of women in the press, was described as "a short pouter pigeon." In his remarkable history of the death of the *New York Herald-Tribune*, Richard Kluger contrasts Ross's height with that of night assistant city editor L. L. Engelking to illustrate her skill as a top reporter in pursuit of major stories:

Engel (as he preferred to be called), big as he was, was slightly intimidated by the cool, correct, and superbly reliable Miss Ross, little as she was, but he knew she was the one to call. . . . Sorry to get you out of bed. . . . Well that's fine. Engel hung up and mopped his brow. "What a woman! she's coming up.[45]

Kluger goes on to describe Ross's efforts in covering a kidnapping:

During the damned cold winter dawn in a place crawling with cops, officials and reporters . . . and there in the middle of all that muck and mire was little Ishbel, wearing her red cloth coat with the little fur collar and her high heeled shoes—no boots or galoshes. She'd worked all the previous day and hadn't slept.[46]

One of the other small females who made a large impact on the world of newspapers as advertising solicitor, manager, and president of the *New York Herald-Tribune* was Helen Rogers Reid. According to Steven D. Lyon, "Her innovativeness and energy were a major influence in the development of current journalism, especially in the field of advertising."[47]

In a pair of biographical sketches of "Queen Helen" in 1944, Mona Gardner refers to Reid's height no fewer than five times: "only five feet one," "little Mrs. Reid's eyes," "little Miss Rogers," "wasn't little Helen a born manager?" and by repeating the oft-repeated quote from her Barnard yearbook:

> We love little Helen, her heart is so warm
> And if you don't cross her she'll do you no harm.
> So don't contradict her, or else if you do
> Get under the table and wait till she's through.[48]

SMALL EDITORS

Also working at the *Herald-Tribune* as one of America's most famous city editors under Reid was Stanley Walker. Described by Kluger as "a sly, sawed-off Texan," Walker was

small, five foot seven or eight and wiry, probably never weighing more than 125 after the biggest meal in his life, and had wavy black hair with auburn tints, a thin aquiline nose, and assertive grey eyes. He smiled mostly with his eyes because he was sensitive about his ugly discolored teeth.[49]

Also described as being "sawed off" is Eugene Patterson, a former editor in Atlanta, Washington, D.C., and St. Petersburg, Florida. "Patterson," wrote *New York Times* man Martin Arnold not long ago, "is stocky, of medium height, barrel chested and walks with the roll and gait of an early James Cagney, whom he resembles in style and shape." The only part of that which he challenged, says Creed Black, is "medium height." When Patterson led an American Society of Newspaper Editors delegation through China in 1975, acting premier Teng Hsiao-ping thought he was tall—but Teng stood only five feet. Fellow Georgian Joe Parham, on the other hand, has written, "Let's face it—he is sawed off, standing five feet seven inches, with all hackles raised."[50]

Along with Patterson, four other ASNE presidents have been described as everything from small to diminutive: founder Casper Yost, Stuffy Walters of the Knight Newspapers, Vermont Royster of the *Wall Street Journal,* and Richard Smyser of the *Oak Ridge* (Tennessee) *Ridger.*

Probably the smallest of these men was Yost, whose height was seldom ignored in discussions about his work as an editorial writer for the *St. Louis Globe-Democrat* or even at his funeral. According to Jim Allee Hart,

A studious little man who weighed scarcely a hundred pounds, Yost added much to the journalistic traditions of St. Louis by his development of professional ethics which he practiced scrupulously in the conduct of the editorial page. His connection with the *Globe-Democrat* could not help adding to the prestige of the paper. Regrettably, he did not value timeliness in editorials and often would allow editorials with a news peg to remain on his desk until after the *Post-Dispatch* had published one on the same subject.[51]

In another summary of his work, Hart says that Yost should not be forgotten:

Little Casper, though tagged "Arsenic-and-old-lace" by his contemporaries, might better be called the father of the modern concept of the responsibility of the press— a concept often lost today in the more dramatic scuffles about freedom of the press. Probably nobody has stated so well as Yost the obligations that the power of the press imposes on itself. And, of course, Yost instigated it, if indeed he did not actually write, the famous "Code of Newspaper Ethics" set up by the American Society of Newspaper Editors.[52]

The editor of a small-town paper, Smyser has also been described as having a "Tom Sawyer" look. Royster's nickname is "Bunny," and the cigar-smoking Walters was referred to as "stocky."

STRIKING PERSONALITIES

Shortness in height has also been associated with a drive for power by some historians and critics. Shortly after his first meeting with Scripps, Howard was named president of the Scripps-Howard League and became one of the most influential and respected journalists of his day. He was despised by critics such as George Seldes who resented his changing the paper's populist thrust after Scripps's death in 1926 and for Howard's union busting activities: "From his youth Howard devoted himself to making money and gaining power. Only so long as old Scripps brand of liberalism paid, did he stick to it."[53]

The son of a tollgate keeper who moved to Indiana, Howard picked up his dry Hoosier twang, a vocabulary of profanity, and a sharp tongue always ready with an insult. He also developed habits of hard work and thrift, which he applied as a reporter and editor in Indianapolis and St. Louis. He was twenty-three years old and working as the president of the Publishers Press Association when Scripps first met him:

He was a striking individual, very small of stature, a large head and speaking countenance, and eyes that appeared to be windows of a rather unusual intellect. His manner was forceful, and the reverse from modest. Gall was written all over his face. It was in every tone and every word he voiced. There was ambition, self-respect and forcefulness oozing out of every pore of his body.[54]

Such confidence is also demonstrated in the lives of other small journalists such as Josephus Daniels, who successfully combined a newspaper career as editor of the *Raleigh News and Observer* with government service, including secretary of the navy and ambassador to Mexico; Joel Chandler Harris, an editorial writer with the *Atlanta Constitution*, better known for his creation of Uncle Remus; and William Burke (Skeets) Miller, a "diminutive" reporter for the *Louisville Courier-Journal*. Articles by Miller won the Pulitzer Prize after he helped to organize rescue crews and crawled into a black, slippery passage to interview a young Kentucky man who was trapped in Mammoth Cave.[55]

CONCLUSION

Being short in height is only one of many attributes that may discourage or motivate journalists to greatness as writers, editors, managers, and publishers. Other physical and emotional handicaps have contributed to success as well as failure in journalism, as in other professions. Although the "traitist" school makes some valid points in explaining success or failure because of biological, genetic, or gender characteristics, leadership in journalism appears to be based more on behavior.[56] Behavioral factors contributing to success and leadership include clarity of purpose and the ability to act decisively, a strong need to succeed and achieve on the job, a desire for responsibility, self-confidence, sound judgment, and writing, editing, and analytic skills.

After gender, race, and physical disabilities, shortness in height is one of the easiest attributes or stereotypes upon which journalists and historians can make decisions. It takes no thinking, analysis, or compassion for others to see and make prejudgments that become prejudice. It is something that many well-known journalists and historians include in their writings as metaphors and as means of comparison. Shortness in height has not always detracted from job performance or the climb to success. Indeed, in the case of many of the personalities discussed in this chapter, it appears to have been a significant force nudging the short to try to make it bigger in a competitive business.

NOTES

1. Joe Alex Morris, *Deadline Every Minute: The Story of the United Press* (Garden City, N.Y.: Doubleday & Co., 1957), p. 26.

2. The politically correct terminology for such people in the 1990s is *vertically handicapped*.

3. For example, see W. D. Dannenmaier and F. J. Thurman, "Authority Status as a Factor in Perceptual Distortion of Size," *Journal of Social Psychology* 63 (2) (1964):361–65; P. R. Wilson, "Perceptual Distortion of Height as Function of Ascribed Academic Status," *Journal of Social Psychology* 74 (1968): 97–102; D. Koulack and J. A. Tuthill, "Height Perception: A Function of Social Distance," *Canadian Journal of Behavioral Science* 4 (1) (1972): 50–53.

4. *Dictionary of Literary Biography* (Detroit: Gale Research Inc., 1984), 29:205.

5. E. C. Lechelt, "Occupational Affiliation and Ratings of Physical Height and Personal Esteem," *Psychological Reports* 36 (3) (1975): 943–46.

6. H. H. Kassarijian, "Voting Intentions and Political Perception," *Journal of Psychology* 56 (1963): 85–88.

7. E. Berscheid and E. Walster, "Physical Attractiveness," in L. Berkowitz, ed., *Advances in Experimental Social Psychology* (New York: Academic Press, 1974), vol. 7.

8. Gay Talese, *The Kingdom and the Power* (New York: World Publishing Company, 1969), p. 186. See also Matthew Josephson, "The Talleyrand of the Times," in *More Post Biographies* (Athens: University of Georgia Press, 1947), p. 136.

9. Retta Blaney, "Anatomy Mattered When Jay Spry Was on the Copy Desk: And Now I Know What to Call a Very Short Person," *Quill* (June 1992): 48.

10. Kay Marie Magowan, *Biographical Dictionary of American Journalism* edited by Joseph P. McKerns (Westport, Conn.: Greenwood Press, 1989), p. 266.

11. Roger Butterfield, "Silliman—He's a Wonder," in *Post Biographies of Famous Journalists*, ed. John E. Drewery (Athens: University of Georgia Press, 1942), p. 48.

12. *Dictionary of Literary Biography*, 25:69.

13. Ibid., p. 503.

14. Richard Kluger, *The Paper: The Life and Death of the New York Herald Tribune* (New York: Alfred A. Knopf, 1986), p. 252.

15. Donald Robinson, *The 100 Most Important People* (Boston: Cardinal Pocket Books, 1952), p. 212.

16. Frank R. Ford, "Vintage Vignettes," *Scripps Howard News* (November 1989): 11–12.

17. Ibid.

18. James William Crowl, *Angels in Stalin's Paradise* (Lanham, Md.: University Press of America, 1982), p. 5.

19. Malcolm Muggeridge, *Chronicles of Wasted Times*, vol. 1, *The Green Stick* (New York: William Morrow and Co., 1973), pp. 254–55. Quoted in ibid., 195.

20. Crowl, *Angels*, p. 194.

21. Ibid., p. 195.

22. Homer W. King, *Pulitzer's Prize Editor* (Durham, N.C.: Duke University Press, 1965), p. 58.

23. Ralph H. Meeker, *Newspaperman: S. I. Newhouse and the Business of News* (New Haven: Ticknor & Fields, 1983), p. 7.

24. Ibid., p. 14.

25. Ibid., p. 20.

26. Ibid., p. 108.

27. Quoted by Clifford G. Christians, *Dictionary of Literary Biography* (Detroit: Gale Research, 1984), p. 169.

28. Charles Long, "Eisenstaedt," *Quill* (December 1973): 21.

29. Associated Press, "Photojournalist Still Loves His Work after Six Decades behind the Camera," *Salt Lake Tribune*, May 3, 1992, A-17.

30. Joseph Goulden, *Fit to Print: A. M. Rosenthal and His Times*, (Secaucus, N.J.: L. Stuart, 1988), p. 14.

31. Goulden, p. 13.

32. Ibid., p. 22.

33. Thomas A. Schwartz, *Biographical Dictionary of American Journalism*, Joseph McKearns, ed., p. 574.

34. Talese, *Kingdom and the Power*, p. 574.

35. Ibid., p. 81.

36. Ibid., p. 61.

37. Frederick C. Painton, "The Hoosier Letter-Writer," in *More Post Biographies*, ed. John E. Drewery (Athens: The University of Georgia Press, 1947), 278.

38. *Dictionary of Literary Biography*, 29:291.

39. Ibid.

40. Ibid.

41. Mary Mander, "American Correspondents during World War II," *American Journalism* (Summer 1983):25.

42. Morris, *Deadline*, p. 250.

43. *Dictionary of Literary Biography*, 73:219.

44. Ibid., 29:330.

45. Kluger, *The Paper*, p. 222.

46. Ibid.

47. *Dictionary of Literary Biography*, 29:301.

48. Mona Gardner in Drewery, ed., *More Post Biographies*, p. 299.

49. Kluger, *Paper*, p. 240.

50. Quoted by Creed Black in *Gentlemen of the Press: Profiles of American Newspaper Editors*, ed. Loren Ghiglione (Indianapolis: R. J. Berg & Company, 1984), p. 316.

51. Jim Alee Hart, *A History of the St. Louis Globe-Democrat* (Columbia: University of Missouri Press, 1961), p. 219.

52. Ibid., p. 248.

53. George Seldes, *Lords of the Press* (New York: Julian Messner, 1938), p. 80.

54. Morris, *Deadline*, p. 27.

55. Louis L. Snyder and Richard B. Morris, ed. *A Treasury of Great Reporting* (New York: Simon and Schuster, 1949), p. 422.

56. For example, see Fred E. Fiedler, *A Story of Leadership Effectiveness* (New York: McGraw-Hill, 1967), and Conrad C. Fink, *Strategic Newspaper Management* (Carbondale: Southern Illinois University Press, 1988).

14

International Aspects of the Disability Issue

Cherie S. Lewis

While traveling through Southeast Asia as a lecturer for the U.S. Information Service, I became interested in international aspects of disability. At the time, I had been a Fulbright scholar in Taiwan and was teaching journalism courses at National Chengchi University. When the opportunity arose to deliver journalism lectures in Thailand, Malaysia, and Singapore, I took up the challenge.

On the second day of my trip, I broke my foot on a Hong Kong street. As a result, I traveled through four Asian nations with a cast on my leg and two crutches. It was a unique opportunity to experience the different ways that cultures relate to disabled individuals.

I soon learned of the gap between my Western viewpoint and that of many East Asians. From my American perspective, I continued to view myself as an independent person but one who had a temporary problem that made it more difficult to be physically active. I certainly was not going to let a broken foot stop my trip and never considered canceling my lecture tour. I continued to take buses, taxis, and airplanes and even hiked in Thailand, helped along by some friendly Israeli backpackers.

My views were at odds with East Asian norms. According to the local physicians with whom I spoke, the typical East Asian with a broken foot would cease most physical activity and return home to his or her parents. The temporarily disabled individual would be considered an invalid who needed the services of a caretaker. I had the chance to discuss this disability issue with many professors and students whom I met on my lecture tour. They were curious about my continuing to travel despite my disability and wanted to learn more about the cultural differences that affected my decision on this matter.

They learned much about how Americans view temporary disabilities, such as mine, and I, in turn, learned about their culture. I saw much to admire in the willingness of Asian families to serve as caretakers for injured individuals. But I also saw that such caretaking, if turned into a life-style, could make it quite difficult for a permanently disabled individual to lead an independent life. I received an unexpected education on the impact of tradition, culture, and education on the perspectives held by people toward disabled individuals.

These perspectives vary from nation to nation and influence both those who reside in a particular nation and those who visit it. Nations vary widely in terms of general attitudes, airline policies, hotel accommodations, and building accessibility. In the past, for example, many airlines declined to transport wheelchairs. Many that did charged for this service. At one point in the recent past, only three international airlines—Air Canada, USAir, and Israel's El Al—boarded wheelchairs without charge.

The nature of these international differences can be summarized as attitude and access. *Attitude* refers to the overall perspective and philosophy concerning disabled people. Are disabled people viewed as "different" or "less"? Is the goal for a disabled person to achieve as much independence, financial and otherwise, as possible? Or is the goal for such an individual to be provided with appropriate care, medical and otherwise? Finally, who decides on an individual's goals: that person or a caretaker? *Access* refers to access to technology. Obviously, I could not have achieved any degree of independence on my trip without crutches. But in some developing nations, even such basic technology as this is not available to the large numbers who cannot afford it.

When I left Taiwan, I donated my metal crutches to the local YMCA, which planned to loan them to individuals who could not afford to purchase them. Other more complex technologies, such as wheelchairs, are less available and often cost more. Wheelchairs also need regular maintenance and repairs, and competent technical help to keep them in good running order may not be available.

In other nations, these technologies are available for a reasonable cost, but cultural attitudes often mandate against their use as tools to enable individuals to develop independent lives. In Japan, for example, the caretaker model is strong, and families often prefer their disabled members to remain within the family system. While the willingness of family members to care for each other is commendable and ensures that disabled individuals will not live in isolation, it often mandates against independence for disabled persons.

These issues of attitude and access, so strongly influenced by education and local culture, form the crux of the international discussion on disability issues.

Two major organizations are involved with these issues on the international level: the United Nations, which works primarily with governments, and Disabled Peoples International, based in Winnipeg, Canada, which works primarily with nongovernmental organizations. Both groups have sought to utilize the mass media in their quest to improve conditions for the world's disabled people. The mass media can be a powerful force to counter the prevalent image of disabled people as individuals who need caretakers rather than as individuals who have the potential to care for themselves.

The United Nations designated 1981 as the Year of Disabled Persons and set up a trust fund with $1 million to pay for projects in various member states. This was the first time that the international community took action on the disability issue, and many governments sponsored some type of activity. Media coverage of these activities raised the international awareness level of this issue.

Many of the events were fund raisers. Although they succeeded in raising needed monies for medical research and care, they also served to perpetuate negative stereotypes of the disabled and promote the image of disabled people as helpless. These functions reflected the charity model, which sees the disabled as individuals to help, not as individuals who can make their own choices. When these charity functions are covered by the mass media, negative stereotypes of the disabled are reinforced.

The United Nations General Assembly voted to proclaim the years 1983–1992 as the Decade of Disabled Persons. Along with the proclamation, the General Assembly adopted a World Program of Action, a set of basic guidelines for decade activities. Few funds were allocated, however, severely restricting the projects undertaken by member nations.

This low level of funding reflects a basic conflict within the United Nations and within individual member nations about the status of the disabled. In the past, some nations, such as the United States and Great Britain, have generally favored the charity model and have advocated that disability issues be considered an internal matter by individual governments. Sweden and Canada, among other nations, have favored a human rights model, advocating that disability rights be placed in the same legal category as rights for women and for ethnic groups.

The United Nations as an organization has straddled the fence on this conflict. It proclaimed both a year and a decade for the disabled but failed to fund the decade fully. In contrast, it allocated $9 million for projects during the Decade for Women.

The world's mass media have also reflected this cloudy status for disability rights. They provided much coverage of international women's conclaves in Mexico City and Nairobi but have not heavily covered international projects and conferences related to disability issues.

This situation may change in the near future. The passage of the Americans with Disabilities Act (ADA) in the United States has changed the legal status of the disabled in the United States, and this will no doubt have an impact on the U.S. stand on this issue in future U.N. discussions. In addition, issues related to disabled people have recently been officially designated as human rights issues by the United Nations Human Rights Sub-Commission. Argentinean attorney Leondro Despouy was appointed by the subcommission to conduct an international study of this issue and submitted his report in February 1992. Despouy found that most member governments were violating international law in this area. Some nations refused to consider disabled refugees as eligible for resettlement. Others denied disabled individuals medical care and food. This report is the first step in a lengthy process of initiating official United Nations involvement and action in this human rights area.

Disabled Peoples International (DPI) has been active in the effort to interpret international human rights law to include issues of disability within its provisions. DPI representatives met frequently with Despouy and played a key role in the drafting of his final report on human rights of the disabled.

Founded in 1980 in Winnipeg by 250 disabled persons, DPI has a network of more than 110 groups worldwide, with a majority of them in the developing world. The world's largest disability organization, DPI is a grass-roots catalyst for change. As one of the world's few cross-disability organizations, it is the sole international representative of the unified voice of persons with physical, mental, and sensory disabilities. It works closely with the United Nations and its various agencies, including the World Health Organization.

DPI favors the full participation of disabled people in society and advocates disabled people's making their own choices and having control over their own lives. The organization is run by disabled people, including its director, Henry Enns, a social worker who has been active in the Canadian disability movement since 1975. The same holds true for DPI's member groups. Any local organization controlled by disabled people can become a member of the national DPI assembly in its home nation. Strong local organizations are active in many parts of the world, including Trinidad, Singapore, and Finland.

As an advocate of independent living for disabled people, DPI has organized educational events, produced resource materials, and helped local groups achieve financial independence by starting their own businesses. Local disabled groups now operate a supermarket in Zimbabwe, a furniture factory in Jamaica, and an agricultural cooperative in Zambia. A wheelchair factory in Nicaragua fulfills the dual goal of providing employment for the disabled and providing needed technology for them.

DPI has been active in the movement to make wheelchairs more available in developing areas. The group has been working closely with Ralph Hotchkiss, who invented a wheelchair appropriate for developing nations. His chair can be inexpensively produced and maintained and performs well on unpaved roads, which are common in developing nations. His wheelchair utilizes inexpensive bicycle tires that are readily available in most parts of the world, especially where bicycles are a chief form of transportation. Hotchkiss has written a manual on starting a wheelchair factory and has conducted seminars on this topic, attended by individuals from many developing nations. DPI itself has also been involved in international training, especially in Africa and Latin America.

As a political organization, DPI has been involved in lobbying efforts with the United Nations and other international groups, such as the International Labour Organization (ILO). Its work bore fruit when the ILO adopted a statement on the employment and rehabilitation of the disabled in 1984. By doing so, the ILO was officially supporting the rights of the disabled in the workplace and publicizing its interest in this issue.

The DPI's political philosophy is reflected in its involvement in the world peace movement. One year after its founding, it adopted an international statement on world peace. At its 1982 meeting in Japan, DPI delegates traveled to Hiroshima to read the group's peace statement at the Peace Memorial Park. At this event, DPI members marched with survivors of Hiroshima and called for peace and nuclear disarmament.

DPI's activity in the peace movement stems from the group's general interest in social justice and the fact that war is a leading cause of disability. In our own era, we can readily see the numbers of disabled individuals created by the wars of the post–World War II era, including the conflicts in Vietnam, Lebanon, and Yugoslavia. By staging a media event in Japan, DPI hoped to raise awareness of the need for peace and the connection between war and disability.

According to DPI director Henry Enns, attitudes toward the disabled can often be the biggest barrier to the full integration of disabled people into society. These attitudes and negative images can be changed through education and positive media coverage. Yet often this coverage is lacking because many editors do not view disability issues as important, ongoing news stories. The DPI's annual convention in Vancouver in April 1992 was covered well by the local press, sporadically by the Canadian press, and hardly at all by the world press. This international gathering of over 3,000 disability activists, the largest such event ever held, was all but invisible to the world's mass media.

DPI is one of several organizations trying to change this situation. It has sponsored seminars to publicize issues that have not yet been part of the world's disability agenda, including the status of disabled refugees and disabled people living in rural areas. In August 1990 in Vienna, DPI cosponsored with agencies of the United Nations a seminar on disabled women. By organizing these events, DPI and the United Nations are seeking to place these issues on the international agenda. In 1992, DPI initiated an international public education campaign and has plans to work more closely with the mass media in the future.

Another Canadian organization, the Disability Network, is working on a similar goal. Known by its nickname, DNET, the Toronto organization produces a thirty-minute weekly news-driven show focusing on disability issues. Because of the program's affiliation with the Canadian Broadcasting Corporation, it can be viewed by audiences across Canada. Regular segments include "Language Watch," which looks at words used inappropriately in reference to people with disabilities, and "Your Rights," which provides legal advice on disability issues. Issues covered in the feature portion of the program have ranged from architectural accessibility to the use of computers to help a deaf woman testify in a Manitoba courtroom. One upbeat story focused on a University of Calgary rock climbing workshop, Climbing the Unseen, for blind and visually impaired people.

Since its debut in March 1990, this show has been produced and hosted by people with disabilities. Employment equity is one of the driving forces behind DNET. The program trains people with disabilities in various aspects of production for future mainstreaming into all areas of television programming. Two members of the production crew use wheelchairs, and one is legally blind. The program is also affiliated with the Centre for Independent Living in Toronto, which helps disabled people find employment after their training period with DNET has been completed. (See chapter 9.)

Increased employment of disabled people within the media industries can help improve the coverage of disability issues, in both quantity and quality of coverage. This is a long-term goal of many disability advocacy organizations. In the meantime, since the mass media generally do not cover the disability issue as an ongoing news story, staged media events are often an effective way to obtain coverage. DPI has been especially active in staging such events on the international level.

Other organizations have been active in staging events on the regional and local level. Over the past two years, I have observed first-hand several such media events and projects. While attending a mass media conference at the Hebrew University in Jerusalem in June 1991, I had a chance to observe Israeli attitudes and policies toward the disabled. As a major tourism center, Israel is particularly hospitable to disabled travelers. The Israeli wheelchair basketball team of the Beit Halochem training and rehabilitation center often holds exhibition games to acquaint the local population with the athletic activities of disabled persons. The team toured North America in 1992, with the high point being a game versus an American team, played in New Jersey's Meadowlands Arena before a Nets-Hawks game. These televised media events are a way to raise awareness of disability issues and to integrate disabled athletes into mainstream athletic events.

In August 1992, while attending a conference in the field of journalism education, I spoke with two administrators in the final stages of planning a disability event in Quebec. As part of the festivities for the 350th anniversary of the founding of Montreal, a disability organization in a local suburb planned an open-air festival to honor the neighborhood's disabled residents and the group's volunteers. The sponsoring organization, Association de loisir des handicapes physiques de Pointe-aux-Trembles et de l'est Montreal, has been working for several years to make its local area accessible and to provide cooperative housing for the disabled. The group has discussed this with many local businesses and has been effective in making many of them wheelchair accessible.

In addition to its goal of honoring volunteers and participants, this event publicized the group's work and the neighborhood's attitude toward the disabled. Not only did this neighborhood accommodate the needs of the disabled, it actively sought them as residents and tried to include them in neighborhood activities. Held in Prince Albert Park on August 26, 1992, the festival, An Accessible Neighborhood, featured a buffet, a speech by Montreal's mayor, a wheelchair basketball game, and a visit by André Viger, a member of Quebec's wheelchair basketball team. Extra wheelchairs were provided for the nondisabled, so that they could participate in the wheelchair basketball games. This event helped Montreal's residents learn more about their disabled fellow citizens.

The Montreal Insectarium also staged a media event in 1992 to honor the disabled. On September 9, the Insectarium's butterfly population was set free for the winter. Called Donnez-Moi Des Ailes ("Give me wings"), the event focused on disabled children and their desire to be mobile. Sponsored jointly with the Société pour les enfants handicapes du Québec (Association for Disabled Children), the event featured Canadian television star Marc-André Coallier.

Much has happened in the international arena since 1981, when the United Nations declared the Year of Disabled Persons and DPI held its first world conference in Singapore. Disabled persons in both developed and developing nations have formed organizations, lobbied for legal and social change, and started their own businesses.

The world's mass media have slowly started to place disability issues on their news agendas. Both major international organizations and smaller local organizations hope this trend continues, for they recognize that the media can do much to publicize their activities and counter negative stereotypes of the disabled. If attitudes toward the disabled are often the major barrier facing them, then the world's mass media can do much to weaken this barrier and help disabled persons achieve full integration into mainstream society.

15

Virtual Reality: The Promise of a Brave New World for Those with Disabilities

Jack A. Nelson

During this century, startling developments in communications technology have changed the world and the way that society functions. The evolution of radio and television, of course, offers the most dramatic examples of media that have helped reshape the world in everything from politics to morality. Nevertheless, a relatively recent development in computer technology has the potential for bringing even more striking changes in the way they affect some people's lives. This is the creation of computer-created worlds called *virtual reality* or *cyberspace,* in which users have the sensation of entering an artificial world and interacting with their surroundings.

The theory behind virtual reality is that humans do not directly experience reality. Rather, they receive external stimuli which the brain interprets as reality. As technology has advanced, a computer can send programmed stimuli that the brain interprets as indistinguishable from actual experience. This requires equipment that is currently very expensive—data helmets that envelop the user with sight and sound, and data gloves or suits that allow the computer to track the user's hand or body movements. At present these presentations are crude and cartoonish, but they may represent the first stages of more complex virtual realities that someday may seem as real as actual experience. In fact, the potential is for it to become indistinguishable from reality.

"This is going to be the most substantial communications technology of the twenty-first century," says neuroscientist David Warner of the Loma Linda University Medical Center in San Bernardino County, California (telephone interview, June 2, 1992). Warner has been active in adapting the technology in its present form to further the quality of life of patients at that facility.

This chapter will explore the benefits that this new communications technology presently offers certain fields, and will focus on its potential for helping those with disabilities in the future to improve the quality of their lives.

The key is that a virtual world can be created any way we want it to be, a fact of major importance to users with disabilities. In this virtual world, we must have the feeling of "presence"—we must feel that we are there. As in the real world, virtual reality allows the user to walk around corners, to pick up objects and examine them, and to open doors and interact with objects of that world. In this environment, some features now being developed will allow the user to feel the weight and resistance of objects being touched. In the future in this virtual world, a user will no doubt be able to pick up a cup of coffee and feel not only the weight of the cup, but the heat emanating from it. In addition, virtual reality offers the capabilities of multiuser capabilities, so that one may bring along a friend to share the experience—even though in reality they could be a continent away from each other.

Even today an architect can enter a virtual building he has drawn, walk through the rooms, examine doorways, move a window if he chooses by simply taking hold and rearranging it to suit himself, and judge the place as if it were already built. Soon armchair business people may be able to visit a virtual conference half a world away. Already the Matsushita Electric Works in Japan invites customers to describe their ideal kitchen, feeds the data into a computer, then asks them to tour the virtual kitchen to see if everything is in the right place, to peek into drawers, to open the doors of the virtual appliances and cabinets to make sure they are unobstructed, and to judge if the cupboards are too high. This allows them to make any modifications desired in their kitchen as if it had already been built (Bylinsky 1991, 142).

This virtual reality is a sensory experience that so totally immerses the users that they can barely distinguish between reality and the artificial experience. As Brenda Laurel explains:

Telepresence means that you take your body with you into another world; you experience from the inside. When you watch a good movie or play a good game you're apt to forget about your body altogether. In telepresence, your body's right there, experiencing sensory immersion. And through a variety of interface techniques, you are also able to do things with your body in virtual environments like walk, fly, or manipulate virtual objects. (Laurel, 103)

At present to enter these virtual worlds, one dons two pieces of equipment. The first is a type of goggles, with two small color television screens mounted side by side in a rubber mask much like a diver's mask. A magnetic sensor atop the mask transmits data to the computer about the wearer's position in space. The other piece of equipment is the data glove, a single spandex glove wired with sensors. As the hand is flexed or moved, the light flow along each finger changes to alert the computer to the movement.

BACKGROUND OF VIRTUAL REALITY

The concept of virtual reality was first presented in 1965 by University of Utah researcher Ivan Sutherland, a computing pioneer, at a conference of the International Federation of Information Processing Societies. He offered the vision of three dimensional images so sharp and true they would be indistinguishable from reality, an ultimate display that would even offer tactile sensations. Three years later Sutherland unveiled the first system of virtual reality. This early effort was cumbersome and used a headband hung with two miniature monitor screens and a huge mechanical arm with sensors (Daviss, p. 40).

It took the U.S. military to more fully develop the concept. Thomas Furness and his team at Wright Patterson Air Force Base in Dayton, Ohio, developed a flight simulator for pilot training for the complex F-16 fighter. It was called the Super-Cockpit and used a helmet in which the trainee looked at a computer-synthesized virtual reality projected onto the inside of the helmet's face shield.

Flying in this virtual world, pilots could control their virtual plane largely with eye movements and simple voice commands. They wore a glove lined with position sensors, so they could point to buttons or instruments displayed on the helmet's face shield. They could launch an anti-aircraft missile, for example, by "pushing" a virtual button. The effect was dramatic: after simulated battles the pilots emerged sweating and with hearts pumping and adrenaline flowing (Daviss, 40). Those who trained in the Super-Cockpit scored well above those who trained in conventional methods.

Jaron Lanier, the head of VPL Research in Redwood City, California, has been one of the moving forces in the development of virtual reality to its present stage. His company has been instrumental in the development of the DataGlove, DataSuit, the Powerglove, Swivel 3-D, and VPL EyePhones. Autodesk, a research company up the road from VPL in Sausalito, has been a leader in virtual reality developments, along with such universities as Stanford, the University of Washington, and the University of North Carolina.

REVIEW OF THE LITERATURE

This technology is new and enough on the fringe of science so that so far little attention has been paid by the academic world in communications. Much of the current thinking about virtual reality systems was proposed by

University of Connecticut researcher Myron Krueger in 1983 in his book *Artificial Reality*, which was updated in a 1991 edition. Krueger distinguishes between virtual reality, which he sees as that system that uses datagloves and goggles, and other systems that give the illusion of participating in a graphic world through other means.

Howard Rheingold's book *Virtual Reality* has been a popular explanation of the technology since 1991. Brenda Laurel, who comes from a background of theater and computers, explores the relationship of these worlds in the 1991 volume *Computer as Theater*. Sandra Helsel and Judith Paris Roth, editors of the journal *Multi-Media Review*, published *Virtual Reality: Theory, Practice & Promise*, also in 1991.

Because the astonishing possibilities of virtual reality have caught the public's imagination, most of the literature has occurred in the popular press in such magazines as *Omni, Mondo 2000*, and *Fortune*. Most attention has been given in the computer and scientific magazines, or those dealing with cultural aspects of society. A segment of the television news show "20/20" was also devoted to the emerging technology of virtual reality. Some of the most valuable sources for this paper were in the proceedings of a conference on Virtual Reality and Persons with Disabilities in March 1992, sponsored by California State University, Northridge, and directed by Harry Murphy.

MEDICAL USES OF THE TECHNOLOGY

In the field of medicine, virtual reality seems to hold new worlds of efficiency and promise. Henry Fuchs, a computer scientist at the University of North Carolina at Chapel Hill, has been a leader in synthesizing diagnostic images of a patient's body using x-rays, ultrasound, and magnetic resonance to create virtual models of the patient. By using the virtual reality model, the radiation therapist will one day be able to walk around the virtual patient to dissect the patient electronically to locate and expose a tumor. The physician could then accurately figure the specific dose and configuration of the radiation. In theory, the physician could shrink himself and enter the patient's body to further assess the proper treatment. "Right now, the technology isn't quite up to it," Fuchs admitted in 1990, but since then major strides have been made (Daviss, 39–40).

Lanier gives a more explicit description of the process:

We take information about the human body from scanning machines and turn it into objects in virtual reality. This means doctors can put their patients through a scanner, then walk into virtual reality and pick up the patient's bones and internal organs. Suppose the patient has a serious deformity or injury. A surgeon could get a feeling for the three-D structure of that person's body to help plan surgery. This is still in the earliest testing phases. . . . We've done one project with the San Diego Super-computer Center where we had people looking at the structure of their brains. You can have two physicians inside the brain at the same time, and they can talk about what they see. One can point to the structure and say, "There's an abscess here." (Stewart, 113–114)

That is not far in the future. Lanier says that Fred Brook and Henry Fuchs at the University of North Carolina have already let chemists pick up molecules whose atoms are portrayed as fist-sized in order to study them better.

VIRTUAL REALITY AND THOSE WITH DISABILITIES

Even for those with disabilities, the possibilities of this new technology seem limited only by the imagination. Thomas Furniss, who pioneered much of the military application of this science, is excited about the possibilities: "With the technology of virtual reality we can change the world." Furniss sees a whole new range of experiences for those with limitations:

Right now, we can build virtual worlds for quadriplegics in which they can move and behave just as well as if they weren't handicapped. We can use whatever movement they have—finger movement, even eye movement—to give them full physical mobility control in a virtual environment. They could meet with other people in virtual worlds. They could do computer-aided design. (Daviss, 38)

Lanier agrees: "You see, in virtual reality the whole world is your body—equally—and everybody shares the same body. Check it out. It's true" (Barlow 1990, 50).

In addition, it need not be a solitary experience. Current technology allows a user to enter a virtual room in which a pair of goggles wait on a table—goggles similar to the ones the user is wearing. They are waiting for a fellow traveler. By putting on a real-life counterpart to those goggles, another person anywhere in the world can join in the action by linking to the same computer and interacting with the original user.

The utility of virtual reality for people with disabilities occurs on several levels. For instance, architects could design buildings and then enter the design to check out matters such as wheelchair accessibility. Planners and those with special needs can "walk through" the planned building and come to agreement on final design issues.

More important, however, virtual reality makes it possible for impaired individuals to accomplish tasks that would otherwise be denied them. For example, NASA engineers control robots that perform tasks in space from remote locations. In much the same way, a person with limited mobility can perform functions in the real world by interaction with the virtual world. That is, the sensors can be hooked to a machine—a robot, for instance—so that the robot moves at a command, a hand movement, or even a voice command. As a medium for remote control, artificial reality bridges the gap between humans and machines.

For the blind, familiarizing themselves with the layout of a building might be accomplished by simply shrinking the building down to a small size, which the person could then explore with his or her hands.

As the next step, the environment can be designed with a particular disability in mind. For example, it might be tailor-made for a person with a visual impairment, who sees only in shadows and light. To teach that person to operate certain equipment, for instance, a virtual world can be set up so that each tool has heavy black outlines that are easily visible while the person learns to operate them safely. The flexibility of virtual reality will allow changes in that environment, so that as the person learns to use one tool, another may be added, and eventually as the person becomes proficient, the outlines will gradually disappear and the environment will become more like the real world. Eventually the person will be able to perform the tasks in the real world (Middleton, 40).

In addition, for a hearing-impaired child a virtual world could be set up to provide valuable cues to help the child to learn. Already voice-recognition technology allows hearing-impaired persons to monitor their speech output on a computer screen. This provides a model of correct sound, a visualization of their own speech pattern so that they can modify it to match the model. In a virtual setting, the whole world could be made to react to the voice— if the words are spoken correctly. Flower gardens will blossom, birds will fly from their nests, and doors may open on command. All of which can certainly be a powerful teaching tool (Middleton, 41).

In addition, the virtual environment allows everyone—regardless of their physical abilities—to move about, to fly through the air, to turn sommersaults, or perform other feats—regardless of the physical constraints of the human body. When one can maneuver through a virtual environment by hand motions or even voice control, it makes no difference if the user is sitting in a chair or in a wheelchair. Through virtual reality those whose mobility is limited in the real world will be able to attend virtual conferences or visit exotic places in virtual travel.

ENTERTAINMENT

Already some arcades across the country have featured crude versions of virtual reality as entertainment for profit. In San Francisco, a theater performance called "Invisible Site: A Virtual Sho" incorporates many virtual reality techniques and has played to enthusiastic crowds.

For the disabled community, the entertainment aspect of this new technology may have powerful therapeutic impacts. With virtual reality technology, people with physical impairments will be able to experience things that have been denied them in the past. Something as routine as throwing a ball or as fantastic as flying through space may be achieved by a hand gesture or a nod, or even by making a sound. This technology will enable them to control environments in which they interact with whatever the designer chooses to make available. Eventually, as tactile feedback is built into the systems, there will be opportunities to experience sensations they have never felt before (Middleton, 42).

Virtual reality pioneer Jaron Lanier of VPL Research in Redwood City, California, believes it will ultimately be used as a form of interactive entertainment. He talks about users being able to "inhabit" the body of a shark or a brontosaurus to see what life is like for those animals (Fritz 1991, 46).

MODIFICATIONS

For some disabilities, modifications of the present virtual reality systems will be necessary—but very feasible—for maximum benefits. For instance, following up on the example of the visually-impaired person, current visual displays are of little value. As Gregg Vanderheiden, John Mendenhall, and Tom Andersen point out, individuals who are blind could have access to the same systems if the underlying concepts being displayed and command structures required for operation were made available. Those who are blind could then use a verbal or other nonvisual mechanism to carry out the same tasks accomplished via the virtual reality visual interface.

As Virtual Realities add sound, touch, and force feedback, the value and accessibility of these environments for people who are blind will increase . . . computer-generated information such as color or visual texture could be presented verbally or converted into tactually discernible information to make it "visible" to the individual who is blind (Vanderheiden et al., 1992, 66).

MENTAL THERAPY

Indeed, even in treatment of mental disorders there seems to be promise in virtual reality. At the Loma Linda University Medical Center near Los Angeles, research is underway in multiple systems environments to work with pediatric psychiatric patients. Using actors, various facial expressions are fed into the data of cartoon characters that can interact with the youngsters. Because the character reacts to the children, a bond is formed. "They will talk to their cartoon friend about things they never would tell a doctor or even an adult," says neuroscientist David Warner (telephone interview, June 2, 1992).

THE NEAR FUTURE

In the near future, according to Middleton, we may expect several improvements in the current virtual reality systems:

1. More realistic display resolution, that is, the virtual worlds created will be less like video games and more like reality.
2. Inclusion of tactile and force feedback sensations. At present, for example, when an object is picked up in a virtual world there is no sense of weight or shape, or of force resistance in pushing a cart.
3. Use of speech and other input devices.
4. Reduction of system delays. At present, delays affect all types of sensory feedback, with visual displays being the most noticeable.
5. An increased mobility. Currently, most systems use a cable tether, limiting the sense of the virtual world that is being explored. This may become unrestricted (Middleton, 44).

Of current virtual reality systems, almost all are expensive enough that access is so far limited to major research centers or to expensive commercial ventures. A single system from VPL costs in the neighborhood of a quarter million dollars (Fritz 1991, 50). Other systems are cheaper but are limited in their ability to create realistic environments.

Currently, the environments are still rather crude, with the animated figures having little texture or subtlety. But researchers are working on virtual reality images that approach the reality of film or video. When those images reach that quality, the virtual reality experiences will be difficult to distinguish from reality itself.

In an interview with *Omni Magazine*, Lanier considered the problem of using virtual reality to help those with disabilities:

You might help people who are paralyzed have the experience of walking in Virtual Reality. Sensors placed on uninjured parts of their bodies could let them control a complete body in virtual reality, allowing paralyzed kids to play sports with other kids. Would this activity keep parts of the brain awake that might otherwise atrophy through lack of use? This is completely unknown right now. I haven't studied it as a scientist; I've only hacked it as a technologist. The field is crying out for more study of phenomena like this. (Stewart 1991, 115)

THE AKINS SURVEY OF FUTURE USAGE

In assessing the future of virtual reality as it pertains to the disabled, A.S. Akins reported in 1992 on research in which 24 experts were surveyed on their perceptions of how virtual reality may impact the lives of those with disabilities in the future. He used two qualitative techniques, the ninebox and the timeline, to assess the results (Akins, 9).

The consensus of these respondents was that the impact of direct mind interaction on society would definitely be high, while at the same time noting that the probability of direct mind interaction through virtual reality would be medium.

Two outlier groups were identified, both indicating a belief that the probability of direct mind interaction is low. The outlier groups commented that direct mind interaction provided numerous opportunities for misuse and the possibility of injury to individuals made this technology too risky to consider. (Akins, 11)

Akins used a two-dimensional timeline chart to have his respondents consider the impact of this technology over time. The following trend was posed to the audience:

Increasing interest in the virtual reality field will lead to inexpensive, and available virtual reality technology that will enhance the lives of the physically handicapped. A total of 24 responses were collected (Akins, 11). Although there was no clear consensus among the respondents, over half of the participants (13) felt that virtual reality could have a very significant impact for those with disabilities by providing an environment—a virtual reality—in which they would not be handicapped. A smaller group (10) agreed that the expense of virtual reality would almost assuredly prohibit this new technology from having much effect on the lives of those with disabilities.

A NEW WORLD WAITING?

"I want to make it clear that virtual reality will not make disabilities magically disappear," says James R. Fruchterman (1992, 19). "However, it will become a powerful tool for many people with disabilities. To a great extent, employment in a virtual office will remove many of the barriers that exist today."

Eventually, virtual reality may be delivered through direct computer-to-brain connections, which seem to be the stuff of science fiction. To overcome the limitations of current virtual reality technology, advanced software will make it possible to understand our speech and analyze scenes effectively. Computers will need to recognize very subtle gestures or voice commands to control virtual reality.

Fruchterman claims that "the voice recognition technologies developed for natural interacting with Virtual Reality systems will deliver the number one technology desired by deaf people: real-time text translation from voice to visual characters. Scene analysis will advance to the point where real-time descriptive video will be generated for blind people" (1992, 18).

In the workplace, the combination of virtual reality and expanded telecommunications will allow anyone to work where they please. The office will become a defined place in cyberspace, where a worker may stroll down the hall to chat with a coworker—who could in reality be located a thousand or twenty thousand miles away (Fruchterman 1992, 18).

In almost any extended conversation of virtual reality the subject of sex comes up. "I don't know what to make of it," writes expert John Perry Barlow in *Mondo 2000*. "As things stand right now, nothing could be more disembodied or insensate than the experience of cyberspace. It's like having everything amputated. You're left underendowed and any partner would be so insubstantial you could walk right through her without either of you feeling a thing. . . . Yes, it will work for that purpose and it will be easy. . . . Even if Virtual Reality turns out to provide the format for the ultimate pornographic film—a 'feelie' with a perfect body—it will serve us better as the ultimate telephone" (Barlow 1990, 42).

The sexual potential of virtual reality has drawn mostly sneers and hoots from observers. Rheingold, the pop-culture expert on virtual reality, has dubbed the topic "Dildonics" and even *Elle* magazine devoted an article to the subject (Dvorack 1992, 78). But most writers so far see such use as on a par with a mail-order sex shop. Nevertheless, for some in the disabled community, such a development might possibly play an important part in fulfilling the quality of full-life experiences.

A FUTURISTIC SCENARIO

Akins proposes a rather startling scenario as a possible alternate future in which the technology of virtual reality could conceivably play a prominent role. Projecting into the year 2013, in which tremendous strides have been made by the medical world to develop virtual reality as a technology that could help those unable to walk, or the blind to see. He proposes it as a liberating technology whose first beneficiaries are those with disabilities. His scenario is summarized as follows:

I can run as fast as any man. . . . I have friends the world over. We meet every Sunday to trade tales of the work week, to remember who we were and to talk about what we have become. . . . I work as a teacher and educator. I use computers to help people experience the joy of learning. They come to my classroom anxious, nervous, afraid. . . . they see how people communicate in the virtual world, and they wish to become a part of it, but they are afraid. Afraid of the companion, the small, no larger than a dime, computer that is placed under the skin. . . . I try to show the worlds that await. Worlds in which they can do things beyond their imagination, worlds unlimited by day to day reality, worlds that will allow their minds to function in new and innovative ways, worlds that will allow them to work in an unrestricted manner, to be as productive as they dare. (Akins, 13)

In this scenario, the narrator finishes by describing how in an accident years earlier he lost an arm and a leg, his spine was severed, and he has lain in a coma for years—to be reborn in a sense only when the virtual reality computer chip was placed in his neck.

I exploded into a new world, a world where I was not bedridden, a world where I was whole again. I could walk, run, laugh, just like any other man. I was freed from the wrecked form of my own body.... through my companion, and in the virtual worlds in which I live, I move without restriction, with freedom. (Akins, 14)

This speculation, of course, proposes major advances that may or may not occur. Nevertheless, given the speed and the effectiveness of technological changes that have occurred in recent years, we are increasingly moving into an age where technology will be able to accomplish almost anything we can imagine. Fruchterman, for instance, proposes that we have moved beyond the Information Age into what he calls the Age of Magic. He sees this brought about by advances in computer hardware and software, nanotechnology, medicine, telecommunications, and virtual reality.

Granted, Fruchterman says, we are going to need a tremendous amount of processing power to deliver the promise of the Age of Magic we are talking about. But he makes the point that by extrapolating current trends, we can predict that by the year 2025 we will be able to purchase a desktop computer with the rough processing power equivalent to a human being. Twenty-five years beyond that, a desktop computer will have the computing power of the whole human race, he says (Fruchterman, 1992, 16).

In addition, nanotechnology—which is the creation of machines the size of viruses—will have the ability to manipulate molecules according to a specified program. This will allow us to grow revolutionary drugs at will, cure genetic diseases by repairing damaged genes, and rebuild the damaged arteries and nerve cells of stroke victims. Eventually, they will be able to modify our bodies by design (Fruchterman, 1992, 17).

DANGERS OF THE TECHNOLOGY?

Some people worry about the downside to the emergence of virtual worlds. "Once that field of view surrounds you and controls everything you see, you're inside," says Furniss.

That paradigm shift becomes absolutely compelling. Even with the crude graphics on some very basic systems, people really get turned on. The social implications are of great concern to us. The downside is the creation of socially immature people. Virtual realities will do what people want them to do, and that's not the way the real world works. This can be a tremendous medium through which to learn, but it can also hinder people from learning other things in the real world. (Daviss, 1990, 41)

Others see less danger. "We shouldn't be so worried about reality that we forget a little fantasy is useful too," says Michael McGreevy, who is in charge of developing virtual realities at NASA's Ames Research Center (Daviss 1990, 41).

CONCLUSION

Will virtual reality create a nation of vegetables unable to deal with other humans? Will it be a Ramboesque version of a video arcade? The implications of such advanced technology as virtual reality will likely remain of concern for some time. Yet the potential for aiding mankind—and in particular in improving the lives of those with disabilities—seems to make this quantum leap forward well worth the risk. "The goal is to see how you can use technology and mold it to a person instead of asking the person to come to the technology," says Lanier. "Again, how do you make things human-centered? What we really need to focus on is not so much the ultimate power of our computer or increasing the ultimate power of our technology but rather us saying how can we empower each other, how can we create bridges between us?" (Lanier 1992, 3).

Overall, there is the haunting attraction of the description of one who experienced virtual reality:

I know that I have become a traveler in a realm that will be ultimately bounded only by the human imagination, a world without any of the usual limits of geography, growth, carrying capacity, density or ownership. In this magic theater, there's no gravity, no Second Law of Thermodynamics, indeed, no laws at all beyond those imposed by computer processing speed—and given the accelerating capacity of that constraint, this universe will probably expand faster than the one I'm used to. (Barlow, 36)

Indeed, the evidence seems to show that new worlds are not only on the near horizon, but—in some form, at least—are already available in a limited form.

REFERENCES

Akins, A. S., "Virtual Reality and the Physically Disabled: Speculations of the Future." In Harry Murphy, ed. *"Proceedings: Virtual Reality and Persons with Disabilities,"* pp. 9–14. Los Angeles, Calif: California State University at Northridge.

Bailey, Charles W., "Intelligent Multimedia Computer Systems: Emerging Information Resources in the Network Environment." *Library Hi-Tech.* Issue 29, no. 1. (1990): 29–41.

Barlow, John Perry, "Being in Nothingness." *Mondo 2000* (Summer 1990): 34–43.

Barlow, John Perry, "Life in the DataCloud: John Barlow Interviews Jaron Lanier." *Mondo 2000* (Summer 1990): 44–51.

Bylinsky, Gene, "The Marvels of Virtual Reality." *Fortune* (June 3, 1991): 140.

Carlson, Shawn, "Science and Society," *The Humanist* (March/April 1991): 43–45.

Churbuck, David, "The Ultimate Computer Game." *Forbes* (February 5, 1990): 154–156.

Daviss, Bennett, "Illusions." *Discover* (June 1990): 37–41.

Dvorak, John C., "America, Are You Ready for Simulated Sex and Virtual Reality?" *PC Computing* 5:5 (May 1992): 78.

Fisher, Scott S. and Jane Morill Tazelaar, "Living in A Virtual World." *Byte* (July 1990): 215–221.

Fritz, Mark, "The World of Virtual Reality." *Training* (February 1991): 45–50.

Fruchterman, James R., "The Age of Magic." In Harry Murphy, ed. "Proceedings: Virtual Reality and Persons with Disabilities," pp. 15–20.

Hecht, Jeff, "Tune in, Turn on, Plug in Your Software." *New Scientist* (August 19, 1989): 23, 30, 32.

Helsel, Sandra K., and Judith Paris Roth, *Virtual Reality: Theory, Practice & Promise.* Westport, Conn.: Meckler Publishing, 1991.

Krueger, Myron W, *Artificial Reality.* New York: Addison-Wesley, 1991.

Lanier, Jaron, "Virtual Reality and Persons with Disabilities," in Murphy, pp. 3–7.

Laurel, Brenda, *Computer As Theater.* New York: Addison-Wesley, 1991.

Laurel, Brenda, "Strange New Worlds of Entertainment," *Compute* (November 1991): 102–104.

Middleton, Teresa, "Matching Virtual Reality Solutions to Special Needs," in Murphy, pp. 37–46.

Murphy, Harry, ed. *"Proceedings: Virtual Reality and Persons with Disabilities,"* Los Angeles, Calif.: California State University, Northridge. 1992.

Rheingold, Howard, *Virtual Reality.* New York: Summit Books, 1991.

Sobchack, Vivian, "What in the World." *Artforum* (April 1991): 24–26.

Stewart, Doug, "Interview: Jaron Lanier," *Omni Magazine* (January 1991): 44–46.

Stone, Judith, "Turn On, Tune In, Boot Up." *Discover* (June 1991): 32–35.

"Through the Computer Screen and into the Wonderland of Virtual Reality," January 13, 1992 *Pittsburg Post-Gazette.*

Vanderheiden, Gregg C., John Mendenhall and Tom Andersen, "Access Issues Related to Virtual Reality for People with Disabilities," in Murphy, pp. 63–70.

Van Name, Mark L., "Virtual Reality Represents New Level of Communication," *PC Week* p. 48.

Appendix 1

Reporting on People with Disabilities: A Glossary of Terms

Afflicted: Connotes pain and suffering. Most people with disabilities do not suffer chronic pain. It is better to be more specific. For example, "He has muscular dystrophy."

Alzheimer's Disease: A progressive, incurable, disabling brain disease leading to severe dementia. But by no means is it a synonym for dementia or senility. The disease is often misdiagnosed, and its name often is misused by laypeople.

Amyotrophic Lateral Sclerosis (ALS): A rapidly progressive neuromuscular disorder in adults. ALS is caused by degeneration of the motor nerves in the spinal cord and leads to atrophy of the muscles. Also known as Lou Gehrig's disease.

Arthritis: Inflammation of the joints. There are two types: osteoarthritis and rheumatoid arthritis. Do not say, "The woman is arthritic," but rather "She has arthritis."

Bipolar Disorder: A mental disorder caused by a chemical imbalance in the brain and characterized by severe mood swings; also known as manic depression. People with this disorder generally are able to lead normal lives when the disorder is kept in remission by drug therapy. Some creative people with bipolar disorder have bursts of creativity during the so-called manic phase. *See* Mania, Manic Depression.

Birth Defect: Try to avoid the term "defect" or "defective" when describing a person. "Congenital disability" is a reasonable synonym. *See* Congenital Disability.

Blind: Describes a person with a total loss of vision. Not appropriate for persons with partial vision. Use "partially sighted" or "visually impaired" in those cases. *See* Visual Impairment.

Cerebral Palsy (CP): A condition caused by damage to the brain, most often during pregnancy or labor or shortly after birth. It is not a disease and is neither progressive nor communicable. Do not refer to a person as "cerebral palsied," or as "a CP." The term "CP" can be used to describe the condition but not a person who has the condition.

Chronic: Applied to a disease that lasts a long time, as distinguished from a short-term, or acute, illness. Beware applying it to mental patients in a pejorative way, however, implying that they are beyond rehabilitation.

Client: A term often used in place of "patient" by health-care practitioners because it puts the service provider and the person receiving the service on a more equal footing. Increasingly, human service agencies are using the word "consumer" in the same way. *See* Patient.

Communicative Disorder: An umbrella term for speech, hearing, and learning disabilities that affect the ability to communicate.

Congenital Disability: Describes a disability that has existed since birth. The term "birth defect" is not appropriate. *See* Birth Defect.

Crippled: Avoid this negative word when referring to a person. Say, "He has a physical disability."

Deaf: Describes a person with a total hearing loss. Not appropriate for persons with partial hearing. It is appropriate to say, "He is deaf." Do not say, "He is profoundly deaf." Deafness is not a disease and is caused by accidents as well as disease. *See* Hearing Impairment; Mute.

Defect: Avoid using this negative term to describe a disability. Bad examples: "She suffers from a birth defect" or "He has a defective leg."

Deformed: Describe the condition rather than using this general, negative term. *See* Disfigurement.

Developmental Disability: A severe mental or physical disability manifested prior to age 22 that is likely to continue indefinitely. The disability may substantially limit major activities such as mobility, learning, language, and self-sufficiency.

Disability: A lack of competent power, strength, or physical or mental ability; a limitation of function imposed by an impairment. The Americans with Disabilities Act defines "disability" as a physical or mental impairment that substantially limits one or more of the major activities of an individual.

Disabled: An adjective that describes a permanent or semi-permanent condition that interferes with a person's ability to do something independently, such as walk, see, hear, learn, or lift. Example: "The amputation of his leg left him partially disabled." Do not say simply, "He is disabled," because no one is totally disabled. And by all means do not use "disabled" as a noun, such as, "The disabled will gather." It can be argued that every human being is disabled in one or more ways. *See* Handicap.

Disease: A sickness; an active ailment. A disability itself is not a disease and does not indicate poor health.

Disfigurement: A scarred, injured appearance. Do not refer to people with disfigurements as "the disfigured," "victims of disfigurement," or "deformed." *See* Deformed.

Down Syndrome: Preferred over "mongoloid" to describe a form of mental retardation caused by improper chromosomal division during gestation.

Dwarf: A medical term applied to some persons very short in stature and not normally proportioned. Dwarfism generally is hereditary, and there are more than 80 different types. Referring to a person of small stature as a "dwarf" or "midget" as general terminology is inappropriate.

Dying: About to die; a person near or at the time of death. Avoid saying someone is "dying of cancer" or "dying of AIDS" at a time when they are, in fact, living with those diseases.

Epilepsy: A disorder marked by disturbed electrical rhythms of the central nervous system resulting in seizures. Do not call someone "an epileptic" but rather a "person with epilepsy" or "person with a seizure disorder." *See* Seizure.

Guide Dog: A dog used by people who are blind or deaf to help guide them. Note that "Seeing Eye Dog" is a trademark; hence, all guide dogs are not Seeing Eye Dogs.

Handicap: Can be used to describe a condition that restricts normal achievement, but such usage has become less acceptable. Except when citing laws or regulations, avoid using "handicap" to describe a disability. The term should be used in reference to environmental barriers preventing or making it difficult for full participation. For example, people who have paralysis and use a wheelchair are handicapped by stairs. Also avoid the expression "handicapped access," which implies that the access is handicapped. *See* Disabled.

Handicapped Person: Use "person with a disability" in most instances. A disabling condition may or may not be handicapping. *See* Disabled; Handicap.

Hearing Impairment: Used to describe loss of hearing from slight to severe. Some people prefer the term "partial hearing." Hearing-impaired or hard of hearing people are not deaf. Some 14 million Americans are hearing impaired, while 2 million are deaf. *See* Deaf.

Homebound: Means "bound for home." Don't apply it to people who, as a result of their disabilities, spend a great deal of time at home.

Impaired: Used when referring to physical impairment. But "a person with partial hearing" is preferable to "he is hearing impaired."

Invalid: Literally means "not valid." Do not use it to describe a person with a disability.

Lame: An old term used to describe a disability. Avoid it, as it is almost always seen as negative.

Learning Disability: A general term that applies to physical or psychological problems that affect learning. Sometimes indicates the existence of minimal brain dysfunction.

Mainstreaming: The principle of integrating persons with disabling conditions into society at large.

Mania, Manic Depression: Mania is a type of mental disorder characterized by impulsiveness and intense craving. Manic depression is a type of psychosis characterized by mood swings from mania to depression. "Bipolar disorder" is the preferred term for manic depression. *See* Bipolar Disorder.

Mentally Ill: A person diagnosed as having a mental disorder. Terms such as "mentally deranged" or "crazy" are inappropriate. "Neurotic," "paranoid," "psychotic," "sociopathic," and "schizophrenic" are specific and technical medical terms.

Mental Retardation: Describes a person with significantly below-average general intellectual functioning, manifested during the developmental period. Can range from mild to profound. Terms such as "moron," "mentally deficient," or "feeble-minded" are very often misused and misunderstood.

Mongoloid: Avoid this term. Rather, use "a person with Down syndrome" or "people with mental retardation." *See* Down Syndrome.

Multiple Sclerosis (MS): An unpredictable, progressive, potentially crippling condition of the brain and spinal cord that generally has its onset in young adulthood.

Muscular Dystrophy (MD): A generally hereditary, progressive condition that weakens the muscles.

Mute: Preferred term to describe a person who cannot speak or chooses not to. Terms such as "deaf-mute" and "deaf and dumb" are inappropriate. "Unable to speak" often is appropriate. Most people who are deaf have healthy vocal cords. If they cannot speak, it is because they do not hear the correct way to pronounce words. Most mute people have been deaf from birth or infancy. *See* Deaf.

Nondisabled: Avoid using "non-disabled" or "able-bodied" to describe people without a disability. Such terms imply that persons with disabilities are generally less able.

Normal: A thing or trait that conforms to a standard or a mainstream pattern; approximately average in a psychological trait such as intelligence or personality. Better to describe the trait, rather than the person, as "normal." Avoid this term when describing a person without a disability.

Paranoid: Deluded, often to the extent of feeling persecuted. Generally, this term is regarded as a symptom rather than a diagnosis.

Paraplegia: Total or partial paralysis of both legs. *See* Quadriplegia.

Patient: Use this term only when referring to someone presently in a hospital or under a doctor's immediate care. Do not say, "He was a polio patient," but rather "He had polio." *See* Client.

Polio: Poliomyelitis; an acute infectious viral disease resulting in paralysis because of damage to the motor nerve cells of the spinal cord. Paralysis caused by polio is stable and not progressive once the infection is over. Do not say "polio victim" or "polios." Say "a person who had polio." *See* Post-Polio Syndrome.

Post-Polio Syndrome: A condition that occurs in adulthood in people who had polio. It is characterized by fatigue and muscle weakness. Many people who had polio as children appear to have experienced post-polio syndrome. *See* Polio.

Quadriplegia: Paralysis of all four limbs. *See* Paraplegia.

Rehabilitation: Attempting to restore a person to an optimum state of health. There is a major emphasis today on "rehab"/vocational training of people with physical and mental disabilities. Those who press for better rehabilitation services are most commonly referred to as "consumer advocates."

Schizophrenia: A major mental disorder characterized by a distortion of reality. It generally results in a "shattered personality," not a "split personality." The clinical term for the latter is "multiple personalities." *Schizophrenia* is not a synonym for *psychosis*.

Seeing Eye Dog: A dog used by people who are blind to help guide them. "Seeing Eye Dog" is a trademark; hence, all guide dogs are not necessarily Seeing Eye Dogs. When in doubt, say "guide dog."

Seizure: An involuntary muscular contraction symptomatic of the brain disorder epilepsy. The term "convulsion" should be reserved for seizures involving contractions of the entire body. The term "fit" is used in England, but it has strong negative connotations in the United States. *See* Epilepsy.

Spastic: An adjective describing a muscle with sudden, abnormal, and involuntary spasms. It is not appropriate for describing a person with cerebral palsy. Muscles, not people, are spastic.

Special: Not an appropriate term to describe persons with disabilities in general. It is seen as patronizing. Some groups have tried to find other terms to describe people with disabilities, such as "physically challenged" or "differently abled." These terms tend to confuse people, often trivialize disabilities, and do not inform the public.

Specific Learning Disability (SLD): Describes a disorder in the ability to learn effectively in a regular educational environment. Does not include persons with vision, hearing, or motor disabilities, those who are mentally retarded, or persons who are culturally or economically disadvantaged. The term "specific learning disability" is preferred because it emphasizes that the disability affects only certain learning processes.

Speech Impaired: Describes persons with limited or difficult speech patterns. *See* Stutter.

Spina Bifida: A congenital condition in which the vertebrae of an unborn child fail to close completely. The condition limits motor activity to varying degrees.

Stricken with: Try saying, "a person who has . . ."

Stroke: Cerebral vascular accident. Most strokes occur when blood to the brain is interrupted by a blood vessel obstruction.

Stutter: Say, "people who stutter," not "stutterers." *See* Speech Impaired.

Suffers from: It is wrong to assume that an individual "suffers from" a disability.

Vegetable: Do not apply this term to a human being. Rather, say, "a person with severe disabilities," or simply describe the person's condition.

Victim: A person with a disability is not necessarily a victim. Do not say "a cerebral palsy victim" or "AIDS victim" but rather a "person who has cerebral palsy" or "a person with AIDS." The term "victim" connotes someone who was in an accident or a war or who generally was violated or deceived.

Visual Impairment: Used to describe a person with a vision that is less than total. A more positive way of putting it is, "a person with partial vision." A person with partial vision is not blind. *See* Blind.

Wheelchair: Do not say that a person is "confined to a wheelchair" or is "wheelchair bound." Rather say, "She uses a wheelchair." Wheelchairs help with mobility; they do not imprison people.

NOTE

Reprinted with permission from the Disability Committee of the American Society of Newspaper Editors, originally published in 1990.

Appendix 2

Serial Publications Dealing with Disabilities

Abilities
Deaf and Blind Children's Center
361–365 North Rocks Road
North Rocks, New South Wales
Australia

Accent on Living
P.O. Box 700
Gillum Road and High Drive
Bloomington, IL 61701

AFB News
15 West 16th Street
New York, NY 10011

Association for Persons with Severe Handicaps Journal
11201 Greenwood Avenue North
Seattle, WA 98133

Careers and the Disabled
Equal Opportunities Publications
150 Motor Parkway, Suite 420
Hauppauge, NY 11788-5145

Closing the Gap
P.O. Box 68
Henderson, MN 56044

Computer Disability News
National Easter Seal Society
70 East Lake Street
Chicago, IL 60601

Direct Link
Center for Computer Assistance to the Disabled
1950 Stemmons Freeway, Suite 4041
Dallas, TX 75207-3109

Directory of Software Data Sources
ISTE Publications
University of Oregon
1787 Agate Street
Eugene, OR 97403

Disability Issues
27–43 Wormwood Street
Boston, MA 02210-1606

Disability Now
Spastics Society
12 Park Crescent
London, WIN 4EQ
England

The Disability Rag
Box 145
Louisville, KY 40201

Disabilities Studies Quarterly
Department of Sociology
Brandeis University
P.O. Box 9110
Waltham, MA 02254-9110

Disabled Outdoors Magazine
2052 West 23d Street
Chicago, IL 60608

Disabled USA
President's Commission on Employment of Handicapped
111 20th St. N.W., Vanguard Building, Room 660
Washington, DC 20036

DPH Journal
1920 Association Drive
Reston, VA 22091

Exceptional Parent
P.O. Box 4944
Manchester, NH 03108

Family Support Bulletin
1522 K Street, NW, No. 1112
Washington, DC 20005-1202

Gallaudet Today
Department of Publications and Production
Gallaudet University
800 Florida Avenue, NE
Washington, DC 20002-3695

In Touch
Box 12927
Austin, TX 78711

Journal of Applied Rehabilitation Counseling
Carey Building, Suite A-305
8136 Old Keene Mill Road
Springfield, VA 22152

Journal of Chronic Diseases
Pergamon Press
Maxwell House
Fairview Park
Elmsford, NY 10523

Journal of Physical Medicine and Rehabilitation
30 North Michigan Avenue
Chicago, IL 60602

Journal of Rehabilitation
633 South Washington Street
Alexandria, VA 22314

Mainstream
Able-Disabled Advocacy
861 Sixth Avenue, Suite 610
San Diego, CA 92101

Moving Forward
Box 3553
Torrance, CA 90510-3553

National Information Center for Children and Youth with Handicaps News Digest
Box 1492
Washington, DC 20013

Palaestra: Forum of Sport and Recreation for the Disabled
Challenge Publications Ltd.
Circulation Department
Box 508
Macomb, IL 61455

Paraplegia News
Paralyzed Veterans of America
5201 North 19th Avenue, Suite 111
Phoenix, AZ 85015

A Positive Approach: National Magazine for the Physically Challenged
Box 910
Millville, NJ 08332

Psychosocial Rehabilitation
Sargent College of Allied Health Professions
635 Commonwealth Ave.
Boston University
Boston, MA 02215

Psychosomatic Medicine
265 Nassau Road
Roosevelt, NY 11575

Psychosomatics
Academy of Psychosomatic Medicine
922 Springfield Avenue
Irvington, NJ 07111

Rehabilitation Counseling Bulletin
2 Skyline Place, Suite 400
5203 Leesburg Pike
Falls Church, VA 22041

Rehabilitation Gazette
4502 Maryland Avenue
St. Louis, MO 63108

Rehabilitation Literature
2023 West Ogden Avenue
Chicago, IL 60612

Rehabilitation Psychology
200 Park Avenue
New York, NY 10003

Sexuality and Disability
Human Sciences Press
72 Fifth Avenue
New York, NY 10011

Technical Aid to the Disabled Journal
P.O. Box 108
Ryde, New South Wales 2112
Australia

Technology and Disability
Andover Medical Publishers
125 Main Street
Reading, MA 02180

Towards Independence
P.O. Box 426
Mellville 2109
South Africa

Appendix 3

Major Organizations Concerned with Disabilities

Alexander Graham Bell Association for the Deaf
3417 Volta Place, NW
Washington, DC 20007

Alliance for Technology Access
(a coalition of people with disabilities, professional organizations, and computer
organizations)
1307 Solana Avenue
Albany, CA 94706

American Association on Mental Deficiency
5201 Connecticut Avenue, NW
Washington, DC 20015

American Cancer Society
777 Third Avenue
New York, NY 10017

American Coalition of Citizens with Disabilities
1200 15th Street, NW, Suite 201
Washington, DC 20005

American Congress of Rehabilitation Medicine
20 North Michigan Avenue
Chicago, IL 60602

American Foundation for the Blind
15 West 16th Street
New York, NY 10011

American Occupational Therapy Association
6000 Executive Boulevard
Rockville, MD 20852

American Physical Therapy Association
1156 15th Street
Washington, DC 20005

American Rehabilitation Counseling Association
5203 Leesburg Place
Falls Church, VA 22014

American Speech and Hearing Association
9030 Old Georgetown Road
Washington, DC 20014

Arthritis Foundation
3400 Peachtree Road, NE, Suite 1101
Atlanta, GA 30326

Bureau of Education for the Handicapped
U.S. Department of Education
400 Maryland Avenue, SW
Washington, DC 20202

Closing the Gap
(source of information on use of computer-related technology for exceptional individuals)
P.O. Box 68
Henderson, MN 56044

Council of Organizations Serving the Deaf
P.O. Box 894
Columbia, MD 21044

Council of State Administrators of Vocational Rehabilitation
1522 K Street, NW, Suite 836
Washington, DC 20005

Disability Network
Canadian Broadcasting Corporation
P.O. Box 500, Station A
Toronto, M5W 1E6
Canada

Disabled American Veterans
3725 Alexandria Pike
Cold Spring, KY 41076

Disabled People's International
101-7 Evergreen Place
Winnipeg, Manitoba, R3L 2T3
Canada

Eastern Paralyzed Veterans Association
75-20 Astoria Boulevard
Jackson Heights, NY 11370-1177

Epilepsy Foundation of America
815 15th Street, NW, Suite 528
Washington, DC 20005

Goodwill Industries of America
9200 Wisconsin Avenue
Washington, DC 20014

IBM National Support Center for Persons with Disabilities
P.O. Box 2150
Atlanta, GA 30301-2150

IBM Program to Train Disabled Persons
    (offers guidance in computer configuration, adaptive devices, setup assistance, and
    telephone support)
IBM Corporation
800 North Frederick Avenue
Gaithersburg, MD 20879

International Association of Rehabilitation Facilities
5530 Wisconsin Avenue, No. 955
Washington, DC 20015

International Center for the Disabled
340 East 24th St.
New York, NY 10010

Job Accommodation Network
    (federally funded information and referral service)
918 Chestnut Ridge Road
Suite #1
P.O. Box 6080
Morgantown, UV 26506

Joni and Friends
    (provides help for people with disabilities and people associated with churches)
P.O. Box 333
Agoura Hills, CA 91301

M.D.F. Technologies
    (develops technology such as stand-up wheelchair)
3427-C Old Frankstown Road
Pittsburgh, PA 15229

Media Access Office
8121 Van Nuys Boulevard, Suite 214
Los Angeles, CA 91402

Mobility International USA
(dedicated to facilitate international educational and community exchanges of disabled)
P.O. Box 3551
Eugene, OR 97403

Muscular Dystrophy Associations of America
810 Seventh Avenue
New York, NY 10019

National Association for the Deaf
814 Thayer Avenue
Silver Spring, MD 20910

National Association for Mental Health
1800 Kent Street
Roslyn, VA 22209

National Association of the Physically Handicapped
5473 Grandville Avenue
Detroit, MI 48228

National Association for Retarded Citizens
2709 Avenue E, East
P.O. Box 6109
Arlington, TX 76011

National Congress of Organizations of the Physically Handicapped
6106 North 30th Street
Arlington, VA 22207

National Easter Seal Society for Crippled Children and Adults
2023 West Ogden Avenue
Chicago, IL 60612

National Federation of the Blind
1800 Johnson Street
Baltimore, MD 21230

National Federation of the Blind in Computer Science
3530 Dupont Avenue, N.
Minneapolis, MN 55412

National Foundation/March of Dimes
1275 Mamaroneck Avenue
White Plains, NY 10605

National Head Injury Foundation
18A Vernon Street
Framingham, MA 01701

National Multiple Sclerosis Society
205 East 42d Street
New York, NY 10010

National Paraplegia Foundation
333 North Michigan Avenue
Chicago, IL 60601

National Rehabilitation Association
633 South Washington Street
Alexandria, VA 22314

National Rehabilitation Counseling Association
8136 Old Keen Mill Road
Springfield, VA 22152

National Rehabilitation Information Center
(offers ABLEDATA, a major information source for products for people with
disabilities)
8455 Colesville Road, Suite 935
Silver Spring, MD 20910-3319

National Spinal Cord Injury Association
369 Eliot Street
Newton Upper Falls, MA 02164

Office for Handicapped Individuals
Department of Education
400 Maryland Avenue, SW
Switzer Building, Room 3106
Washington, DC 20202

Office of Special Education and Rehabilitation
Apple Computer Incorporated
20525 Mariani Avenue, M/S 43S
Cupertino, CA 95014

Paralyzed Veterans of America
7315 Wisconsin Avenue, Suite 300W
Bethesda, MD 20014

Partners of America, Rehabilitation Education Program
2001 S Street, NW
Washington, DC 20009

Prentke Romich Company
(a leader in augmentive and alternative communication and computer access for
the disabled)
1022 Heyl Road
Wooster, OH 44691

President's Committee on Employment of the Handicapped
111 20th Street, NW
Vanguard Building, Room 660
Washington, DC 20036

Rehabilitation International USA
20 West 40th Street
New York, NY 10018

Rehabilitation Services Administration
Department of Education
330 C Street, SW
Washington, DC 20201

RESNA
(information exchange organization dealing with disability)
1101 Connecticut Avenue, Suite 700
Washington, DC 20036

Royal Association for Disability and Rehabilitation
25 Mortimer Street
London, W1N 8AB
United Kingdom

Society for the Advancement of Travel for the Handicapped
(provides information for disabled travelers)
26 Court Street
Brooklyn, NY 11242

Technology Information Project
(provides information on assistive technology)
P.O. Box 341
Lincoln, MA 01773

Technology Related-Assistance Project
State of Maryland
Office for Handicapped Individuals
Box 10, One Market Center
300 West Lexington Street
Baltimore, MD 21201

Trace Research and Development Center
(specializes in communication aids and use of computers)
S-151 Waisman Center
1500 Highland Avenue
Madison, WI 53705

Travel Information Service
Regional Resource and Information Center for Disabled Individuals
Moss Rehabilitation Hospital
12th Street and Tabor Road
Philadelphia, PA 19141

United Cerebral Palsy Association
66 East 34th Street
New York, NY 10016

Veterans Administration
810 Vermont Avenue, NW
Washington, DC 20420

World Institute on Disability
  (concerned with integration and independence of persons with disabilities)
510 16th Street, Suite 100
Oakland, CA 94612

World Rehabilitation Fund
400 East 34th Street
New York, NY 10016

Worldwide Disability Solutions Group
  (offers computer solutions for specific problems for disabled Macintosh computer
  users)
Apple Computer, Inc./MS 2SE
20525 Mariani Avenue
Cupertino, CA 95014

Selected Bibliography

BOOKS

Barish, Frances. *Frommer's Guide for the Disabled Traveler: The United States, Canada, and Europe.* New York: Frommer/Pasmantier, 1984.

Basore, P. "Barriers to Education." *News Media and Disability.* November 1988.

Bernotavicz, W. A. *Changing Attitudes toward the Disabled Through the Media: What the Research Says.* Portland, Maine: Research and Advanced Study, University of Southern Maine, 1979.

Biklen, Douglas. "Framed: Print Journalism's Treatment of Disability Issues." In Allen Gartner and Tom Joe, eds., *Images of the Disabled: Disabling Images*, pp. 31–46. New York: Praeger, 1987.

Bryant, Jennings, and Dolf Zillman. *Responding to the Screen: Reception and Reaction Processes.* Hillsdale, N.J.: Lawrence Erlbaum Associates, 1991.

Cain, E. J., Jr., and F. M. Taber. *Educating Disabled People for the 21st Century.* Boston: Little, Brown, 1987.

Campling, Jo. *Images of Ourselves: Women with Disabilities Talking.* London: Routledge and Kegan Paul, 1981.

Clogston, John S. *Disability Coverage in Sixteen Newspapers.* Louisville, Ky.: Advocado Press, 1990.

Couch, Gordon. *Nicholson's Access in London: A Guide for Those Who Have Problems Getting Around.* London: Nicholson, 1986.

Cylke, F. K. *That All May Read: Library Service for Blind and Physically Handicapped People.* Washington, D.C.: Library of Congress, 1983.

Disability Resource Centre. *Into the Streets: A Book by and for Disabled People.* Collingwood, Australia: Disability Resources Centre, 1981.

Driedger, Diane. *The Last Civil Rights Movement: Disabled People's International.* New York: St. Martin's Press, 1989.

Durgin, Rod, and Norene Lindsay. *The Physically Disabled Traveler's Guide.* Toledo, Ohio: Resource Directories 1986.

Editor and Publisher International Yearbook, 1989. New York: Editor and Publisher Co., 1989.

Elliott, Deni. "Media and Persons with Disabilities: Ethical Considerations." In Mary Johnson and Susan Elkins, eds., *Reporting on Disability*, pp. 59–66. Louisville, Ky.: Advocado Press, 1989.

Freedman, Jacqueline, and Gersten, Susan. *Traveling, Like Everybody Else: A Practical Guide for Disabled Travelers.* New York: Adama Books, 1987.

Gartner, A., and Tom, Joe, eds. *Images of the Disabled, Disabling Images.* New York: Praeger, 1987.

Gerbner, T. "Stigma: Social Functions of the Portrayal of Mental Illness in the Mass Media." In J. G. Rabkin, L. Geib, and J. B. Lazar, eds., *Attitudes toward the Mentally Ill: Research Perspectives: Report of an NIMH Workshop, January 24–25, 1980.* DHHS Publication No. (ADM) 80-1031. Washington, D.C.: U.S. Government Printing Office, 1980.

Gliedman, John, and William Roth. *The Unexpected Minority: Handicapped Children in America.* New York: Harcourt Brace Jovanovich, 1980.

Goffman, Erving. *Stigma: Notes on the Management of Spoiled Identity.* New York: Simon & Schuster, 1963.

Guidelines for Reporting and Writing about People with Disabilities. Research and Training Center on Independent Living. Lawrence: University of Kansas, 1991.

Johnson, Mary, and Susan Elkins, eds. *Reporting on Disability: Approaches and Issues, A Sourcebook.* Louisville, Ky.: Advocado Press, 1989.

Kirschner, C. *Data on Visual Impairment in the U.S.: A Resource Manual on Characteristics, Education, Employment and Service Delivery.* New York: American Foundation for the Blind, 1985.

Kubey, Robert, and Mihaly Csikszentmihalyi. *Television and the Quality of Life: How Viewing Shapes Everyday Experience.* Hillsdale, N.J.: Lawrence Erlbaum Associates, 1990.

Leonard, B. D. "Impaired View: Television Portrayals of Handicapped People." Ph.D. dissertation, Boston University, 1978.

Lichter, Robert S., Linda S. Lichter, and Stanley Rothman. *Watching America: What Television Tells Us about Our Lives.* Englewood Cliffs, N.J.: Prentice-Hall, 1991.

Liebert, R. M. *Television and Attitudes toward the Handicapped.* Albany, N.Y.: New York State Education Department, 1975.

National Advisory Commission on Civil Disorders. *Report of the National Advisory Commission on Civil Disorders.* New York: Bantam Books, 1968.

Noble, Cinnie. *The Handicapped Traveler: A Guide for Travel Counselors.* Toronto: Canadian Institute of Travel Counselors, 1986.

Padden, Carol, and Tom Humphries. *Deaf in America: Voices from a Culture.* Cambridge: Harvard University Press, 1988.

Perske, Robert. *Unequal Justice? What Can Happen When Persons with Retardation or Other Developmental Disabilities Encounter the Criminal Justice System.* Nashville, Tenn.: Abingdon Press, 1991.

Reporting on People with Disabilities. Washington, D.C.: Disabilities Committee, American Society of Newspaper Editors, 1991.

United Nations. *World Program of Action.* New York: United Nations, 1983.

United States. *Access Travel: Airports.* Booklet 580Y. General Services Administration. Washington, D.C.: Government Printing Office, 1991.

U.S. Congress. House. Committee on Labor and Human Resources. *Assistive Technology for Persons with Disabilities.* Hearings. 100th Cong., 2d sess., May 19–20, 1988.

Weiss, Louise. *Access to the World: A Guide for the Handicapped.* New York: Holt, 1986.

Wood, Michael. *America in the Movies.* New York: Basic Books, 1975.

PERIODICALS AND NEWSPAPERS

"Advocates for Disabled Actors Still Fighting Casting Barriers." *Hollywood Reporter,* April 8, 1991.

Barlow, W. E. "Act to Accommodate the Disabled." *Personnel Journal* (November 1991):119–24.

Bates, Rebecca. "The Oppressed as Oppressor." *The Disability Rag* (July–August 1990):23.

Biklen, Douglas, and Robert Bogdan. "Media Portrayals of Disabled People: A Study in Stereotypes." *Interracial Books for Children Bulletin.* Vol. 4:6, 7 (1982):4–9.

Bogdan, R., and D. Biklen. "Handicapism." *Social Policy* (March–April 1987).

Breisky, Bill. "Diversity and Disabilities." *ASNE Bulletin* (September 1990):13–22.

Byrd, E. K. "Television Programming: A Rating of Programs Depicting Disability." *Alabama Personnel and Guidance* 5:2 (1979):19–21.

———. "Magazine Articles and Disability." *American Rehabilitation* 4:4 (1979):18–20.

———. "Television's Portrayal of Disability." *Disabled USA* 3:1 (1979):5.

Byrd, E. Keith, and Timothy R. Elliot. "Disability in Full-Length Feature Films: Frequency and Quality of Films over an 11-Year Span." *International Journal of Rehabilitation Research* 11:2 (1988):143–48.

Byrd, E. K., and R. B. Pipes. "Feature Films and Disability." *Journal of Rehabilitation* 47:1 (1981):51–53.

Clogston, John S. "Fifty Years of Disability Coverage in the New York Times." *News Computing Journal* 8:2 (1992):39–50.

Cooke, Annemarie, and Neil Reisner. "The Last Minority." *Washington Journalism Review* 13:10 (December 1991):14–18.

Covington, George. "The News Media and Disability Issues: A National Workshop—News Media Education Project." Washington, D.C.: National Institute on Disability and Rehabilitation Research, 1989.

Cox, Meg. "Show with Retarded Actor Breaks New Ground on TV." *Wall Street Journal,* July 19, 1989, p. B-1.

Dahlgren, Peter. "What's the Meaning of This? Viewers' Plural Sense-making of TV News." *Media Culture and Society* 10 (1988):288.

Dalton, L. "At Gannett, Workforce Diversity Means Including the Disabled." *Gannetteer* (May 1989):6–9.

Davidson, Bill. "Are All Cripples Bad Guys? How Films and TV Shape the Way We Think." *McCalls* (September 1987):67–68.

Dietl, Dick. "They Won Anchor Roles With Talent." *Worklife* (Summer 1988):4–5.

"Disabled People Gain Roles in Ads and on TV." *New York Times,* September 23, 1991, p. 14.

Donaldson, J. "The Visibility and Image of Handicapped People on Television." *Exceptional Children* (March 1981):413–16.

D'Souza, D. "Illiberal Education." *Atlantic* (March 1991):52.

Edwards, Clark. "Integration of Disabled Students in Classroom with New Technology." *Journalism Educator* 47 (Spring 1992):85–87.

———. "From the Editor: The Americans with Disabilities Act." *News Computing Journal* 7:3 (October 1991):i–x.

Elliott, Timothy R., and E. Keith Byrd. "Media and Disability." *Rehabilitation Literature* (November–December 1982):348–51.

Glasser, T. L. "Professionalism and the Derision of Diversity: The Case of the Education of Journalism." *Journal of Communication* 42 (Spring 1992):131–140.

Goltz, Gene. "Disabled Are Knocking at the Door." *Presstime* (January 1991):54.

Hahn, Harlan. "Disability and Rehabilitation Policy: Is Paternalistic Neglect Benign?" *Public Administration Review* (July–August 1982).

Haller, Beth. "Paternalism and Protest: The Presentation of Deaf Persons in the *New York Times* and *Washington Post*." Paper presented at the Meeting of the Association for Education in Journalism and Mass Communication, Montreal, Quebec, August 1992.

Hartinger, Brent. "Gays on Film." *Spectrum Weekly*, June 5–11, 1991, p. 17.

Hembree, D., and R. Sandoval. "RSI Has Become the Nation's Leading Illness." *Columbia Journalism Review* (July–August 1991):41–46.

"The ICD Survey of Disabled Americans: Bringing Disabled Americans into the Mainstream." Louis Harris and Associates, p. 4. New York: ICD-International Council on the Handicapped, March 1986.

Jackson, Nancy Beth. "Potential Physical Disabilities in Computerized Journalism Education." *News Computing Journal* (December 1992):33–43.

Jankey, Les. "Illusion and Reality: Coming Together during 'Coming Home.' " *Disabled USA* 1:16 (1978):4–6.

John, Jeffrey Alan. "Covering Disabled America: Media Face the Challenge of Change." *Editor and Publisher*, December 28, 1991, pp. 12–13.

Johnson Mary. "Life Unworthy of Life." *The Disability Rag* (January–February 1987):24–30.

———. "Journalists with Disabilities Have Access to a Growing Array of Helpful Devices." *ASNE Bulletin* (July–August 1992):12–15.

———. "Opportunity Lost." *The Disability Rag* 11:3 (May–June 1990):30–31.

Kalter, Joanmarie. "Good News: The Disabled Get More Play on TV, Bad News: There Is Still Too Much Stereotyping." *TV Guide*, May 31, 1986, p. 43.

Keller, Clayton E., Daniel P. Hallahan, Edward A. McShane, E. Paula Crowley, and Barbara J. Blandford. "The Coverage of Persons with Disabilities in American Newspapers." *Journal of Special Education* 24:3 (1990):271–282.

Krossel, M. " 'Handicapped Heroes' and the Knee-jerk Press." *Columbia Journalism Review* (June 1988): 46–47.

Lattin, D. "Whose Life Is It Anyway?" *Disabled USA* 3:3 (1980): 7–18.

Ledbetter, S. "Journalism: A Rewarding Career." *Careers and the Handicapped* (Fall 1990): 62–66.

Longmore, Paul K. "A Note on Language and the Social Identity of Disabled People." *American Behavioral Scientist* (January–February 1985): 419–23.

———. "Screening Stereotypes: Images of Disabled People." *Social Policy* (Summer 1985): 31–37.

———. "Mask: A Revealing Portrayal of the Disabled." *Los Angeles Times Sunday Calendar*, May 5, 1985, pp. 22–23.

McKee, B. "What You Must Do for the Disabled." *Nation's Business* (December 1991): 36, 38–40.

Marsano, William. "The View from the Wheelchair." *Traveler Magazine* (December 1990): 133–35.

Martin, T. A. "Plan Now for Americans with Disabilities Act." *Newspapers and Technology* (June 1991): 12, 41.

Miles, Mike. "Why Asia Rejects Western Disability Advice." *Quad Wrangle* (December 1983): 27–29.

Mitchell, L. R. "Beyond the Supercrip Syndrome: It's Time for a Disability Beat." *Quill* (November 1989): 18–23.

Nelson, Jack A. "A Step Forward in the Portrayal of Those with Disabilities on Television." *News Computing Journal* 8:3 (December 1992): 43–52.

———. "Access to the Media for the Disabled: Changing Public Perceptions." Paper presented to the Association for Education in Journalism and Mass Communication, Boston, August 1991.

O'Connor, John J. "TV and Civil Rights: The Media Still Is the Message." *Perspectives: The Civil Rights Quarterly* 14 (Summer 1982): 39.

Ostrow, Joanne. "Handicapped Actors Hurt by TV Stereotypes." *Denver Post*, February 19, 1989.

Owen, Mary Jane. "News about People with Disabilities Interests a Growing 'Minority.'" *ASNE Bulletin* (May–June 1989): 34–35.

Parette, R. B. "The Importance of Technology in Education and Training of Persons with Mental Retardation." *Education and Training in Mental Retardation* 26 (1991): 165–78.

Pritchett, K. "Disabilities Act Poses Enigmas for Many Firms." *Wall Street Journal*, November 29, 1991.

Rehabilitation International. "Rehabilitation International: 60 Years as a World Organization." *International Rehabilitation Review* (first quarter 1982).

Rosenberg, J. "ANPA Issues Alert on Disabilities Act." *Editor and Publisher*, August 10, 1991, p. 17.

Rovner, J. "Promise, Uncertainty Mark Disability Rights Measure." *CQ*, May 12, 1990, p. 1477.

Sandovsky, R. "Can Media Improve Rehabilitation Services?" *Journal of Rehabilitation* 37:2 (1976): 8–9.

Self, William, and Marian Huttenstine. "ADA: The Civil Rights Act for All." *News Computing Journal* (December 1992): 9–33.

Shapiro, Joseph P. "A New 'Common Identity' for the Disabled." *U.S. News & World Report*, March 29, 1988.

Slate, Libby. "The Able Disabled." *Emmy Magazine* (November–December 1985): 28–33.

Smith, Michael. "Language Use Affects Coverage of People with Disabilities." *Journalism Educator* (Winter 1991): 4–11.

———. "Professors Must Be Part of the Team That Helps Students." *ASNE Bulletin* (September 1990): 22.

Treesberg, Judith. "That Wasn't for Deaf People!" *The Disability Rag* (January–February 1987): 22–23.

Wall, O. "Mental Illness and the Media: An Unhealthy Condition." *Disabled USA* 2:2 (1978): 23–24.

Weinberg, N., and R. Santana, "Comic Books: Champions of the Disabled Stereotype." *Rehabilitation Literature* 39: 11–12 (1978): 327–31.

Winfield, Betty Houchin. "FDR's Pictorial Image: Rules and Boundaries." *Journalism History* 5:4 (Winter 1978–1979): 110–14.

Wood, Daniel B. "Redrawing US Portrait of Disabled." *Christian Science Monitor*, March 2, 1989.

Worthington, Bob. "Are Media Organizations Prepared to Comply with the Employment Provisions of the ADA?" *News Computing Journal* (December 1992): 53–63.

Yoshida, Roland K., Lynn Wasilewski, and Douglas Friedman. "Recent Newspaper Coverage about Persons with Disabilities." *Exceptional Children* 56:51 (February 1990): 418–23.

Zola, Irving Kenneth. "Depictions of Disability—Metaphor, Message, and Medium in the Media: A Research and Political Agenda." *Social Science Journal* 22 (1985): 5–17.

BOOKS DEALING WITH DISABILITY

Access Travel: Airports. Booklet # 580Y. Washington, DC: General Services Administration, 1991.

Barish, Francis. *Frommer's Guide for the Disabled Traveler: The United States, Canada, and Europe*. New York: Frommer/Pasmantier, 1984.

Bruck, Lilly. *Access: The Guide to Better Life for Disabled Americans*. New York: Random House, 1978.

Byrd, E. K., P. D. Byrd, and R. R. Elliott. *Attitudes toward Persons with Disabilities*. New York: Springer, 1989.

Campling, Jo. *Images of Ourselves: Women with Disabilities Talking*. London: Routledge and Kegan Paul, 1981.

Couch, Gordon. *Nicholson's Access in London: A Guide for Those Who Have Problems Getting Around*. London: Nicholson Publications, 1986.

Disability and Rehabilitation Handbook. New York: McGraw Hill, 1978. Covers various disabilities, rehabilitative services, and role of the family.

DeLoach, Charlene and Bobby Greer. *Adjustment to Severe Disability: A Metamorphosis*. New York: McGraw-Hill, 1981. For professionals and families dealing with disability.

Driedger, Diane. *The Last Civil Rights Movement: Disabled People's International*. New York: St. Martin's Press, 1989.

Durgin, Rod and Norene Lindsay. *The Physically Disabled Traveler's Guide*. Toledo, Ohio: Resource Directories, 1986.

Freedman, Jacqueline and Susan Gersten. *Traveling, Like Everybody Else: A Practical Guide for Disabled Travelers*. New York: Adama Books, 1987.

Gartner, Allen and Tom, Joe, eds. *Images of the Disabled, Disabling Images*. New York: Praeger Press, 1987.

Hale, Glorya, ed. *The Source Book for the Disabled*. New York: Bantam Books, 1981. A guide to more independent lives for those with disabilities.

Into the Streets: A Book by and for Disabled People. Collingwood, Australia: Disability Resources Center, 1989.

A Manual for Integrating Persons with Disabilities into International Educational Exchange Programs. Eugene, Oreg.: Mobility International USA, 1986.

McNeil, Ian. *Disabled Travelers International Phrasebook*. London: Disability Press, 1979.

Miller, Kathleen and Linda Chatterton, eds. *A Voice of Our Own: Proceedings of the First World Congress of Disabled Peoples International*. East Lansing, Mich.: Center for International Rehabilitation, Michigan State University, 1982.

Miller, Kathleen, Linda Chatterton and Barbara Duncan. *Participation of People with Disabilities: International Perspectives*. East Lansing, Mich.: Michigan State University, 1982.

Noble, Cinnie. *The Handicapped Traveler: A Guide for Travel Counsellors*. Toronto: Canadian Institute of Travel Counsellors, 1986.

Nussbaum, Ruth. *Information for Handicapped Travelers*. Washington, D.C.: National Library Service for the Blind and Physically Handicapped, Library of Congress, 1987.

Power, Paul W. and Arthur Dell Orto. *The Role of the Family in the Rehabilitation of the Physically Disabled*. Baltimore, Md.: University Park Press, 1980. Describes how the family influences the adjustment of the disabled.

Shapiro, Joseph. *No Pity: People with Disabilities Forging A New Civil Rights Movement*. New York: Times Books/Random House, 1993.

Support for the Disabled in Sweden. Stockholm: Swedish Institute, 1981.

The Trace Resource Book. Madison, Wis.: Trace Research and Development Center. An annual directory of products and resource information on assistive technology.

Viscardi, Henry. *A Man's Stature*. New York: John Day, 1952. Personal account of one born with underdeveloped legs who helped society to realize the worth of those with disabilities.

Walzer, Mary. *A Travel Guide for the Disabled: Western Europe*. New York: Van Nostrand Reinhold, 1982.

Weiss, Louise. *Access to the World: A Travel Guide for the Handicapped*. New York: Henry Holt and Co., 1986. Valuable guide for the wheelchair traveler and others with special needs.

World Program of Action. New York: United Nations, 1983.

Zola, Irving Kenneth. *Missing Pieces: A Chronicle of Living with a Disability*. Philadelphia, Pa.: Temple University Press, 1982. A personal odyssey of a disabled professor.

Zola, Irving Kenneth. *Ordinary Lives: Voices of Disability and Disease*. A collection of personal histories of people with disabilities. Cambridge, Mass.: Applewood Books, 1982.

Index

About the Editor and Contributors

JACK A. NELSON is an Associate Professor of Journalism in the Department of Communications at Brigham Young University in Provo, Utah. He also taught at California State University/Humboldt and the University of Utah. He worked as a reporter for the *Deseret News* in Salt Lake City and since 1981 has been part-time Utah editor for *Western Outdoors Magazine*, which serves the eleven western states. He has been a paraplegic since the age of seventeen.

BILL BREISKY has been editor of the daily *Cape Cod Times*, Hyannis, Massachusetts, since 1978. He is the author of a 1974 book, *I Think I Can*, concerning his daughter's struggle to surmount the effects of a brain injury, and he served for two years as chair of the Disabilities Committee of the American Society of Newspaper Editors.

JOHN S. CLOGSTON is an Assistant Professor in the Department of Journalism at Northern Illinois University, DeKalb, Illinois. He has worked as a radio news reporter and news director. His doctoral dissertation examined newspaper coverage of persons with physical disabilities.

JOE COUGHLIN is an educator, broadcast journalist, and author. He lectures extensively on media, human rights, and disability issues. Through his management consulting practice, he provides timely advice to some of North America's finest companies on how to manage a diverse work force.

He is best known for his role as anchor of two award-winning television shows in Canada, "Challenge Journal" and "Disability Network."

JOHN M. CRANDELL is Professor of Educational Psychology at Brigham Young University. He serves as a member of the Utah State Library Board and on numerous state and national advisory committees.

CLARK EDWARDS worked for more than twenty years as a journalist after the amputation of his left leg. Edwards worked his way up through the industry from weekly newspapers and 500-watt daytimer radio to the position of network producer and correspondent. Edwards has taught news writing, editing, and television news at the University of Missouri and the University of New Mexico. He is currently Professor-in-Charge, Journalism, Department of Communication, Duquesne University, Pittsburgh.

DENI ELLIOTT is the Mansfield Professor of Ethics and Public Affairs at the University of Montana and is a full professor in the Department of Philosophy there. Prior to that, she was the Director of the Institute for the Study of Applied and Professional Ethics at Dartmouth College. She was also tenured in the Department of Communication at Utah State University.

JAMES A. FUSSELL is a reporter for the *Kansas City Star*.

TOM GREIN is former senior editor for Ingersoll Publications Co. and now owns a weekly newspaper in Herndon, Virginia.

MARY JOHNSON edits *The Disability Rag*, which she founded in 1980. Her articles and commentary about disability issues have appeared in many publications including the *New York Times*, the *Nation*, the *Village Voice*, and the *Progressive*. She is editor of the book *People with Disabilities Explain It All for You: Your Guide to the Public Accommodations Requirements of the Americans with Disabilities Act* (1992).

DAVID LAWRENCE, JR., is publisher and chairman of the *Miami Herald*.

CHERIE S. LEWIS, an Assistant Professor at Syracuse University, was a Fulbright Scholar in Taiwan and a speaker for the U.S. Information Service from 1989 to 1991. She is currently an officer of the People with Disabilities interest group of the Association for Education in Journalism and Mass Communication and is committed to helping journalism students learn more about disability issues. Her doctoral dissertation at the University of Minnesota dealt with legal tactics used by women's groups to improve coverage of women's issues and to improve employment opportunities for women in television.

ALF PRATTE is a Professor in the Department of Communications at Brigham Young University, where he teaches mass media history, opinion writing, and other graduate and undergraduate classes. A former reporter for the *Honolulu Star-Bulletin*, Pratte has also taught at Shippensburg University, Hawaii Pacific College, and the Kapiolani Community College of the University of Hawaii. He is one of the founders of the American Journalism Historians Association (AJHA).

KEN RAINS is a reporter at the *Journal and Courier* in Lafayette, Indiana.

LILLIE S. RANSOM is a Ph.D. student in journalism/mass communications at the University of Maryland–College Park. She interned in the newsroom at a Baltimore television station and at several radio stations. In addition, she worked for several years at Gallaudet University and as a freelance interpreter and Basic Sign Language instructor. She is a member of the Board of Trustees, Maryland School for the Deaf.

LEE W. ROBINSON is Assistant Superintendent of the Utah Schools for the Deaf and the Blind. He was the initiator of the National Association of Parents of the Visually Handicapped and has directed federally funded projects.

JOSEPH P. SHAPIRO is Senior Editor at *U.S. News & World Report*. He is the author of the 1993 book, *No Pity: People with Disabilities Forging a New Civil Rights Movement*.

MICHAEL R. SMITH, Assistant Professor of Mass Communications at Lycoming College in Pennsylvania, works with several organizations committed to people with disabilities. A writer and editor for more than ten years, he has written about the news coverage of people with disabilities, technology, and other journalism issues for magazines and journals. He recently published a book on church history.

JOEL TORCZON is chief copy editor for the *Bakersfield Californian*.